Southern Sons

Southern Sons

Becoming Men in the New Nation

LORRI GLOVER

The Johns Hopkins University Press

Baltimore

© 2007 The Johns Hopkins University Press
All rights reserved. Published 2007
Printed in the United States of America on acid-free paper

2   4   6   8   9   7   5   3   1

The Johns Hopkins University Press
2715 North Charles Street
Baltimore, Maryland 21218-4363
www.press.jhu.edu

Library of Congress Cataloging-in-Publication Data
Glover, Lorri, 1967–
Southern sons : becoming men in the new nation / Lorri Glover.
p. cm.
Includes bibliographical references and index.
ISBN-13: 978-0-8018-8498-6 (hardcover : alk. paper)
ISBN-10: 0-8018-8498-5 (hardcover : alk. paper)
1. Young men—Southern States—History—18th century. 2. Young men—
Southern States—History—19th century. 3. Boys—Southern States—History—
18th century. 4. Boys—Southern States—History—19th century. 5. Men—
Socialization—Southern States—History. 6. Boys—Education—Southern
States—History. 7. Southern States—Social conditions—18th century.
8. Southern States—Social conditions—19th century. I. Title.
HQ1090.5.S68G56 2007
305.242'1097509034—dc22   2006016501

A catalog record for this book is available from the British Library.

For Chris, Erin, and Zack Lier

CONTENTS

ACKNOWLEDGMENTS

I started research on this project through a grant from the office of Lynn Champion, Director of Academic Outreach in the College of Arts and Sciences at the University of Tennessee, and I have waited a long time to be able to publicly thank Lynn for all the support and kindness she has shown throughout my time at UT. Matt Schoenbachler encouraged my foray into the early Republic, and then read an early draft of the manuscript, offering excellent advice that greatly improved the finished version. Craig Friend helped me work out many of the foundational ideas in this project during our collaboration on another book, and still happily agreed to read this manuscript. Steve Ash has been friend, editor, and mentor. His example and encouragement remain invaluable to me.

In addition to generous support for research from the University of Tennessee, grants from the Filson Historical Society and the North Caroliniana Society enabled me to study the rich collections at those repositories. I owe many thanks to the archivists and staff at the Duke University Special Collections Library, the Filson Historical Society, the North Carolina Collection and the Southern Historical Collection (both at the University of North Carolina–Chapel Hill), the South Carolina Historical Society, the South Caroliniana Library, the Tennessee State Library and Archives, the Virginia Historical Society, and the special collections libraries at the University of Kentucky and the University of Tennessee. Carrie Galliford and Amy Looney worked as stellar research assistants on the project. I profited immensely from presenting early findings from my research at the Southern Historical Association and the Society for Historians of the Early American Republic. Michael Zuckerman and Toby Ditz provided particularly constructive commentary on papers I read, and I am grateful for the critiques they offered. Jennifer Green and Bruce Wheeler read chapters in the early stages, and their questions and comments shaped my subsequent writing. Theda Perdue remains unfailingly generous with her time and wise counsel; she and

Michael Green also opened their home to me when I researched in North Carolina.

Bertram Wyatt-Brown read the entire manuscript—rigorously, twice. This is a far stronger work because of his careful and sophisticated assessment. It was, well, an honor to have him evaluate my work and share his ideas about this generation of men. I am also grateful to Robert J. Brugger, Juliana McCarthy, and the staff at the Johns Hopkins University Press for the support and care they showed the book.

My family and friends provided both encouragement for and breaks from research and writing. Debbie Blackwell, Mary Block, Lynn Sacco, Betsy Sutherland, and Cynthia Tinker helped me think through conceptual and writing difficulties, and they all made time away from work a great pleasure. Jeff Norrell was a true friend throughout the project, and his example has taught me to be a better teacher and, I hope, a more courageous person. Encountering the parents in this book gave me an even deeper appreciation for my own mother and father, Jackie Mansell and Gerald Glover, and the values they taught my sister and me. I wrote part of the book while on a semester leave from UT, frequently staying with my niece and nephews. By 3:30 on those days, I could not wait for the bus to bring Erin, Chris, and Zack home. The book is dedicated to them, because I said I would. Dan Smith offered endless support for the book and then reminded me when it was time to move on—he is my best critic, trusted friend, and treasure.

Southern Sons

Introduction

In 1806, Samuel DuBose, a prominent South Carolinian, wrote his younger brother William, a student at Yale, to tell him about the untimely death of a young kinsman. The letter Samuel wrote, which conveyed disgust rather than grief, could also be read as a cautionary tale for the teenage William—a model of everything a young man ought to avoid and the price he could expect to pay if he did not. According to Samuel, their recently deceased relative Isaac "had given up himself for several years past to every excess and extravagance." Isaac was "half of his time drunk," unable to succeed in a career, wasteful with his father's money, and a burden to his mortified relatives. The DuBose family endured these heartaches for several years, until Isaac's debauchery brought on his passing. "I believe at his death," Samuel told William, "the only regret was that he had lived so long. Such was the end of a young man who might have been an ornament to his country and a comfort to his relations."[1]

Isaac DuBose had squandered his potential and did not merit forgiveness, even in death. Dutiful, upstanding boys who died prematurely provoked far different responses from their grieving relatives. William Barry, for example, lovingly eulogized his brother Leonard, who died at age sixteen, as "the most accomplished man in the country of his age . . . [with] an open countenance; polite, dignified and manly in his appearance." William proclaimed Leonard "the pride of his family [and] had he lived, he would no doubt have been the proudest ornament of his country." That language—of loss to family and country, of exceptionality, and of defining sons as "ornaments"—appeared consistently in literary discussions of deceased young men who, unlike poor Isaac DuBose, earned their relatives' affections.[2]

In describing the deaths of adolescents, southern elites of the early national period demonstrated that they held clear and unwavering expectations of what made a boy a man. Successful boys devoted themselves to family, distinguished themselves in society, and shone as "ornaments" in the young Republic. Manhood required nothing less. But as Isaac DuBose's short, dissolute life indicated, not every southern son born of privilege became a respected man. Boys earned their manhood only after navigating elaborate, exacting tests and proving themselves worthy of being called men. Those who faltered lived (and died) in ignominy.

For better than two decades, honor, rather than manhood, has been the dominant approach to understanding the lives and culture of nineteenth-century southern men.[3] While scholars investigating the North in recent years have used gender analysis to interrogate masculine ideals, family relationships, and middle-class values, the emergence of men's studies exerted little influence on southern historians.[4] The honor ethic has certainly provided a compelling analytical model for understanding the culture of the Old South. But that framework emphasizes a set of values that persists over time and throughout the South—an interpretation that calls for further interrogation.[5] It is time to revisit the honor thesis, to treat the early South with greater chronological specificity, and to analyze the effects of gender values on the lives of the region's leading men.

This book uses manhood as the framework for exploring the lives of young men of the southern gentry who came of age between the 1790s and the 1820s, in the shadow of the founders. Although honor accurately denotes a primal, perhaps the quintessential southern value, this concept does not explain what adolescents in this cohort, who hailed from Georgia, South Carolina, North Carolina, Virginia, Maryland, Kentucky, and Tennessee, were striving to become. Manhood is a less static concept, which more effectively captures the journey these boys—not yet southern and not yet men—undertook. They were and understood themselves to be part of a significant and distinctive generation, the first born to the American Republic and specially called to prove themselves as men. Honor was an important component in their coming to manhood; they responded quickly and often violently to character aspersions, feared shame, and obsessed over communal evaluation of their conduct.[6] But they also embraced an Atlantic enthusiasm for refined culture and found British conduct literature central to their pursuit of manhood. They closely identified with the Republic, and imagined they could not be men without fulfilling the demands of citizenship and service to the new nation. And their transition to manhood played out against a backdrop of bondage; they became men in part by personifying the antithesis of their slaves and became southern by protecting that institution. Their changing status, then, emerged from a complex mix of influences—national, Atlantic, and local—which included but transcended honor. Manhood was ultimately what adolescents and their families sought. It was, rather than a cultural value like honor, the culmination of a process, a series of tests that these boys faced in the early national era.

In the minds of southern elites, manhood was a social, not simply a biological, designation, and it required testing. To be a man in this society was to be male, white, and elite *and* to embody the proper gender attributes. A male lacking any of these qualities was not fully a man in the eyes of the region's ruling class. (Without wishing to concur with or reify this circumscribed vision of manhood, throughout the book I have, for concision of phrasing, used the term "southern men" as shorthand for white, elite men from the southern states.) Although acknowledged as males, poor whites seldom and slaves never gained affirmation as men from the gentry. And boys of the elite class did not automatically become men after achieving a particular age or accomplishment. A boy became a man only when he convinced his community that he was one.[7]

Becoming recognized as men required gentry boys to put away their personal predispositions and put on the comportment and character of an ideal gentleman —to become what their society deemed manly. Women faced a similar burden, and thanks to several decades of sophisticated scholarly inquiry we know quite a lot about the rigid societal expectations that they confronted in early America.[8] This study shows how adolescent boys met a parallel code of manliness or forfeited their respectability. In the early South, masculinity required boldness and autonomy, whereas femininity demanded submission and selflessness. But for both men and women of the southern gentry, gender was exacting. Successful boys learned to adeptly perform the prescribed role, grooming their education, appearance, relationships, lifestyle, careers, and even emotions to, in an oft-repeated phrase, "act the part" of men.[9]

For this first generation of intentionally American sons, learning to play the part of men was equally vital and vexing. Whereas the founding generation had identified as Virginians or Carolinians or more commonly as Britons before the American Revolution, their sons learned from the earliest stages of life to think of themselves as Americans first. Raised as self-consciously and proudly American, this cohort grew up being told that the destiny of the Republic depended on their virtue, their dutifulness, their leadership as men. Unless they proved themselves worthy citizens, they would be not just the first but tragically the last generation of American sons. Thus the early national era was marked by anxiety about the future of the republican experiment and, in particular, fears that this rising generation might betray the founders' remarkable achievements. The fathers of this cohort had, after all, triumphed over the British Empire and forged an independent America. In the process of overthrowing colonial rule, the revolutionary generation also upset the traditional ordering of society. In the early Republic, young men whose families had long enjoyed prominence because of their names and wealth now needed to compete in the new American meritocracy. What had been a birthright became a test. And their fathers set an overwhelmingly high standard. How could any boy hope to match the valor, wisdom, and renown of men such as George Washington, James Madison, and Thomas Jefferson? And how could the Republic endure if they did not?[10]

In the fullness of time, sons raised to emulate the achievements of Jefferson, Washington, and Madison turned into southern nationalists like John Calhoun and James Hammond. This generation's story reveals not only the hopes and anxieties of the Republic but also the seeds of its unraveling. Between the 1790s and the 1820s, the South and these boys came of age together. Although charged with replicating the character and accomplishments of the founders, elite sons from the South grew up to self-consciously identify as southerners and as guardians of the region's increasingly peculiar racial order. While their fathers had replaced their local and imperial identity with an American one, these sons, as men, moved from national to sectional allegiance. As they took responsibility for leading the South in the antebellum era, instead of bringing their parents' republican ideals to fruition, they promoted southern nationalism and laid the foundation for the Civil War.

This book answers two interrelated questions: What did it take to be a man in the early national South? And how did these republican sons become southern men? Part 1 investigates the foundational values of autonomy and duty taught to boys in childhood—expectations that would trouble southern sons throughout their coming-of-age experiences. The first test of manhood commenced when boys pursued higher educations and genteel reputations. Part 2 begins by exploring the clash of familial plans and peer influences during the college years and charts the evolution of distinctly southern schools and educational values. Simultaneous to their formal education, boys honed their skills as gentlemen. Part 2 also follows their quest for refinement and explains how youth culture transformed parental ambitions for gentility and respectability. As revealed in Part 3, manly status also required winning a desirable wife. Success in courting flowed from proper refinement and education and marked a man as capable of leading a household. After preparing themselves intellectually and socially and then marrying reputable women, young men needed only to prove their capacity for leadership—over businesses, politics, and slaves—to fully validate their manhood. Part 3 concludes by surveying young men's forays into community and civic leadership and racial power and explains how they reconciled the call for manly autonomy with the expectation of public duty.

Time and time again these adolescents heard that their own fates along with that of their families and the American Republic depended on their proving themselves worthy of being called men. Anxiety about these boys and the future of the nation pervaded the private writings of early republican southerners, and for good cause. In response to nearly ceaseless familial pleas to study carefully, spend wisely, walk gracefully, speak eloquently, court confidently, lead judiciously, and a hundred more suggestions, boys often acted impertinent, extravagant, awkward, and violent—as out of control and childish as one could imagine. But as they, alongside their nation and region, matured, these southern sons turned into adept, committed stewards of their gentry families and the southern way of life. Their successes, not their failures, would be their undoing.

PART ONE

SONS

CHAPTER ONE

The First Duties of a Southern Boy

When his eldest and much beloved son James turned sixteen, Tennessean Francis Ramsey confessed that since the boy's birth he had "almost dayly and hourly felt anxiety of mind."[1] In that brief passage, Ramsey articulated the apprehensions of a generation of parents and kinfolk who tried to turn boys into gentlemen in the early national South. Like Ramsey, most southern elites delighted in the arrival of a new son, but they also felt a great weight of responsibility. A newborn son inaugurated a twenty-odd-year-long ordeal of turning a male child into a southern patriarch, and families felt nervous about boys' prospects. Parents, siblings, and kin oversaw this often daunting project during the first decade or so of a boy's life. Later on, conduct experts, educators, the boy's peers and girlfriends, and family friends and business associates would aid (and contradict and thwart) them.

Parents worried so much about their sons because they expected so much from them. In the first place, southern elites felt certain that their boys held a particular responsibility to lead. They believed, as Virginian John Randolph explained to his young kinsman Theodore Dudley, "the richer, the wiser, the more powerful a man is, the greater is the obligation upon him to employ his gifts in lessening the sum of human misery."[2] The American Revolution intensified this perceived call to service. Indeed, the revolutionary cohort thought that the persistence of the Republic depended on the talents and diligence of this generation of American sons. Elites also needed their boys to preserve family wealth and prominence. Without dutiful, accomplished sons, families foundered. For these sons, then, good was never good enough. Boys hoping to earn affirmation as men had to be great—precociously talented, devoted to family, and, in a phrase repeated countless times, ornaments to their nation.

Elite families drilled boys on the imperatives to ready themselves for civic service, since these first American sons carried the future of their families and the Republic on their narrow shoulders. Boys were constantly prompted to work hard, develop respected talents, educate themselves, refine their manners, and learn to act confidently in the world—so that they could be acknowledged as worthy men.[3] Southern elites shared these hopes and anxieties with northerners who also raised young sons to confidently assume political and social preeminence. Although the Revolution had challenged elite social dominion, many of the self-styled "better sort" still believed that their sons, aided by family wealth and sophistication, should rise to the top of America's emergent meritocracy. Southern elites certainly kept far tighter limits on membership in their region's "better sort" and for far longer, but they and their northern contemporaries held in common a mission to groom their sons for civic leadership and social renown and to thus be known as American gentlemen.

Sacred Civic Responsibility

Southern gentry families in the early national era, just like their colonial predecessors, believed that wealthy boys bore a special obligation to lead. Edward Rutledge, of the prominent South Carolina family, explained for his son the connections between family lineage and public duty. It was, he avowed, "absolutely incumbent on Men of talents, and independence, and virtue, to participate in the affairs of the Republic." Henry Rutledge was a young man destined for such service: "The family my Son from which you have descended; the style of your education; . . . the early acquaintance which you have formed with public men; the habits to which they themselves are accustomed of considering your nearest connections, as the property of their Country, form such a combination of circumstances as forbid the idea of private Life." Serving honorably was not then a privilege, but a responsibility that boys expecting to be southern gentlemen could not ignore. Kentuckian Thomas Todd directed his young son Charles to focus all his energies on meeting societal expectations: "Recollect the honor, the character & reputation of your Country for talents & genius is in some measure resting on you—pride, ambition, nay duty, demands of you an exertion."[4]

The American Revolution infused those paternalistic attitudes with patriotic meaning at the same time that it called on prospective leaders to prove their civic merits. Only the landed, the truly independent, could exercise the virtue essential to a successful Republic, but preparation for leadership was also vital. Raising capable citizens became paramount in the early Republic. Sacrificing throughout his adult life to properly educate and raise his twelve children, Kentuckian Richard Anderson prized civic responsibility. His son Charles recollected: "His sole personal effort was to make his sons first patriots and good citizens."[5] Mothers also felt a strong calling to raise republican sons—honorable, virtuous, and capable of leading the nation into the future.[6] Adults paid the greatest attention to this civic charge when they began formally educating their sons and then shepherding them into suitable careers. But the seeds were sown in childhood.

Devoted to the republican experiment and proud of the young nation's accomplishments, southerners trumpeted revolutionary heroes as models for their young sons. George Washington became the archetype of manly character for many boys. Charles Anderson remembered that throughout his boyhood "George Washington was ever held up to us all as an object-lesson, or as our exemplar." Like many schoolboys, Noah Jones wrote compositions on George Washington. His 1805 essay explained Washington's virtuous ambition: his accomplishments derived from patriotism and courage, not any quest for personal wealth or power. In a subsequent composition Jones enumerated Washington's exemplary character traits: "a general philanthropy, a clemency towards his enemies; an humanity ever active to relieve the miseries of his fellow creatures; a veracity unimpeached; a prudence which never forsook him, even upon the most trying occasions; a cool, undaunted courage in the hour of danger; and a modest opinion of his own actions." Washington's behavior at the close of the war, particularly his call to the unpaid, unhappy troops for submission to civil leadership, exemplified "magnanimity . . . unequalled in the annals of mankind."[7] Southerners also admired Benjamin Franklin for his multifaceted accomplishments and international renown. Richard Bennehan, like many southern fathers, heralded Franklin as a great American whom his son should strive to emulate. Young Arthur Morson assured his mother that he lived by Franklin's adage: "Early to bed and early to rise makes a man healthy, wealthy, & wise. These two things I am now in the habit of practising every day." St. George Tucker pointed to both Washington and Franklin as models for his sons and stepsons.[8]

Sometimes, the revolutionary heroes that adults wanted boys to emulate were closer to home. Martha Ramsay hoped to raise her son David to be "a citizen worthy of the new nation and of his distinguished Laurens and Ramsay bloodlines."[9] Martha's father, Henry Laurens, headed the Continental Congress, her brother John was a Revolutionary War hero, and her husband became one of the first historians of the American Revolution. John Eppes likewise reminded his son Francis of the necessity of trying to live up to the reputation of his grandfather, Thomas Jefferson. (John Eppes married Maria Jefferson in 1797.) John told young Francis, "The elevated station held by your Grand Father as a philosopher and statesman ought to stimulate you to great exertion—Render yourself if possible worthy of him." And, John reasoned, "If you are not inclined to be his equal in Talents be not his inferior in every manly virtue—The last depends entirely on yourself."[10]

Young David Ramsay and Francis Eppes faced the unenviable, perhaps impossible, tasks of living up to their ancestors' political, military, and intellectual distinctions. The pressure to match the heroic accomplishments of their ancestors weighed heavy on adolescent boys coming of age in the early national period. Henry Clay Jr. articulated this anxiety as he considered his efforts to become the son his famous father wanted: "How difficult it is for a young tree to grow in the shade of an aged oak."[11]

In most cases, sons of the early Republic did not literally descend from prominent Revolutionaries, but they nevertheless felt tremendous pressure to duplicate their valor and achievements. Several of the most influential founders never fathered sons. James Madison was childless (and his efforts rearing Dolley's son from her first marriage, John Payne Todd, failed miserably). Thomas Jefferson acknowledged fathering only daughters. And George Washington, while caring for Martha's children and grandchildren and becoming the metaphorical father of his country, produced no biological offspring. Rather, an entire generation found itself symbolically descended from and expected to fulfill the promise of that quickly deified generation of "founding fathers." At public festivities throughout the young nation, speakers exhorted, "Sons, remember the glory of your fathers."[12]

Boys coming of age in the wake of the American Revolution learned from early childhood that they faced a sacred duty to their nation. And they knew that family loyalty mattered just as much as civic leadership.

Family Sentiment and Service

Just as parents trained boys to revere the Republic, they also sought to inculcate in sons an abiding sense of family loyalty. Elite southern children generally grew up in emotionally expressive families, surrounded by affectionate kinfolk. Parents wrote openly about their love for their offspring. Since mothers oversaw young children on a day-to-day basis, they had less time and reason to commit their feelings to paper, but those who did write often doted on their children and bragged to relatives about their babies' early accomplishments such as walking and talking. Mothers often described the "amusements" and "diversions" their children provided. (No doubt gentry women enjoyed mothering so much in part because household slaves freed them from many arduous tasks.) Fathers traveled from home far more often, so they wrote more frequently and expansively to their offspring about their feelings. When he went abroad in 1803, Virginian Robert Carter wrote a lengthy letter to his children, ages three to seven, whom he left in the care of relatives. Carter referred to the children as his "Beloved little group" and tenderly recollected, "How often has your bewitching prattle enlivened the fireside of your indulgent Parents, and made their anxious hearts heave alternate with joy and hope." Carter assured his young children that he "would not see a hair on your head injured . . . [and] would die for you ten times over." Andrew Jackson felt as loving toward his adopted son, Andrew Jackson Jr. When wartime events delayed his return home to Tennessee, he worried that Andrew Jr. would "think I am runaway from him," and he asked Rachel to "kiss him for me and say to him truly, that in all my life I never wanted more to see you & him than I do at present."[13]

The affective ties in southern families transcended the parent-child bond. Siblings developed especially close connections, and extended kin blurred the emotional and physical boundaries of households. Julia Mordecai of the prominent North Carolina family articulated the sibling bonds of many southerners in a letter to her brother Solomon: "How constantly you occupy my thoughts my beloved Brother, you who so well know all my feelings can only tell—you are entwined in all my affections and every pulsation of my heart is regulated by hopes, fears, and prayers for you." When the Mordecai siblings' mother died, their father married his late wife's younger sister and fathered children with her. Alfred Mordecai remembered that the stepsiblings viewed one another as "all strictly one family, & the confidential & affectionate relations of brothers & sisters, between us, were never disturbed."[14]

Parents actively encouraged such sibling devotion, knowing that connections between brothers and sisters met important emotional needs as well as providing advice and assistance later in life. South Carolinian Jane Ball championed close connections between her sons. "Nothing," she insisted, "could give greater pleasure than . . . Brothers united by the strictest friendship." Both she and her husband, John, taught their sons the importance of "brotherly love and affection." Sterling Ruffin similarly urged his son to correspond often with his sister "as it would not only greatly improve you both, but would tend to keep alive that tender Brotherly affection." Siblings so expected each other to honor their connections that boys complained if their brothers and sisters ignored them. When his elder sister failed to write as often as he expected, young Henry Izard wondered, "Have you entirely forgotten that there exists a Brother who tenderly loves you . . . [and] stands in need of a little notice from you?" And he used guilt to attract her attention: "Does the gentle strings of fraternal love no longer vibrate in your heart?"[15]

Cousins, uncles, aunts, nieces, nephews, and extended kin also professed their love and sense of responsibility for one another. Hugh Grigsby's uncle, the father of eleven children including five sons, wrote Hugh that he and his wife "have very often thought of you with the same affection that we would have felt for an absent and only son." Hugh grew up very close to his cousins, and the young people wrote of their abiding attachments to each other.[16] Conjugal family members encouraged these bonds and often sent young children on extended visits in order to promote family affections and allegiances. Mary Adair and her sister sent their young sons to each other's homes, temporarily trading children. Alicia Middleton also sent her young son to visit an aunt in Rhode Island, directing him to "act well all the time you are away that you may be a comfort and a pleasure to Aunt Russell instead of an anxiety."[17] Adults routinely encouraged young kinfolk to work together and shun conflicts. South Carolinian John Rutledge prompted his children and grandchildren "to love each other, sincerely & affectionately, & to render good Offices, reciprocally."[18] That is not to say that sibling and kin relationships never turned contentious. The literary evidence no doubt under-represents family conflicts, for estranged kinfolk did not correspond. And since early southerners seldom kept personal letters private, preferring to share them with kin and friends, correspondents probably downplayed conflicts. Occasional references to tensions do appear in the historical record. But southern gentry families placed a premium on family duty and avoided feuds whenever possible.

Boys clearly imbibed this culture of family devotion. Very young children obviously could not write about their feelings for their relatives, but commentary from mothers and fathers intimated their love. For instance, according to his parents, at age five Andrew Jackson Jr. slept with a letter his father sent him and longed for his father when he got sick.[19] Once boys grew old enough to write, they put their fondness for family members on the page. The letters written by sons separated from their families provide compelling evidence of the close emotional attachments between boys and their kin. George Henry Calvert, scion of the prominent Maryland family, was just nine years old when his parents sent him to boarding school in Pennsylvania. As an adult he vividly recollected, "I have hardly one pleasant memory of those school-days." While he made new friends at the school, this little eased "the heart-ache caused by being snatched from a warm partial home, and thrown suddenly among cold indifferent strangers. But there were hours when the wound of the affections would not be staunched, when I would quit the play-ground and go off to the southwest corner of the limited lot, the point nearest to my home, and there weep alone, looking wistfully down the road from Philadelphia for relief." William Ruffin longed for his parents and siblings when he left home around age thirteen. Writing to his sister Catherine, he confided, "Oh Dear Sister . . . I would give all the world if I had it just to see home." Age only modestly tempered the melancholy that young men felt at being separated from kin and home. Teenager James McDowell, a Virginian studying at Yale in the 1810s, found the nights most disheartening: "When the shades of evening and glimmering twilight surround me when every foot is still and all the world is 'left to solitude and to me' 'tis then that memory . . . transports me to C. Grove and Abingdon where the ties of nature and affection bind me."[20]

While they promoted such close attachments, elites also made certain that sons understood that family love was not unconditional and that families were centers of reciprocal duties as much as emotional havens. Andrew Jackson doted on Andrew Jr., but he also expected loyalty from their bond. Before Andrew Jr. turned five years old, his father and mother already anticipated that he would "take care of us both in our declining years" and "with a carefull [*sic*] education reallise [*sic*] all our wishes." Writing three years later, Andrew Jackson asked Rachel to tell young Andrew Jr. that "papa hears with pleasure that he has been a good boy & learns his Book[.] Tell him his sweet papa labours hard to get money to educate him, but when he learns & becomes a great man, his sweet papa will be amply rewarded for all his care, expence, & pains."[21]

Boys who failed to fulfill their obligations to kin could expect the withdrawal of approval and love. Fathers in particular made clear that paternal warmth depended on filial behavior. Georgia native Lemuel Kollock on several occasions indicated that his affections hung on his son George's actions. For example, in 1820 he wrote the ten-year-old that he should "be a good boy & a good scholar [and] I shall love you very much as will every one else." John Ball Sr. directly informed his teenage namesake, "As you increase in wisdom & learning so may you expect my affection to increase."[22] Elder kinsmen who served as mentors to their nephews or cousins adopted the same stance: affection flowed from dutifulness and could be destroyed by waywardness. Georgia planter Seaborn Jones advised his nephew William Hart that he loved him, and to "be a good boy—be attentive to your studies—do your best to please every one—and you may then safely confide in the continuance of that regard." And families followed through on these lessons: boys who squandered their potential forfeited their relatives' affections. John Ball Sr., for example, told his son the sad tale of a chronic ne'er-do-well from Charleston who so alienated his family that, when he died, his father refused "to put on mourning for him."[23]

Southerners considered duty to family and community inviolable responsibilities of gentry children, and the prospect that sons might not live up to these standards caused great unease. Adults notified children early in life of the requirement to become respectable and perpetuate the status of their families in society or suffer dire consequences. Robert Carter cautioned his four young children about "the disgrace and ignominy which will await you in this life, and of the evils that may be denounced against your poor, frail, impotent Father as well as yourselves in the life to come, if you fail to do all on your part to become worthy members of society."[24] Girls became "worthy members of society" by practicing deference, social graces, and compassion, which allowed them to eventually become dutiful kinswomen and genteel ladies. Boys grew up to fill more public roles, as politicians, slave masters, and businessmen, as well as refined gentlemen. Success in meeting these standards would determine the prominence of their families—a fact kinfolk never let children forget.

Adults placed enormous pressure on young sons, repeatedly telling them that their actions affected their relatives' future. Virginian John Ambler's father cautioned him that everything he did would reflect on the Amblers. He beseeched the boy to remember that he descended from "a *respectable & worthy family,* who have preserved their reputation, for three or four *generations blot it not my son,* for recollect it would take the same time to *regain it,* if ever." Kentuckian Henry Clay similarly explained how much of his happiness and reputation turned on his sons' behaviors. Since his elder sons dashed all his hopes with their erratic, dissipated behavior, his fifteen-year-old namesake bore an even greater burden: "If you too disappoint my anxious hopes," he wrote Henry Jr., "a Constitution, never good, and now almost exhausted, would sink beneath the pressure. You bear my name. You are my son, and the hopes of all of us are turned with anxiety upon you."[25]

Adults charged future patriarchs with taking responsibility for their kinfolk, and, again, predicted shame and disgrace for boys who failed. When James McDowell traveled from his Virginia home, he expected his son to "lighten the cares of his mother," remain focused on his studies, and appear "Honorable, Social & manly among his fellows." McDowell warned that "a different course would bring shame on himself & disgrace upon his family." Parents particularly charged sons with setting examples for and taking care of younger siblings. Francis Ramsey reminded his elder son James, "You are naturally an Example to your dear little Brother Billy." And, in a typical letter, Edward Campbell counseled his nephew Phineas Kollock to consider himself "doubly responsible, as not only your own reputation is to be supported, but a younger Brother will probably model his character by yours." After widower John Eppes remarried and started a second family, he wanted his teenage son Francis to feel responsible for watching out for his young half-siblings. Mindful that his own age (forty-six) threatened orphanhood for the offspring of his second union, John informed Francis: "To you I look as the friend protector and guardian of those who according to natures laws will be deprived of the advantages of my assistance long before they can arrive at an age to take care of themselves." In other words, these children's future depended on Francis's conscientiousness.[26]

John Eppes's letter to his son not only explained the necessity of family loyalty but also hinted at the priorities of this patriarch as he contemplated his own mortality. Like most southern gentlemen, John focused his energy on his family's future in this world but expressed little concern for his own fate in the next.

Godliness versus Manliness

Religion was the only major area of southern life that elite men did not groom their sons to dominate. The men who first made the South showed little interest in church matters and expressed outright hostility to evangelizing in their families and communities. Women, however, embraced evangelical Christianity earlier on and in greater numbers. As they sought to spread the word to their children, women often subtly contradicted and occasionally even denounced what fathers taught boys. This was the only important issue regarding the rearing of their sons about which southern mothers and fathers disagreed. The Harden family of Georgia illustrates the gendering of religious values in the early national era. When the teenage Edward Harden left his Savannah home to attend the University of Georgia, both of his parents worried about his behavior and character. But his mother emphasized the importance of religion while his father stressed secular morality. Edward Harden coached his son and namesake on matters as diverse as courting, forming friendships, family duty, the importance of college, and the value of good humor, but he ignored religion. Mary Ann Harden, however, tried to instill religiosity in her son and upbraided him when he questioned faith. While she sent the young man a Bible and urged him "to read it methodically, and follow the precepts laid down there," Edward's father sent him a copy of an advisory letter written by Thomas Jefferson that outlined the ideal youth and directed him to read it every Sunday and follow it through the week. In the father's eyes, typical of the values of southern patriarchs, reputation formation should be his son's religion.[27]

Gentlemen in the early national South typically found evangelicalism antithetical to their manhood.[28] Self-critical soul-searching and submission to an omnipotent God ran counter to men's zeal for mastery and self-confidence. Evangelicals also tended to attribute worldly accomplishments to divine intervention, which further challenged gentry convictions of what made a southern male "manly." And they valued overt emotionalism and self-reproach; true believers acknowledged their sinfulness and powerlessness and acted contrite— behaviors no gentleman could afford to display. Evangelicals disapproved of drinking, gambling, dueling, horse racing, and dancing—activities at the core of genteel masculinity. They condemned slavery, which underlay patriarchs' power, as immoral. And they rejected the leisured, luxurious lifestyle of southern elites and encouraged "industry, thrift, and modest living."[29] In an advisory letter typical of evangelical women, Mary McDonald warned her son Charles against "sins" such as gambling, drunkenness, and extravagant spending.[30] In the late eighteenth and early nineteenth centuries, then, evangelicals defined southern men's leisure pursuits as sinful and rejected the authority of men to regulate themselves and master others.

The words of the converted are sufficient to explain patriarchs' disapproval. Daniel Penick, a young Presbyterian minister from North Carolina, manifested the character attributes that made evangelical Christianity unacceptable to most southern gentry men. In his 1821–22 diary, he repeatedly expressed self-doubt, inadequacy, and anxiety. He found himself constantly distracted by "the pollution of my own heart—the number of my sins—their heinous & aggravated nature," and a sense of failure pervaded his writings: "My faith is weak, my hope slight, fears many, & love cold." David Rice, another evangelical, similarly epitomized the adversarial relationship between religious enthusiasm and southern gentry manhood. He condemned slaveholding as ungodly and railed against the sins of drinking, swearing, greed, and extravagance. Rice believed that men were, by nature, "polluted" and "depraved"—that "Man is an impotent creature" incapable of anything without the intercession of God. And when Richard Watkins explained his conversion experience to his mother, he remembered, "I then began to feel my dependence, and to feel that I had a depraved heart." Watkins thought first of concealing his concerns, for he knew that the other students at Hampden-Sydney would ridicule him. But, he explained, "after some reflection, I thought how foolish it was to suffer myself to be laughted [*sic*] out of heaven," and so he resolved to face the rebuke of his classmates.[31] In Watkins's case, both

the language of conversion and his postconversion behavior repudiated masculine values and the class prerogatives enjoyed by patriarchs. His flouting of
peer perceptions threatened the young man's reputation and that of his entire
family.

Gentlemen wanted the rising generation to shun religious excesses and to
pursue instead a secular code of morality. Religious indifference was pervasive
among the revolutionary generation; many fathers ignored religion entirely in
their advisory correspondence. When men did discuss religion, they generally
took one of two approaches. Some ridiculed those they considered excessively
religious, labeling converts as feminine, socially dangerous, even mentally ill.[32]
Other men adopted a more ecumenical stance, emphasizing open-mindedness
and toleration and thereby more subtly conveying their opposition. For example,
Georgian Seaborn Jones encouraged a young kinsman to attend church and
discouraged taking God's name in vain, but he also noted, "I do not expect you to
be forced into any particular mode of faith." In the rare instances in which
Thomas Jefferson discussed religion with his nephew Peter Carr, he urged ra-
tionalism. He counseled Peter to first "divest yourself of all bias in favour of
novelty and singularity of opinion. . . . On the other hand shake off all the fears
and servile prejudices under which weak minds are servilely crouched. Fix
reason firmly in her seat, and call to her tribunal every fact, every opinion."
Religion, like any other field of study, should be approached through critical
analysis and strict application of existing knowledge.[33]

Southern patriarchs' clear preference for civic morality and reasoned skepti-
cism over faith infuriated evangelicals. Presbyterian minister David Rice abandoned Virginia in the 1780s, disgusted with elites, who, Rice insisted, scoffed at
religion and taught their children to do the same. If gentlemen ever bothered to
show up at church services, they "come to ye House of God with much the same
Seriousness & Gravity that they carry to a Race or Dance. . . . The great care of
many seems to be to see fine Faces and show their own; to let their Neighbors see
they have a fine Coat or Gown, a new Wig or an elligent [*sic*] head Dress." Young
men, apparently schooled in sacrilege and indulgence, were "drinking down
Iniquity like water" and doomed "if possible, to be worse than their fathers."[34]

Worshiping at the altar of reputation, southern gentlemen, especially those
from the established coastal regions, raised their sons to judge the morality of
behavior not by religious tenets but according to public perceptions. For example, they valued honesty for its reputational significance. Fathers wanted boys to
evince integrity in society and develop the confidence to declare themselves
publicly; the spiritual or moral implications of dishonesty seldom concerned

them. Upon sending his sons from their home in Kentucky to boarding school, Richard Anderson directed them to, above all else, seek truthfulness. Singling out veracity as the most important "duty and conduct," Richard counseled the boys "never to tell a lie and never to suffer anybody to call you a liar." Mendacity, if made public, destroyed reputations. Thomas Jefferson also warned Peter Carr about the essentiality of veracity and the dire consequences of dishonesty to one's reputation: "It is of great importance to set a resolution, not to be shaken, never to tell an untruth. There is no vice so mean, so pitiful, so contemptible" as lying.[35] Reputation, not salvation, was paramount.

Southern mothers sometimes saw things differently, however, embracing evangelicalism and questioning the secular morality men promoted. At the turn of the century, evangelical denominations welcomed female converts, and women saw in revivalism their chance to demonstrate moral leadership while ensuring personal salvation. Mothers, far more than fathers, directed sons to attend church, pray, and study the Bible. Jane Ball hoped that her son Isaac attended St. Philip's church while a student in Charleston and recommended: "Follow your pursuits with virtue & integrity, not forgetting your Creator, but pray for his Grace to assist you & be your Guide & protector." Elizabeth Peyton praised her son Robert upon learning that the student regularly went to church. Anne Hart also wrote extensively to her son William about religious observances: "Again, let me beg of you, attend the worship of Almighty God—break not the Sabbath in diversions—in party pleasures."[36]

But pious women faced an uphill battle in their attempts to convince their sons, because religious devotion seemed antithetical to masculinity. The close association between women and religious enthusiasm hurt the efforts of women to convert men, for it made men who embraced faith seem less manly. One of Kentuckian Micah Taul's earliest memories centered on his childhood friends' gendered responses to religion enthusiasm. Perhaps only five years old, Micah attended a Baptist service. The next morning at school, he recounted, "I separated myself from the boys, and joined the little girls at play. . . . I preached them a sermon and baptized them, one and all. Of course the boys heard of it, and I did not hear the last of it for years." As the Taul memory reveals, evangelical Christianity was equated with femininity in men's minds, and boys learned to avoid religious activities that called their manhood into question.[37]

Beyond the perceived link between faith and femininity, religious women sometimes challenged masculine values. For example, whereas men emphasized personal accomplishments as markers of status, women often attributed success to God's grace. Maria Campbell wanted her nephew George Kollock to know that his accomplishments were not of his own making: "Remember from whence you derive those very powers of mind" and praise "Him, who is the author of your happiness in affording you these means of improvement." Similarly, in letters to her son Charles, Mary McDonald paraphrased biblical passages that contradicted masculine ambitions for self-sufficiency and mastery. She directed Charles to "trust in the Lord with all thine heart; & lean not to thine own understanding. In all thy ways acknowledge him & he shall direct thy paths." Frances Pinckney directed her son Roger to ignore other boys who derided piety: "Should any Boy make a ridicule of [you] . . . pay no regard to it but mind your Mothers Instructions . . . it is for your good that she reminds you of your duty to your Maker." And Ann Hart told her son to read the Bible daily and "make it the Man of your counsel."[38] Such maternal calls to focus on the hereafter rather than peer expectations, to accept the limitations of knowledge and power, and to submit to God promised to make young men spiritually fulfilled but compromised their claims on southern manhood.

Not surprisingly, the great majority of gentry boys modeled themselves after their elder kinsmen, embracing their masculine values and rejecting evangelicalism. Those few who did convert typically confided first (and sometimes exclusively) to sisters and mothers. Richard Watkins, for example, proudly proclaimed his conversion to his mother, but in a series of letters to his father made no mention of religion, concentrating instead on his desire to fulfill filial duties and succeed in his studies.[39] More often than they were pious, boys were grossly irreverent, even sacrilegious, like the students at William and Mary who attacked a Williamsburg church, destroying the communion table and a stained glass window and smearing feces on the pulpit. Others openly derided religious friends or relatives.[40] But most boys acted like their fathers: simply indifferent. These sons understood that embracing the evangelicalism of the early national era meant disavowing the social life of men and walking away from societal recognition of manly status. Only in the antebellum period, once the evangelical denominations had capitulated on some of their values, namely their criticism of slavery and masculine privileges, did many gentry men join the fold.

While the next life appeared to attract little concern, southern sons learned to devote considerable attention to family and country, their sacred duties. Many recorded in their youthful writings aspirations to become worthy heirs to the Republic and "ornaments" to their country. Boys also showed early signs of building identity around family responsibility. The young Georgian John Wallace, for example, was just thirteen when he began to look forward to taking care of his "dear relations." When his sister delivered a child, he reported: "I take a little credit to myself on being an Uncle. I begin to feel myself as somewhat like a man."[41] Had civic and familial obligations been all that confronted them, sons and their relatives might have viewed maturing to manhood with less trepidation than they did. But these foundational duties were only half the story. Manhood required boys to fulfill these obligations while simultaneously appearing autonomous in spirit and action.

CHAPTER TWO

Raising "Self Willed" Sons

In the summer of 1807, John Ball Jr., an inexperienced father from South Carolina, confessed to his brother William that his two-year-old son seemed already "much spoiled, or self willed." William dismissed any concern, reminding his brother, "You would not count him a true *Ball* if he was not a little headstrong." In a subsequent letter, William went even further, congratulating John on having a son who "takes so much after his relations in that characteristic of our Family, the virtue of being a self willed fellow." William assured John that the boy would turn out fine and suggested he "make great allowances for him."[1] John apparently followed his brother's advice; he dropped his initial concern about the headstrong toddler and fell in line with the child-rearing ethic of his fellow elites, who prided themselves on raising independent-minded sons.

The "anxiety of mind" that parents of southern sons so often felt derived not simply from the great responsibilities they expected boys to meet. It came also from the contradictory character trait that the Ball brothers' conversation revealed: manly independence. Families in essence tried to raise sons who were at once deferential to societal expectations and assertively autonomous.

Being a man in the eyes of southern elites demanded independence: of economic circumstance, conscience, and action. This intense—and racialized—zeal for independence was rooted in slaveholding, and it set southern elites on a course apart from their northern contemporaries. Southern gentry men defined their distinctive independence in contrast to slavery. Whites compelled submissiveness from their slaves and defined slaves as dependent and therefore debased; white men considered dependence and submission anathema for themselves. Southern boys thus learned to privilege independence—the antithesis of enslavement—above all other attributes and to publicly exercise their prerogatives as elite white men.

That autonomy, however, was supposed to be revealed in a highly ritualized, scrupulously regimented fashion. Simply being wealthy, white, and independent did not make a boy a man. He had to learn to perform the elaborate conventions of southern masculinity if he wanted public affirmation of his manhood. But because southern manhood required independence, boys needed to decide to satisfy those obligations; adults could coach and cajole, but would not compel. Growing up as a southern son in the new nation was therefore a negotiated affair, with lenient parents hoping willful boys would somehow decide to fulfill towering expectations. Not surprisingly, this enterprise often left boys and their relatives beset by "anxiety of mind."

The Ideal, Independent Southern Boy

Southern elites had very precise, if complicated, plans about what kind of boys they wanted to raise, and they felt certain that starting early was their only chance of making their ideals a reality. Along with their northern contemporaries, southerners adopted John Locke's perspective on parenting: children represented a "tabula rasa." Character was not inherent in Locke's conception, but rather externally molded. Experiences and education determined character, so boys needed to enjoy proper influences and avoid the insidious, and they needed to do so in early childhood.[2] Elites throughout the South understood that childhood was the time for a boy to get on the right path. As one Georgian explained to his ten-year-old nephew, "By being a good boy, you lay a sure foundation on which to become a good man." Virginian Harmer Gilmer, writing in 1806, provided another typical commentary on youth: "The future destiny of the man depends in a great measure on the habits which he contracts during youth[;] if they are of a vicious nature, he will be totally incapable [unable] to shake them off[.] [T]hey will invest him during the rest of his life[;] . . . if on the contrary he forms correct habits during his youth as he advances in life they will become expanded & matured, and be the chief promotion of his happiness." Penmanship exercises pressed this on the minds of young boys. North Carolinian Thomas Lenoir, for example, honed his writing skills by copying an essay on the importance of boyhood: "in short we may say that man[']s future happiness altogeather [*sic*] depends on how he spends his youthful days."[3]

The language used in these illustrative cases is worth further consideration: in each instance, the emphasis centers not on parents, and what example or discipline they might provide, but on sons, and what they would choose to do. In the early national era families believed their greatest accomplishment would be realized if boys learned to make wise choices that promoted their autonomy and success in society.

Independence was the central character trait southern elites tried to instill in boys. Their commitment to independence in sons did not, however, mean that parents allowed boys to behave as they pleased—quite the contrary. They held very specific expectations of how independence would be performed and spent much time and energy trying to teach sons their ideals. As one father explained to his son, boys needed to learn to "put away" their "natural turn" in order to act the part of and be known as men.[4] Adults knew that a boy could never grow up to be a gentleman in the South unless his community recognized his worthiness. And that did not happen until boys learned to be the right kind of independent men. Concern for public perceptions therefore shaded every lesson families taught young sons, and parents began to cultivate desirable qualities in their sons during infancy. Shortly after the birth of his nephew, for example, Charles Harris wrote his brother, Robert, congratulating him on the arrival of a son and reminding him to be sure that his parenting of the baby would "harden both his body and mind for the rough vicissitudes of manhood."[5]

The autonomy parents nurtured in their sons stood in diametric opposition to their (ideally) deferential, docile daughters. Girls learned from childhood to focus their energies on dutifulness, obedience, and care giving, while boys manifested self-determination and autonomy. Boys could no more easily skirt the expectation that they would be bold and active than girls could escape the role of being deferential and compassionate. Boys did different chores from their sisters, reinforcing gender distinctions from the earliest stages of life. Their educations, while similar to their sisters' in early childhood, diverged from and eclipsed that of girls after about age ten. Leisure activities were also gendered, and boys who displayed talents in orations, horseback riding, or other manly pursuits earned the admiration of their kinfolk.[6]

Adults also hoped that sons, early in boyhood, would publicly distinguish themselves by demonstrating precocious exceptionality. Gentry boys could not be ordinary, but needed public validation of their specialness as soon in life as possible. Praise for precocity instilled a strong sense of self-importance in boys. Hoping to chide his brother Peachy toward proper improvement in oratory, Francis Gilmer used himself as an example. A family friend, Francis bragged, "has often told me that when I was 4 years old, I spoke with as much distinctiveness, precision, & even elegance as one of almost any age, & with a flowing sweetness which astounded him." Alfred Mordecai proudly remembered learning to read at age four. Precocity was the rule rather than the exception, and parents sent boys from home at surprisingly young ages to pursue their studies and ready themselves for leadership. John Palmer enrolled in Pineville Academy at age nine and remained there until he moved to South Carolina College the same month he turned fifteen. Daniel Horry was only eleven when he went to England for his formal education.[7]

But boys' specialness, just like their independence, needed to conform to societal norms. As they searched for unique talents in their sons, adults pressed even toddlers toward particular manly attributes. When Kentuckian Joel Lyle described his two young sons, he both affirmed their distinctive personalities and revealed his ambitions for them. Lyle bragged that his namesake "Little Joel" already "knows all his ABCs by his own industry. He gets his book and asks the letters over until he knows them." Son John, meanwhile, seemed reluctant and fearful. He appeared, his father explained, "lazy about commencing a letter to you, I suppose for a fear that he would not succeed well in the attempt." Moreover, this son, unlike young Joel, seemed less than vigorous and forceful—traits his father prized: "I hope he [John] will become more robust and healthy than he has hitherto been." In 1807 South Carolinian Elias Horry wrote thorough descriptions of his two young sons, eight-year-old William and twenty-month-old Thomas, that also suggested the masculine values parents looked for in their young sons. William appeared "very hearty, and improving both in growth and in his Education." Elias boasted of the boy's intellect, physical prowess, and forcefulness: "His mind is strong and retentive. . . . No Boy of his age surpasses him in bodily Strength, but tho' he has a quick temper . . . he is not quarrelsome." The infant Thomas seemed "also very hearty and is certainly a very fine, promising Boy. . . . His features are more delicate than William's, and his Countenance is less Stern—and rather more open. . . . He can say as yet but a few words, but comprehends every thing, and more than the ordinary Children of his age, and delights in being with his Brother and other Boys, and in all kinds of Mischief."[8]

Both the independence and the special talents that parents desired in their sons were intimately linked to the gentry's racial power. Parents like Horry and Lyle bragged about inclinations in their boys that society found estimable in white men—initiative, vitality, accomplishment—while they deplored attributes deemed unmanly and associated with slaves—docility, self-doubt, and reticence. Such qualities seem obviously racialized: slaves acting boldly imperiled the social order whereas white boys appearing timid merited rebuke. In short, what white parents wanted in their sons they feared in their slaves, and vice versa. And no quality mattered more to elite men or stood in starker contrast to the lives of slaves than independence.

To be a man in the eyes of southern elites was to be white, autonomous, and the master of others, and boys learned to communicate that racial authority early in their lives. For example, when directed by a visiting relative to polish his shoes, six-year-old Lucian Fletcher refused: "He says he is no negro to do such work." As young Lucian demonstrated, sons of elite families aspired to be not simply men, but *gentlemen*. To that end, they needed to demonstrate their superiority over slaves as well as non-elite white boys. Certain chores, including polishing shoes, fell beyond the bounds of acceptability. Such attitudes also shaped leisure interactions between boys. Although gentry sons played with slaves and poorer white boys in the community, all parties knew to acknowledge the social hierarchy, their interactions anticipating adulthood.[9] In fact, parents began training their sons in childhood to manage slaves. Relatives often gave comparably aged slaves to their young kin both as playmates and as the means by which to model the adult power dynamics. Some teenage students carried slaves with them to campuses, particularly those in the South.[10]

Daily witnessing the power of race exerted terrific force in the lives of white boys. Whiteness automatically afforded them authority over nonwhites, and, as explained by historian David Roediger, "had a value as property."[11] When boys played with or were attended by slaves, they experienced this power. Watching owners intimidate and whip slaves reinforced the link between color and authority. Because boys learned these lessons experientially and at such young ages, there is scant evidence of it in the available sources. Correspondents and diarists seldom put into words such overt racial identity. It was rather an unspoken assumption, hardened by the routine, even reflexive, exercise of power over African Americans. One clear indication in the evidentiary base, however, is the frequency with which whites described character deficiencies in racial terms. Gentry boys who misbehaved were often described as having "blackened" their reputations. Moreover, slights to their personal autonomy were characterized as "enslavement."

Independence was, then, at once an ideal masculine attribute and a reality, built on elites' domination of slaves. It was essential, in the minds of southern parents, that their boys understand both the importance and the proper style of manly independence. Learning to meet that ideal, of acting autonomously but according to societal expectations, of living independently while being dutiful, was the central struggle in this generation's coming to manhood. The early signs of their progress were not encouraging. The very quality that adults wanted to cultivate worked against them. Elites' zeal for manly independence meant that parents chose to coax, rather than compel, sons. And boys told so often to act independently actually listened to their elders.

The Reality of Raising Saucy Boys

Predictably, southern scions did not always appreciate the nuances of acting independently yet according to strict parameters. Instead, they usually behaved the way they were raised: with a strong sense of self-satisfaction and little inclination toward obedience. Obstreperousness and truculence ran rife among southern gentry sons. Relatives, tutors, and visitors seldom saw an acquiescent boy in the early South. Even George Washington could not control his stepson, John Parke (Jacky) Custis. Jacky's tutor wrote Washington, complaining that he "never did in my life know a youth so exceedingly indolent or so surprisingly voluptuous."[12]

Enthused with young boys' expressions of autonomy, family members, like John Ball's brother, often dismissed concerns about misbehaving young boys and even took pride in their willfulness. South Carolinian Alice Izard maintained that "great excuses are to be made for youthful follies," and she counseled her daughter Margaret Manigault not to worry about her wayward son Harry, because he was very handsome and charming. Alicia Middleton embraced her young boy's cheekiness as well. In 1817, she wrote her son Nathaniel that his younger brother, Izard, having recovered from an illness, "is in very good health, grown quite fat again and . . . is very noisy, and very saucy."[13]

Adults actually seemed surprised at the entirely predictable consequences of allowing boys to be independent, headstrong, and "saucy." When his sons were eleven and nine, George Blow extolled their willfulness and his lenience. He even bragged about how he liked Robert and Richard "to run wild with delight." But just two years later, he complained that he could "do nothing" with the boys and that "Robert's perversity is unmanageable." After Richard and Robert went away to college, the problems increased, and George regretted that the boys acted "too full of their pleasures and amusements." Astounded at his adolescent sons' refusal to follow paternal advice, Blow failed to see how his approach to parenting nearly guaranteed such obstinacy.[14] Blow belonged to the mainstream of southern families, allowing great liberties in his boys and teaching them to be self-governing. Not surprisingly, then, many parents found themselves in George Blow's circumstance: dismayed that fostering self-determination produced unmanageable sons.

When boys took their independence to extremes, relatives struggled to find ways to correct sons without cowing them. For example, Daniel Horry's chronic misbehavior worried his famous relatives, including his grandmother Eliza Lucas Pinckney and uncle Charles Cotesworth Pinckney. Sent to school in

Charleston around age eight, Daniel much preferred to play with "his pets, his puppies, his Possums." His uncle Thomas warned his mother, Harriott, that Daniel spent his time "rioting with all the little dirty Boys in Charles Town" instead of tending to his studies. The family's varied but ultimately ineffectual responses were typical. Daniel's uncle Charles Cotesworth tried positive reinforcements; for even the slightest effort he praised the boy. Grandmother Eliza prodded Daniel to emulate his esteemed uncles. After his father died, Daniel's relatives tried to embarrass him into living up to the elder Horry's legacy. Nothing worked. The older Daniel got, the less he listened to his kinfolk.[15] As the Horry case indicates, although deeply concerned about boys' future reputations in southern society, adults proved reluctant to force sons to act suitably. Instead, they preferred to try to inspire dutifulness while allowing independence.

Commanding correct behavior through physical force or threats (not coincidentally the lynchpins of slave mastery) simply did not fit with southern family values. Slaves, not future patriarchs, were commanded, threatened, and physically compelled to action. Force was racialized in the ethics of southern elites, and was thus an inappropriate tactic for rearing white children. As Virginian Ralph Wormeley put it, he wanted his son Warner to be "led by silken cords, not driven; induced, not compelled." John Ball Sr. taught by word and deed that boys needed to be won over to reputable behavior. After asking his eldest son to correspond with his younger brothers, John Sr. suggested that John Jr. point out any epistolary mistakes "with mildness, so as rather to encourage than disgust them from writing to you in future." Of course, as boys got older and more out of control, adults sometimes applied a firmer hand. When Warner Wormeley proved chronically truculent, his father reluctantly decided that "if gentle methods, and mild parental exhortation will not [work], contrary to my nature, other means must be adopted."[16] "Other means" (such as reproach, rejection, and threats of disinheritance) were never the first or best options, however.

Negotiation, not deference and force, became the preferred approach to rearing southern sons. Letters to and from young men provide ample evidence of this give-and-take pattern. As boys left home to attend school, relatives wrote extensively, even exhaustively, to them, but those letters almost never struck a demanding tone. Like many fathers, Edward Rutledge was loath to dictate to his son. Instead, he rationalized why son Henry should follow his counsel rather than demanding he do so. At the close of a long advisory letter, Rutledge added, "I hope you will not think I have said too much. If you should be inclined to differ with me on this point—recollect that I have had the advantage of great experience," and he reminded him that "the experience and observation of an affectionate Father, transmitted to an admired Son, is sometimes the fairest part of his inheritance."[17] Thomas Jefferson's letters likewise typified the tenor of writings to boys. While taking great interest in Peter Carr and providing extensive advice from his nephew's childhood through his settlement in a career, Jefferson never commanded. In 1783, he wrote the thirteen-year-old boy, "You are now old enough to know how very important to your future life will be the manner in which you employ your present time. I hope therefore you will never waste a moment." Sixteen months later Peter thanked his uncle for that and the other "good advice" he provided, which Peter intended to follow. Clearly, however, both uncle and nephew viewed Jefferson's remarks as advice, not enforceable demands.[18]

Unwilling to force boys to behave properly, adults turned to guilt as a favorite motivational tactic. Martha Ramsay encouraged her son's diligence in school by reminding him that the family had forgone saving for their daughters' weddings to fund David's education. He thus owed his sisters and parents a solid performance. In order to get her son Robert to write more frequently, Elizabeth Peyton asked him whether he "forgot that he has a father, mother & sister who are all anxious to hear from him. . . . Your long silence has created in me a thousand fears for your health, which can only be dissipated by a letter from you." Calling up the memories of deceased ancestors, especially fathers, was a common variation on this guilt tactic. Roger Pinckney's benefactor invoked the boy's late father to prompt Roger toward honorable behavior: "Embrace it as part of your Inheritance & practice it thro' Reverence to the Character of so good a Man as your Father." John E. Colhoun Jr. also lost his father as a child, and a family friend similarly reminded him that his late father "left a highly honored name behind him; and left too a duty on his sons to emulate his course & to uphold that name."[19]

Relatives also straightened out chronically naughty boys by threatening the withdrawal of affection, which could be heartrending to youngsters. Alicia Middleton manipulated her son with this tactic before he was even ten years old. When he visited relatives, she reminded Nathaniel to write every week, or "we shall think you have forgotten us all, and do not want to come back to us."[20] Boys who failed to honor their kinfolks' wishes knew that they risked family censure. And parents followed through on these threats if boys continued to disappoint. While never a first resort, it proved quite effective in rare cases. After John Jones's father threatened to expel him from the family home, the boy confessed his overwhelming grief: "Language grows feeble in attempting to express the emotions of my soul. To have incurred the displeasure of a Father [would] have been sufficient[,] but to hear him utter those words clutched my heart in a manner ever unknown before."[21]

Families seemed reluctant to go much further than using appeals, guilt, or manipulation at the early stages of a boy's life. Moreover, because of their belief in manly independence, adults saw limits to what they could be expected to accomplish with individual boys. If sons determined to squander their potential and abrogate societal norms, that choice was ultimately theirs. Adults therefore felt responsible for launching sons, but not accountable for all the choices that boys made. William Cumming reminded his father of the limits of his responsibilities: "If one of them [your children] by the waywardness of fortune or nature adopts a course you can not approve; the consciousness of having fulfilled every parental duty should at least console you. Every duty you have fully performed. You have given me sentiments of honour & an education which if they can not confer happiness enable me to bear the privation. You gave me ample pecuniary means & were willing to give more. . . . What more you could have done I am unable to conceive. My errors are on my own head." Sarah Gibbes offered a similar assessment of parental responsibilities and their limits: "As parents let us perform our duty: and should we be so unfortunate as to see our Children not prove so good . . . yet let our conscience acquit us[,] let us have the heartfelt satisfaction to say we have fulfill'd our part."[22]

The attitudes of fathers played a particularly critical, and not always helpful, part in shaping the "self-willed" spirit of southern sons. Public obligations frequently called prominent politicians and professionals away from their homes and left them only sporadically engaged in rearing pre-adolescent boys. William Wirt, for instance, focused so much energy on career advancements and providing for his household that virtually all other parenting responsibilities besides the fiduciary fell to his wife Elizabeth. John Eppes and his second wife were both too busy to spend Christmas with his twelve-year-old son Francis, who resided at a boarding school. A year and a half later, little had changed. John wrote his son, "I have been so much occupied in the election that I have not had an opportunity of writing to you for some time."[23] Even fathers who could be around their children assumed that their parenting duties really commenced as sons approached adolescence. Consider the case of Robert Carter, whose wife died in 1803 and left him with four children, the oldest only seven. Rather than raising them himself, the widower traveled to London to pursue medical studies and left the children with Virginia relatives. He loved the children very much, but he felt his obligation was not to tending to toddlers but to pursuing a better career "that I might render myself more useful to you at an age when you stand more in need of me." Mothers, then, fulfilled the primary child-rearing roles before the teen years, when fathers took the lead.[24]

When boys reached adolescence and fathers decided to involve themselves in shepherding them toward manhood, they discovered their sons well versed, even reveling in their independence. The teenage years proved a less than ideal time to check boys' autonomy. That fathers often wanted to be friends as much as parents further weakened their authority. John Grimké asked his son to "consider me as your friend, as well as Father." John Ball Sr. wanted the same relationship: "Write to me with the freedom of a friend, as well as with the duty and respect due from a son to a father."[25] How exactly sons should parse this, the fathers left unexplained. But such language surely added to boys' notions of self-importance and autonomy. So too did the desires of fathers to, whenever possible, avoid conflict with their sons.[26] Patriarchs did not want to advertise their lack of influence over their children, and they really did believe in the value of boyhood autonomy, so while often frustrated and anxious, fathers only reluctantly rebuked sons and rarely quarreled with them publicly.

Most southern families ultimately produced the autonomous and confident sons they desired, but that independence was not always performed according to adult expectations. Certainly some southern boys navigated the demands of dutifulness, autonomy, family devotion, attention to reputation, and preparation for leadership. Others worked to merit their relatives' love and attention, but felt every bit as anxious as their kinfolk about their prospects. Birthdays, by providing a natural time for boys to evaluate their progress (or lack thereof) toward manhood, seemed particularly angst ridden. On his eighteenth birthday, for example, John Palmer wrote a reflective letter to his mother in which he admitted he saw no cause for optimism: "I have arrived at an age when youth begins to think on what they have done and what they must do. I look back and discover a life of almost useless inactivity. I look forward and anxiety clouds my anticipation."[27] More commonly, boys in this cohort appeared cocksure and entitled, or, to use John Ball's words, "spoiled, or self willed."

Boys who met familial expectations often demanded and got recompense. When ten-year-old John Ramsey learned his catechism, his family bought him his first saddle as a reward. After passing his exams at Princeton in the 1780s, John Randolph notified his mother, "I expect the watch you promised me." Boys learned as much from adults who were not above bribing them to act right. When trying to coax his lackadaisical nephew William Hart into better attention to his studies, Seaborn Jones promised William that if "you continue to progress in your learning, you shall be more and more indulged with what you may want."[28]

Southern sons often exhibited early in boyhood the arrogance, self-indulgence, and violence that critics considered hallmarks of their region. Outside observers, especially teachers who tried to train these boys, routinely blamed the deplorable behavior of gentry sons on permissive parents. South Carolina College president Thomas Cooper and Yale president Timothy Dwight commiserated about "the parental indulgence to the South," which derailed their efforts to educate boys. Azel Backus, a tutor for the Rutledge family, warned John Rutledge that his twelve-year-old son Robert seemed particularly spoiled: "He has acted to my view as if he expected to be little handsome Robert Rutledge forever . . . that his father & friends would be immortal supports . . . [and] that he had nothing to trouble himself about but to learn to dance & get a few Chesterfieldian airs, and be carried in a bandbox to all the Balls, Bath & Theatres of the World."[29] Backus was one of the many northern young men who traveled south to tutor on plantations and recorded their antipathy toward overly tolerant parents and their undisciplined sons. Amos Kendall failed abysmally in his efforts to tutor Theodore and Thomas Clay. At the ages of thirteen and twelve, the brothers appeared to Kendall as too indulged by their parents and suffering from neglected educations. (Kendall rightly predicted that nothing good would come of these Clay boys.)[30] While less condemnatory than visitors, some southerners reluctantly acknowledged these same concerns. Martha Laurens Ramsay, for example, worried about the materialism encouraged by southern society and absorbed by boys. She chastised her son David for appearing "to wish at least to be *richer* than your father and mother, without caring whether you are as wise or as good." Jane Ball also feared that her sons Isaac and William had been "brought up too much in the lap of indulgence" and "their mind is quite occupied with trifles."[31]

Slaveholding not only created the wealth and power of this class of boys but also shaped their "self willed" attitudes. Americans, North and South, recognized that slavery exerted an insidious effect on the character of white children. Surrounded by slaves and the violence necessary to command them, boys in particular grew lazy, arrogant, and cruel. Timothy Ford, a visitor to South Carolina in the 1780s, reported that among elites "every body must have a vast deal of waiting upon from the oldest to the youngest." Slaves constantly attended to children, "& whenever the whim takes it the servant is dispatched on its service." Ford concluded that "the multiplicity of servants & attendance" explained the "dronish ease & torpid inactivity which are so justly attributed to the people of the Southern States, accustomed to have every thing done for them they cannot or will not do anything for themselves." Ebenezer Hazard also complained that the sons of slaveholders never forgot the lessons of entitlement and violence they learned in childhood: "Accustomed to tyrannize from their infancy, they carry with them a disposition to treat all mankind in the same manner they have been used to treat their Negroes." Even southerners committed to and enriched by slavery occasionally admitted that witnessing the mastery of slaves corrupted boys. In Jefferson's oft-quoted words, slavery taught white children "perpetual exercise of the most boisterous passions."[32] As these sons came of age, their early experiences with slave mastery continued to shape their attitudes and behaviors. In time, this generation would shift from lamenting the insidious effects of slaveholding to defending the South's racial order and come to understand how thoroughly their identity as men depended on dominion over slaves. But first, they had to navigate the arduous process of becoming men and figure how to balance dutifulness with autonomy.

In the early years of their lives, these southern sons enjoyed exercising their independence and following their inclinations. At the same time, male children saw that they had to learn to lead their families and honor the Republic. Boys carried these foundational values with them, along with their velvet waistcoats and copies of Euclid, when they left home to attend college and begin the first real test of manhood. For sons, the full expression of independence was about to commence. For parents, the real "anxiety of mind" lay just ahead.

PART TWO

GENTLEMEN AND SCHOLARS

CHAPTER THREE

The Educational Aspirations
of Southern Families

In 1808, as he sent his son Charles to William and Mary College, Supreme Court Justice and Kentuckian Thomas Todd described the possibilities and perils of university education:

> This my dear Son is the golden period for improvement, the succeeding four years, will be the most important to you, in the course of your whole life, you are now laying the foundation on which your future prospects thro life depend, the more solid the foundation, the greater certainty in supporting & rearing the superstructure. This period is to form your character—habits of industry & study are now easily acquired and pursued, which will become familiar & easy & last you forever—If on the contrary; you now neglect them, you fall into idleness, which begats sloth, that engenders dissipation & finally all energy of thought, of Character, & of respectability is forever gone, no exertion can produce a reformation and you will sink into contempt & misery.[1]

A generation of white southern boys, sent to colleges and universities in the early Republic to become men, received similar admonitions from their nervous relatives.

Family ambition combined with civic-mindedness to fuel these anxieties. Americans North and South took great pride in the accomplishments of the founding generation. The valor of Americans during the Revolutionary War was, in popular perceptions, matched only by the virtue of citizens after peace. But the rising generation left many Americans feeling skeptical. Could boys born to the generation after the founders live up to the high standards set by their fathers? Would they be faithful stewards of the Republic?

Americans turned to formal education to answer these questions: education, they decided, would help ensure the worthiness of the next generation of men and thereby protect the future of the Republic.[2] In 1805 South Carolinian Henry DeSaussure captured this sentiment perfectly: "We have lost a few of our venerable men, the remains of the revolution—By degrees they are removed, and a new generation occupy the stage of life. . . . [T]he diffusion of education gives the hope that we shall have able & worthy men for every department of government." Such beliefs in the power of education to produce proper heirs to the Revolution transcended regional boundaries. In an essay on education in the Republic, Benjamin Rush argued for the creation of a federal university that would "convert men into republican machines" capable of cooperating together with "their parts properly in the great machine of the government of the state." University of Georgia founder Abraham Baldwin similarly linked education to national interests, and he believed that the University of Georgia could mold boys "in a manner honorable to their Country and to the general advantage of mankind."[3]

Southerners saw college as the first real test of a boy's ability to be known as a man and respected as a republican. Because of their enthusiasm for manly independence, adults offered advice but allowed students to make their own (often terrible) choices. Gabriel Manigault worried so much about the friendship his son formed with Pinckney Horry, a notoriously dissipated South Carolinian, he passed information he collected in South Carolina to his son's guardian in Europe. Yet as much as he hoped his son would form more reputable connections, Gabriel Manigault viewed the friendship as an important test: "We cannot expect that my Son is to escape bad examples. He must be exposed to them, as he must be to various kinds of temptation. If he has good sense he will escape them. They may even be a service. . . . I will caution him about this young man, & that being all that can be done, we must hope for the best." Richard Beresford put things more bluntly: "Much of the success attendant upon Education depends upon the Knowledge of the Student's Character; even his vices may be productive of valuable Ends, corrupted Substances may form a rich Manure."[4]

Unfortunately, manure abounded. High-minded ideals about educating boys for their own advancement and the preservation of the Republic collided with southerners' dedication to youthful autonomy. Although convinced that injudicious students would do themselves irreparable harm, adults felt bound to indulge their sons' independence. Relatives monitored choices about finances, studies, friends, and behavior but ultimately left decision-making to teenage students. For their parts, college students enjoyed great liberties but exercised them under close adult scrutiny and, their kinfolk continuously reminded them, with profound consequences.

Education in the New Nation

Changes in the economy, values, and especially the political culture in the young nation made Americans put greater stock in formal education than ever before. The Enlightenment stressed individual effort in the acquisition of knowledge for the improvement of society and placed a premium on education. The American Revolution advanced an ideology of personal rights and self-determination and challenged lineage and class entitlement. And the transition to a market economy in the early nineteenth century reinforced this cultural trend toward individualism and competitiveness.[5] In the colonial era, a man's family name and his inherited wealth assured his social status and his claim to political power. Only the wealthiest of Americans received a formal education, and most traveled to Europe for their schooling. Attendance at university, while signifying a man's refinement and worldliness, was by no means a requirement for inclusion in the colonial gentry.

In the early Republic, however, much of that changed. While family and class still played important roles in social standing, they no longer guaranteed a man's position. Instead, men needed to prove their worthiness by competing with others for power and wealth. Future leadership still required the right gender and race (and, in the South, lineage), but individual initiative, of the sort that formally educated men manifested, also became ever more important. Writing a young cousin in 1809, St. George Tucker explained how the rising generation's status would depend on individual talent and hard work: "If there was a period in the History of Man which demonstrated the necessity of a Man's being able to place his reliance on *Himself*, the last thirty years may be considered as furnishing the most awful and instructive Lessons upon that Head."[6] Education allowed boys to ready themselves for the duties of manhood and citizenship in the young Republic.

Southern families, no less than their northern counterparts, infused their educational ambitions with admiration for and duty to the nation. In the years after American Independence, many parents associated Europe with decadence, which they juxtaposed against the virtues of America. Thus they concluded that a more appropriate education could be found at home, in the United States. In 1785, Thomas Jefferson articulated the perceptions of many proud citizens when he contended that "of all the errors which can possibly be committed in the education of youth, that of sending them to Europe is the most fatal." (Jefferson insisted that no man under thirty should even go to Europe!)[7] Moreover, since Americans believed that the success of their republican experiment required an educated, virtuous citizenry, colleges and universities represented important centers for teaching national responsibilities. As one southern educator explained, America triumphed because of "principles and accomplishments established in the minds of her sons, rather than in her property and external resources." The United States could persist only by instilling those same values in each succeeding generation through education. Inculcation of those national ethics must begin in youth, since "there is no place in which the forming hand of Society may be more conspicuous than upon their youth, and more thoroughly pervade and insinuate itself into every part."[8]

Southern elites expected formal education to turn their boys into self-conscious and eminent Americans. When, for example, wealthy South Carolinian John Ball Jr. headed off to Harvard in 1798, his parents urged him to conduct himself so that the Ball family would be respected and "your country will be ornamented by you." Fellow Carolinian Ralph Izard similarly longed to see "my Sons so educated as to afford me a prospect of their being Men of abilities, & honour, & their becoming useful, valuable Citizens of their Country." And Virginian Daniel Guerrant urged his younger brother to excel in his studies for the same reasons: "We hail the day when you will return to your native soil, aquiting yourself with honor at School and qualified to render Services to your Country."[9]

Beyond their republican ambitions, politics did not play a significant role in shaping parents' educational choices. In the first place, political tensions were not especially pronounced among southern elites. Moreover, parents believed that if they raised the right kind of man, he would make proper political choices. Likewise, religion rarely influenced parents in the schools they selected or the lessons they wanted instilled. Parents certainly knew about the denominational origins of most American universities, but the religious affiliations or leanings of those schools seldom informed the educational plans of the southern gentry until after the 1820s.[10] Making their sons into respectable republican leaders occupied their energies instead.

Since the most prestigious American universities were in northern states, southern boys traveled there to pursue their patriotic, manly educations in the decades of the 1790s and 1800s. Harvard, Yale, and Princeton attracted students from throughout the nation. The University of Pennsylvania medical school supplanted schools in Edinburgh and London as the most popular choice for American students. John Ball Sr. selected Harvard for his namesake because the school enjoyed the finest reputation in the young United States and because he wanted his son "educated in America upon patriotic principles." Marylanders Rosalie and George Calvert also chose Harvard for their eldest son because it "is, according to everybody, the best university in America." Students felt proud of attending such renowned schools. South Carolinian and Harvard student John Colhoun Jr., for example, proclaimed, "I have every reason to rejoice that I came here[,] for this *University* is without exception far superior to any *College* in the United States."[11]

Southern Exceptions

Despite their strong identification with the Republic, southern elites also held several regionally distinctive ideas that distinguished their sons' schooling from that of northern boys. To begin with, they remained deeply committed to protecting their place at the head of society, and they used education to ensure their power. Formal schooling remained the prerogative of southern elites in the early Republic, while the proliferation of opportunities for acquiring knowledge in the North—in academies and military schools and through apprenticeships— more thoroughly democratized manly power there. That is, as more northerners of the middling and lower ranks educated themselves, they enjoyed status as men and citizens. Middle-class self-made manhood, predicated on individual initiative and improvement, predominated in the North. Southerners modified this emphasis, touting individual preparation and education but retaining a tight elite monopoly over higher learning.[12]

During the early national era, northerners and southerners also diverged in their calculation of the balance between image and accomplishment in deter- mining a man's position in society. Middle-class northerners typically educated their sons for careers that would ensure their economic viability and social respectability. Since these upwardly mobile men would need to work for a living, professional proficiency was essential. In the minds of southern aristocrats, con- versely, the ultimate value of a university education derived from its capacity to promote public status. Intellectual edification, although a useful consequence, was seldom the primary purpose of attending college. Southerners emphasized the reputation enjoyed rather than the knowledge acquired by a man of educa- tion, and they prized preparation for future leadership more than scholastics. In short, southern elites sent their boys to college to become manly. For instance, when Richard Bennehan made plans to attend his son's public examinations at Chapel Hill in 1795, rather than anticipating a display of the fourteen-year-old's mastery of Greek and Latin, he hoped "to find you in perfect health & more of a Man than I have ever yet seen you." Georgian Edward Harden similarly ex- plained to his namesake, a new student at the University of Georgia: "You have now entered college—it is an important crisis in your life, and from it you may date the commencement of your manhood." And when reflecting on his studies at a Parisian military academy, George Izard valued that experience because it marked a milestone in his coming to manhood: "At Metz, I began to feel that I was what I had hitherto only affected to be, a man."[13]

Although southern parents calculated education more in reputational than in intellectual terms, perhaps appearing more superficial than northern parents, they felt no less anxious about the test confronting their boys. Ralph Izard, for one, felt it vital for his son to understand: "This is the time of Life, in which by proper, or improper management, the foundation will be laid for his becoming either a very useful, & valuable Member of Society, or the contrary." Southerners repeatedly wrote to students explaining the necessity of using their time at college to ensure future success as genteel men. John Eppes warned his seventeen-year-old son Francis to remember that college was the place to mold himself into a man: "The next five years of your life will be the most important—On the manner in which you employ them must depend your future station in society." Charles Goldsborough strongly advocated his cousin Henry Harrington's attendance at a college, for such an education would enable Henry to "become a useful and valuable member of society . . . [and provide] a fair opportunity of gratifying his honorable ambition by improving and enlarging his mind."[14] In these directives, which typified advisory letters to southern sons, the counsel appears vague— future status, value to society, a broadened mind—rather than specific to a base of knowledge or career preparation, which predominated in northerners' letters to college boys.

The infrequency with which southerners discussed academics is striking. Most concentrated on writing about the social contacts their young relatives formed and their grace in society instead of ideas and skills. Kinfolk almost uniformly encouraged boys to, in the words of Virginian Sterling Ruffin, "be not only attentive to your books, but particularly so to your manners." While Marylander Richard Hopkins studied medicine in the 1780s, his cousin noted that learning could be pleasant, distracting, and conducive to a gentlemanly reputation. But, he warned, "books dont do alone," and he urged the young man to devote himself to mastering social skills. Virginian Theodorick Bland went even further, concluding that "the Paltry Jargon of schools constitute the smallest part of a Gent[leman']s Education."[15]

The assessments made of students and schools provide added confirmation that southern elites valued reputation over the practical dimensions of education. Arthur Morson's guardian at school reported to the boy's father, Alexander

Morson, that young Arthur thrived: "[Arthur] continues to merit the esteem & confidence of the faculty . . . his deportment is amiable & manly & his progress in his studies such as to compensate you for your expence & the loss of his society." Although studies appeared last on his list, Arthur's guardian at least mentioned academics among the boy's accomplishments. Many other southern elites ignored scholastics. Alice Izard went so far as to complain that northern schools paid too much attention to academic matters at the expense of refinement: "The Graces are not cultivated, nor even those elegant manly plays, & exercises which developes [*sic*] the human figure advantageously."[16]

There were, to be certain, occasional exceptions to this pattern. Some fathers did direct sons to master skills practical to running the plantations and businesses they stood to inherit. Attention to finances particularly concerned planters training their successors. John Ball Sr. wanted his namesake to understand that "there is perhaps no one branch of your Education that will be so usefull to you through life as that of a perfect & quick knowledge of figures." Richard Bennehan seconded John Ball's emphasis on arithmetic. He advised his son Thomas to study mathematics in order to succeed in future business affairs. John Ball Sr. also complimented his son's decision to study anatomy, for it too would enable John Jr. to manage family "assets." According to John Sr., if a man understood basic medical skills he could care for his slaves with less expense and greater ease.[17]

Moreover, up-and-coming families, particularly those from the interior states of Tennessee and Kentucky, tended to show more interest in academics than did established tidewater elites. The early migrants to the southern frontier, like their northern contemporaries, knew that their sons could not necessarily fall back on land and slaves and would need to rely on their own training to make a living.[18] These Kentucky and Tennessee families wrote more frequently and specifically about academic matters, and their boys often sent home descriptions of their coursework and routines. Some even provided hourly breakdowns of their schedules. For example, Kentuckian George Corlis mailed his father a description of his daily activities and lectures attended while studying medicine in New York. Kentuckian Charles Thruston similarly kept his father apprised of his progress through Cicero and Horace. Later, when he moved to West Point, Charles continued this close accounting of his class work, explaining to his family back home precisely what he learned in geometry and how much he read in Euclid.[19] But as the number of families able to claim gentry status in the interior South expanded after the turn of the nineteenth century, the values of these parents and the behaviors of their boys increasingly replicated those of their tidewater contemporaries. The wealthier the family, the greater the attention paid to refined education. Henry Clay, for example, who surpassed the accomplishments and matched the wealth of many tidewater gentlemen, duplicated the attitudes of his coastal peers when he tried to educate his sons. The more that elites in Kentucky and Tennessee, like Clay, acquired the values of coastal gentlemen, the closer they paralleled their educational expectations.

Throughout the early national South elite men's passion for independence—deriving from their class and racial power—altered their sons' educational experiences. Even though adults vigilantly counseled students, they rarely interceded in boys' lives at college. For example, when Virginian Thomas Armstrong cautioned his son Martin against improper friendships and leisure pursuits, he quickly added: "I don't wish to be understood as forbidding innocent amusements, which are perhaps necessary for the health of the body, and the recreation of the mind. But I wish to inculcate that you avoid such practices that you would in your own sober judgment condemn in others." Of course, egregious inattention to educational standards raised the ire of parents because it belittled familial sacrifices and portended weak character in boys. Virginian Ralph Wormeley complained that, despite many years and much money expended educating his son, the boy remained ignorant of basic spelling and grammar. John Grimké reluctantly chastised his dilatory son Henry: "I am sorry to observe such an apathy, such a disinclination to read or to any thing like study, that I cannot pass it over with silence, but I must endeavour to fix your attention on it."[20] But adults extended great latitude to gentry sons. Only repeated and grossly aberrant behavior provoked such rebukes—and rebukes were about as far as any parent was willing to go. Southerners shared Thomas Armstrong's priorities: they ultimately wanted their sons to make their own, good choices at college, thereby exercising the autonomy that their definition of manhood required.

While kin provided extensive counsel, they hammered away at the necessity of individual effort. Like many other southern fathers, John Haywood devoted himself to providing each of his sons a good education, reminding the teens that their efforts in college would surely "avail you when you become Men." But he also acknowledged the limits of his money and advice: "As to the rest, it must depend on themselves." Boys heard such directives often enough that many parroted the language back to their kin. While attending the University of Virginia, Richard Watkins assured his father that he understood the necessity of personal initiative: "If I do not now make good use of those advantages, which you have so kindly bestowed on me . . . the whole fault rests upon my own shoulders—Rest satisfied that you have done your part."[21]

When they wrote about their sons' self-determination, southern elites absolutely did not mean that boys could behave any way they liked. Personal accomplishments or failures echoed beyond the reputations of individual boys, altering the prospects of families. So at the same time that they encouraged autonomy, older kin religiously reminded young men that the future of their families depended on their reputations. This intensified emphasis on responsibility and diligence left young men nonplussed. Given their first chance to live the independence they learned in boyhood, adolescents found themselves inundated by appeals for duty and assiduousness. Under the sudden scrutiny (but not the authority) of relatives, boys were expected to balance family duty with personal autonomy and learn how to exercise restrained independence. Relatives, meanwhile, struggled to teach family duty without compromising manly autonomy.

Parental Tactics

Compelling obedience, through manipulation, force, or threats, was not an option for southern gentry parents. Submission was a highly racialized trait in the minds of southern elites, and tactics reserved for dominating chattel were antithetical to rearing white sons. Future patriarchs learned *to* command, never *by* command. So in their quest to raise autonomous yet respectable men, gentry families relied on inspiration rather than coercion. Furthermore, parents found it necessary to seek the help of kin and friends as they tried to entice their often errant boys to behave responsibly and respectably.

The proving ground of college afforded southern parents numerous opportunities to test sons' decision-making skills as well as their own abilities to coach rather than dictate. Parent-child correspondence over money provides a revealing look at parental values concerning the education of sons. Many parents used college allowances to teach sons about and test them on money matters. Boys often oversaw all their funds for the academic year, reporting on their expenses in letters back home. Such record keeping gave sons practice for future financial responsibilities, and by checking those expenditures fathers encouraged fiscal conscientiousness. Parents and guardians adopted the same attitude toward academic matters, allowing students liberty in choices in order to test their decision-making abilities. In a letter from his mother, Princeton student and South Carolinian John Gibbes learned that he should determine the length and course of his studies: "We put so full a confidence that you will most certainly act for the most advantage for Yourself; that we leave it to yr. opinion." Georgian John Stacy echoed those same sentiments in a letter to his son: "I have no wish to control you in staying or returning, and I feel unwilling to advise . . . as you are of sufficient age to exercise reason in forming a judgment of the conduct you ought to pursue, I am willing to leave it to your own discretion & free choice." Young men characteristically enjoyed the prerogative of determining their living arrangements as well. Relatives felt obligated not only to encourage such independence but also to fund all reasonable choices. Like many other fathers of college students, George Jones left educational decisions in the hands of his son, while requesting only, "Let me know your determination as soon as possible that I may make you the necessary remittances."[22]

If students made bad choices, parents counseled and complained, but seldom went any further toward correction. When, in September 1808 Charles Todd had still not informed his father about the outcome of his July examinations, Thomas Todd chided the William and Mary student. But reluctant to take any real action, he impotently complained that if Charles failed at school "my pride will be wounded."[23] Like many other fathers, Todd wanted his son to be respectable and responsible but declined giving force to his words. Most parents, despite their attentiveness and anxieties, neither would nor could exert their will over boys studying great distances from home. Those few adults willing to issue commands typically found them unproductive, as boys simply ignored them.

Guilt was the favored tool of parents seeking to influence sons away at college. John Grimké provides an illuminating example. Upon learning of his son Henry's suspension from college, John traveled to the school to appeal for the boy's readmission. Reminding Henry of those efforts, John Grimké wrote: "I shall think but lightly of all the bodily trouble & fatigue, great as it was, at so inclement a season of the year, & through such dreadful roads, which I underwent" so long as Henry returned to college. Some correspondents even intimated that filial irresponsibility could imperil the health of loved ones. While John Stacy left it to his namesake to decide whether he remained in school, he was not above using guilt over the boy's ailing mother to encourage a return home: "Her anxiety of mind [about young John] may be a disadvantage to her in her weak state of health." And George Jones explained that his son's successes would "afford me very great pleasure . . . [and] lessen the pangs of death."[24]

Although not always so dramatic, family members regularly reminded college boys of the sacrifices they made on their behalf. George Swain explained to his son David that funding his education would "give me a considerable scuffle," but that David's hard work would make the sacrifice worthwhile. Similarly, Martha and David Ramsay struggled financially throughout the early national period, but they fully funded their son's education at Princeton. Martha maintained that David Jr.'s prospects depended on securing a gentleman's education, and she would bear any burden, financial or emotional, to properly launch him into manhood.[25] Reminders of the emotional costs parents paid in parting with beloved sons likewise reinforced calls for filial dutifulness. George Jones insisted that in sending his son to Princeton he felt "a severe conflict between affection and duty." Alice Izard also dreaded living apart from her youngest son, Ralph Izard Jr., and reconciled herself to their separation only because "my reason is satisfied that he is better where he is."[26]

Relatives begged boys not to engage in behaviors that betrayed their sacrifices. The prominent North Carolina planter Charles Pettigrew, for example, beseeched his teenage sons: "Don't disgrace your *father* & render abortive the pains he has taken to make you useful[,] *praise-worthy* & immitable characters . . . [do] not be *triflers*, but men in respect to close application to your studies,— men in prudence,—men in patience and christian benevolence." John Randolph insisted that he lost sleep worrying about his young relative Theodore Dudley. Randolph regretted his own educational limitations, and he implored the boy to take another path. Adopting a typically deferential tone, Randolph asked Dudley, "Will you accept a little of my experience, instead of buying some of your own at a very dear rate?"[27]

Adults continued to rely on these tactics even in the face of chronic youthful disobedience. Georgian Seaborn Jones, for his part, tried mightily and failed utterly to prompt his nephew William Hart to pursue his studies. After six years of study at the Richmond Academy, William remained unprepared to enter a university. Seaborn insisted that most boys readied themselves within two years, and he felt stymied: "How . . . am I to account for your unaccountable backwardness?" Reluctantly, he could only conclude that his nephew was "addicted to idleness, play, and obstinacy."[28] But for Jones, as for most benefactors of southern students, diagnosing the problem proved much easier than remedying it. Unwilling to disinherit the boy or to deny him future educational opportunities, Seaborn Jones could only complain and ask his nephew to try to improve. John Ball Jr. fared no better with his wayward half brothers. Exasperated with their extravagance and truculence, he complained that he sent the three teenagers to school to "become useful & respectable citizens . . . but of this I hear nothing or a syllable of your improvement, but an incessant call for money accompanied by the most unbecoming threats." But even he felt bound to continue to subsidize the boys' bad choices, which included abandoning schools, drunkenness, and squandering enormous sums of money.[29]

Although occasionally relatives felt pushed toward more drastic actions, such as threatening disinheritance, few chose to give force to their words. Southern patriarchs' reputations were bound up in the behaviors of the members of their households, and the future of southern families depended on sons. So financially cutting off boys compromised a father's status as well as a family's prospects. Virginian John McDowell demonstrated the hollowness of this ultimate threat. After quarrelling with his son about the boy's "impertinence and undutiful conduct toward me," McDowell confessed to his brother, "Although I threatened to withdraw my Patronage from him if he did not mind I will furnish him with money to complete his Education."[30]

Choosing advice, guilt, and pleas over coercion, parents of college students found it beneficial to collaborate with relatives and friends. Fathers generally oversaw the guidance of young students, but they seldom worked alone. Southerners had a long history of emotional and practical reliance on siblings and kin, and these relatives actively participated in the education of southern sons. Kentuckian and doctor William Short took responsibility for helping his nephew through medical school. South Carolinian John Rutledge oversaw the education of his wife's half-brothers, Robert and William Smith. Spier Whitaker, of Halifax County, North Carolina, supported his brother, Matthew Whitaker, while Matthew studied medicine in Baltimore. Matthew's cousin, Cary Whitaker, also encouraged the medical student to work hard and show his respect for the Whitaker family.[31] Siblings in particular provided support and encouragement to their brothers as they pursued higher education. The North Carolina Mordecais provide a revealing example of the sibling bond in action. These sisters and brothers wrote each other regular, copious letters, encouraging, cajoling, and chastising one another when necessary.[32] In some cases, the early death of a father necessitated greater intercession by siblings and kin. In others, business and politics distracted fathers who shared son-rearing duties with other relatives. But generally the aid given to fathers as they shepherded their sons toward manhood was simply a part of southern family values.

Since those networks of kin could reach only so far, parents sometimes sought out guardians, who provided additional guidance to boys attending distant universities. Living in closer proximity to the student, a local guardian ideally acted as a surrogate father. Alexander Morson asked a friend in New Haven to look out for his son Arthur as the boy studied at Yale and to "advise, council & direct him on all occasions, as you would your own Son . . . [and] in every want act towards him as a Father." And Ralph Izard promised his friend Edward Rutledge that if Rutledge sent his son to New York to school, Ralph would "pay the same attention to him, as to my own Son. . . . The education of a Son is certainly an object of the first magnitude."[33]

At the very least, parents hoped, guardians might keep students from the worst mistakes. When Ralph Izard's son George studied in London, Ralph sought out a guardian because he suspected that "if he is left to his own Master without restraint, at his age, he would be exposed to probable ruin." Indeed, George got into plenty of trouble even under the care of a guardian. In 1793, Ralph Izard apologized for the aggravation George caused: "I am sensible that you must have a good deal of trouble about him, for which I am much obliged to you, & which I would prevent if I could." While both men seemed unable to convince the boy to behave, Izard asked the guardian to persist, fearing things might get even worse. Thomas Todd felt the same way about his son, William and Mary student Charles, who resented the idea of a guardian: "You are young & inexperienced—at a very considerable distance from me, and of your near relations—entering on scenes of life new and fascinating—to form an acquaintance among Strangers and in fact at the time when you are to form the Character which is to support you thro life—I should have been devoid of Affection, nay of common prudence . . . had I omitted such precautions."[34]

The case of William Page and Benjamin Cater of Georgia demonstrates how seriously guardians took their duties and how difficult that obligation could be. Georgian William Page assumed guardianship over Benjamin Cater when the boy's father died. The first hints of trouble came in 1812, when a friend of Page's informed him that Cater wanted to transfer to a boarding school where "the boys are uncontrolled and do pretty much as they please." Over the next few years, Page struggled with the teenager's fiscal extravagance and chronic truculence as he tried to raise Cater "as I would my own Child." Page felt exasperated upon learning that Cater charged coats that he resold to classmates for pocket money; but he was mortified to hear the teenager had impregnated a servant in his boarding house. Endless appeals to Cater's duty to his family and his future standing in society went unheeded; Page struggled with the boy for years before Cater's repeated career failures led him to give up on the young man.[35] As poor Page's tale reveals, guardians, like relatives, encouraged good choices, scrutinized behavior, and reminded students of their responsibilities to themselves, their families, and their country—but few kept chronically obdurate boys from making bad choices.

The strategies southern families used inadvertently fed the entitlement of students and the anxieties of adults. Families held immense expectations of what education would mean for their sons but depended on ineffectual approaches to bring those hopes to fruition. Parents tried to coax proper behavior from sons whom they had raised to resist authority, and sought to inspire dutifulness and compliance at the time they exerted the least influence over them. They hoped for virtue, diligence, and respectability but relied on letter writing campaigns and the intermittent oversight of surrogates to engender these qualities. Given these tactics, southerners found teaching sons to balance dutifulness and autonomy far more difficult than they imagined when they first sent their sons to university to become men. The institutions these boys attended further complicated their passage to manhood, for at college, local and national allegiances collided with emergent sectionalism and helped make them into southern men.

CHAPTER FOUR

Creating Southern Schools
for Southern Sons

Between the 1790s and the 1820s, southerners' hopes that prestigious northern universities would turn their boys into respectable men were eclipsed by their fears about elite sons abandoning the region's slaveholding tradition. Their experiences with educating their sons pushed state loyalties and then regional distinctions to the forefront of elite consciousness. No one more evocatively articulated this move toward sectionalism than the sage of Monticello. In the 1780s, Thomas Jefferson's primary concerns regarding the education of American boys centered on the subversive consequences of sending them to Europe. By the 1810s he argued that Virginians needed to fund local educational enterprises to "rescue us from the tax of toryism, fanaticism, and indifferentism to their own State, which we now send our youth to bring from those of New England."[1] In 1821, in the wake of the Missouri Crisis, Jefferson went further in his condemnation of having southern sons educated outside the region and linked educating boys with defending slavery: "We are now trusting to those who are against us in position and principle, to fashion in their own form the minds and affections of our youth. . . . [W]e must have there five hundred . . . imbibing opinions and principles in discord with those of their own country. This canker is eating on the vitals of our existence, and if not arrested at once, will be beyond remedy."[2]

Early national southerners increasingly wanted a southern educational system that confirmed their racial values as well as their masculine ethics. "My God can't we be educated at the South," demanded one North Carolinian. "We have worshiped their literary deities, Princeton, Yale & Cambridge long enough. . . . Let the Yankees manufacture woolen clothing, let us manufacture men."[3]

Southern State Universities

In the 1790s the North all but monopolized prestigious universities. While some Virginia aristocrats educated their sons at William and Mary, elites from other states in the South tended to prefer the young nation's most prominent schools: Yale, Harvard, and Princeton for general education and the University of Pennsylvania for medical school.[4] At such institutions, southern boys could become American men of virtue, respectability, and patriotism. Young southerners attending these northern schools also stood the best chance of acquiring the reputation essential to leading the South. Thus in the early years of the United States, most scions of powerful southern families spent part of their formative years living in the North, studying at esteemed colleges in order to secure their claim on manhood back home.

But as much as southern parents wanted to buy the best for their young sons, state pride and sectional defensiveness shifted their focus toward local education in the early decades of the nineteenth century. Thomas Jefferson's prediction about students "imbibing opinions and principles in discord" with southern values voiced the sentiments of many of the region's leading families, who saw the creation of state universities as a means to advance their states, their sons, and their increasingly peculiar institution of slavery. Southerners appreciated the many benefits of state education. Closer schools meant less expense and more effective monitoring. School friendships could more efficiently turn into business partnerships and political alliances. Local education enhanced local reputations. George Swain advised his son David on the practical merits of studying in his home state: "As North Carolina is your native State and I hope will be your future station I conclude it will be much better in respect to future popularity to receive your education in your own University."[5] Most importantly, state schools alleviated growing fears, particularly among men from the areas most invested in slavery's continuation, about the nature of the education southern boys received when they traveled north. Samuel DuBose, for example, felt much relieved about the opening of several academies and the new South Carolina College: "For some time past, it must be regretted S.C. has been beholden to some of her sister states and to Europe for the education of her young men; the evil consequences of this, she has suffered severely from." Echoing Jefferson, DuBose worried that "young men then sent off at an early age are very apt to imbibe habits and principles not at all calculated for the country they are to live in."[6]

This was no mere paranoia. Edmund Ruffin Sr. sent his fourteen-year-old namesake to a Connecticut boarding school, only to learn that the headmaster took his son to hear a recently liberated "African Prince" recount his harrowing experience in bondage. Edmund Jr. praised and identified with the speaker, Ibrahima Abdul Rahhaman, whose freedom had been purchased from Mississippi slaveholders by the Tappan brothers of New York. The next year young Ruffin enrolled at the University of Virginia.[7] Although not often so overt in antislavery evangelizing, northern school officials did seek to expand their schools' reputations and the status of their states by attracting and influencing future leaders from the South. In one instance, a 1796 request for additional monies from their state legislature by administrators at the College of New Jersey (Princeton) pronounced the benefits of educating southern sons. Since southern families often sent boys out of the region for education, "It would be the interest, and would certainly be no inconsiderable glory to New Jersey, to be the fountain of education to so large a portion of America, and to furnish those States with their Legislators and their Judges, and be able to infuse her spirit into the politics and councils of our country."[8]

Southerners, of course, wanted to infuse their own spirit into the nation's future leaders. Local pride, coupled with an emerging interest in protecting slavery, pushed southerners to open state universities, most prominently South Carolina College (1805) and the Universities of North Carolina (1795), Georgia (1801), and Virginia (1825).[9] Seven of the first ten state universities founded in the young United States were in the South. Six of the seven states included in this study, Georgia, South Carolina, North Carolina, Tennessee, Maryland, and Virginia, chartered schools in that period. (Alabama created the seventh.) Transylvania, while a private institution, served the state of Kentucky in this capacity during the early national era. Thus, practically speaking, every state in the early national South supported a school.[10] State pride and a perceived need to protect southern sons from the rising chorus of northern critiques of slaveholding underlay the founding of these institutions.

The first hints of the sectional identity and protectionism that would split the nation in the 1860s came as adults in the early national era considered the future of the most vulnerable and most important members of society: the next generation of leaders. Many scholars date the emergence of sectional tensions to the 1819–20 Missouri crisis. And certainly, as Jefferson's comments about education indicate, the rhetoric of sectionalism escalated after this incident. But by the time of this national struggle over Missouri statehood, federal authority in territories, and the extension of slavery into the West, the foundation of southern nationalism already existed. Several decades before Congress first debated the issues that would eventually rend the nation, southern elites already thought of themselves as distinctive and felt chary about northerners. In their view, the first line of defense lay in the education of the rising generation.

Anxious about their far-off and impressionable sons, southern families feared, justifiably, that young men attending northern schools might develop allegiances to that region rather than their southern homes. After two years studying at Harvard, South Carolina native John E. Colhoun Jr. suspected that "the Yankee girls . . . would make much better wives." Although he missed his family while studying in Philadelphia, Marylander Richard Hopkins dreaded returning to his rural home: "I feel much anxiety of mind when I contemplate spending my life confined to the narrow limits of a Neighborhood to be rusticated among unlettered and unpolished rustics."[11] Apprehensions about sons such as Colhoun and Hopkins falling under the sway of urban culture and northern women doubtless kept parents up at night.

But the most pronounced anxieties about southern sons succumbing to northern influences centered on northern questions about slaveholding. Beginning in the 1770s and inspired by the values of the American Revolution, northern states adopted programs of gradual emancipation. During this same era, the South intensified its reliance on slave labor and commitment to the westward expansion of slavery. As early as the 1790s southerners, led by large slaveholders from the South Carolina lowcountry, protested northern criticisms of their "peculiar institution." Although he praised Harvard as the best education for his namesake, John Ball Sr. also worried about the insidious effects of living in New England on so impressionable a young boy as sixteen-year-old John Jr. Shortly after the young man left South Carolina for Harvard in 1798, his father warned: "You are in danger of imbibing principles . . . that will be against the interest of the southern states, tending to the ruin of your own family & fortune—however liberal those ideas may appear, the carrying of them into practice would be attended with the most direful effects." Avoiding any possible ambiguity, John Sr. continued with as emphatic a statement as he ever made in four years of writing to the college student: "Carry in mind that whenever a general emancipation takes place in So[uth] Carolina & Georgia you are a ruined man and all your family connexions made beggars."[12]

Southern colleges and universities succeeded at insulating adolescent boys from "direful" northern influences and served as powerful symbols of state pride. Edmund Hubard articulated as much in his description of the University of Virginia: "Every thing that I saw surpassed my most sanguine expectations. . . . Every gentleman of talent that has visited this place since I have been here, pronounces without hesitation that, there is no institution in the United States at which a Student could derive more benefit than at this." Moses Waddel likewise bragged that at the University of Georgia, "some young men of uncommon promise have graduated here within the last three years, who are industriously ascending the hill of fame." And Charles Wilson Harris felt proud to help hire a mathematics professor for the University of North Carolina and be "useful to an institution which was zealously patronized by the whole state."[13]

The significance of these universities proved so great that few men deigned to publicly criticize them. When David Swain questioned the morality of Chapel Hill students and the educational benefits of attending the university, his father urged him to be "silent as possible on the subject of Chapel Hill . . . every North Carolinian feels interested in its welfare and so strong is the partiality . . . that the least imprudent expression may raise you a host of adversaries and injure your popularity during life." Similarly, after condemning the waywardness of Chapel Hill students, John Pettigrew asked his father to keep their discussions private, for "I should be sorry to be the means of spreading a report which might injure the University."[14]

Prominent men in the southern frontier states of Tennessee and Kentucky joined their tidewater counterparts in resolving to create reputable state universities that would validate their region and make their sons worthy political leaders and refined gentlemen. Henry Clay, for example, promoted the establishment of Transylvania University in his hometown of Lexington, Kentucky, because he believed it could be a key marker of the state's respectability. "All whose eyes are turned to the West, regard it as a distinguished object," insisted Clay, and the school "is not merely destined to shed particular lustre upon that State, but . . . holds the torch of science and literature to all the States and Territories around that senior member of the western family." Men seeking to establish other schools in the southern interior echoed Clay's sentiments. As locals tried to found a medical school in Kentucky, one booster explained that it would "tend to show an air of polish, and refinement over the minds, and the manners of the Citizens, and thereby exalt us in the estimation of our sister States." Tennesseans similarly sought to strengthen their educational institutions in the 1810s and 1820s. Prominent East Tennesseans envisioned an institution in Knoxville that would "raise our noble fountain of literature, and all the country may be watered by the pure stream of science. Fruits delicious will grow where hitherto has been but dry and barren waste."[15]

Few boys from outside the South attended any of these southern state universities. Instead, by the 1810s and 1820s these institutions became exclusive havens for state pride and regional defensiveness. No school created to fulfill these ambitions succeeded more than South Carolina College (later the University of South Carolina). South Carolinians took the reins of leadership of the South from Virginia in the early decades of the nineteenth century, and throughout the early national and antebellum eras Carolinians promoted an increasingly aggressive proslavery, pro-southern political agenda.[16] South Carolina College symbolized and reified the ideals of the state's gentry. In large part, the school emerged out of elite slaveholders' fears about New England educators promoting antislavery among Carolina's sons. Curricular requirements affirmed this agenda: the course in moral philosophy introduced students to proslavery arguments, and students left school steeped in proslavery rhetoric. According to historian Wayne K. Durrill, professors' reliance on recitation and their discouragement of argumentation also facilitated an intellectual conformity that served to solidify consensus in state politics. Moreover, the curricular commitment to classical literature "qualified students for membership in a very select group and provided them with skills and ideas vital to the exercise of political power in the broadest sense."[17] Founders envisioned the school promoting solidarity among South Carolina's ruling class. As Governor John Drayton explained in an 1801 address to the state legislature, "the friendship of our young men would thence be promoted, and our political union be much advanced thereby." The proximity of the college to the state legislature—only a brief walk separates the two institutions—was clearly not coincidental. The school more than met the expectations of its boosters by "properly" training future leaders. Between the 1820s and 1865, twelve of that state's twenty-one governors, five of six state judges, and the majority of U.S. senators representing South Carolina had studied at the college.[18]

The Universities of Virginia, Georgia, and North Carolina repeated the pattern of South Carolina College (along with the South's only colonial college, William and Mary) in attracting students from their respective states, facilitating elite solidarity, and training future leaders. Founders of all these state schools shared Jefferson's vision for his University of Virginia: "To form the statesmen, legislators, and judges . . . to harmonize the interests of agriculture and commerce . . . to develop the reasoning . . . cultivate the morals, to enlighten . . . and finally to form the habits of reflection and virtuous conduct which lead to happiness. In other words . . . to make leaders and citizens."[19]

In all of these early southern schools, far more than at those in the North, elites dominated education. The price of attending these schools ensured a gentry clientele. Virginia ranked as the most expensive school in the United States by 1840; North Carolina charged more than any northern school except

Harvard.[20] Southern elites showed little interest in public education and allowed only limited opportunities for advanced schooling beyond their own ranks. Military academies did develop in the early-nineteenth-century South, but they catered primarily to the middle ranks of society. Some denominational schools also emerged in the early South as well, Hampden-Sydney among the most prominent.[21] But state schools attracted more attention and more scions from gentry families, for they offered the greatest chance to mingle with similarly circumstanced boys and acquire the reputation of a man. Southern elites also remained indifferent to if not opposed to funding primary educational opportunities for those outside the gentry ranks, even as public schools for children proliferated throughout northern states in the early nineteenth century. Wealthy southern families continued to hire private (usually northern) tutors to teach their young children at home instead of encouraging public schools. This practice promoted gentry monopolization over education and visibly affirmed the status of the family; only the wealthy could contract for such services.

The southern gentry's determination to use education to groom future patriarchs and affirm class status even shaped the curriculum and rituals of university life. Boys studied subjects and performed rites that exhibited their status, using school as a training ground for manly power. Greek and Latin and oratory formed the cornerstones of southern education in the early national era, and these fields verified a man's class and his refinement in the minds of elites.[22] Classical studies remained central to most southern universities' curricula even as scientific and practical instruction supplanted it in European and northern schools. This persistent curricular emphasis on classics and oratory affirmed the southern conviction that education should be less practical than ornamental; for elites, classical training marked a man's elegance and respectability.[23] Throughout the early national era the University of North Carolina, like its sister institutions, required student proficiency in Greek and Latin before admission. In the first class, boys studied grammar, Roman antiquities, Greek, and English. If students passed examinations, they proceeded to the second class, in which they added arithmetic and geography. From its founding through the 1830s, South Carolina College required students to spend most of their time on Greek and Latin texts. And oratory, particularly mastering the speeches of Cicero, occupied parts of all four years of study.[24] Neither shifts in European and northern educational practices nor occasional criticisms from within the South did much to alter the classical emphasis of southern universities, because mastery of Greek and Latin and of oratorical arts still affirmed men's refinement and helped validate claims to manhood and power in elite circles.

Academic rituals reinforced the exclusivity of attending university in the South and underscored the link between education and political power. For example, during graduation exercises at South Carolina College, the president presented students to state leaders who sat in the front row and, with ritualized handshakes, welcomed young men into South Carolina's ruling class.[25] Public examinations allowed boys to demonstrate their erudition and confidence and provided vital practice for future careers in politics. Boys regularly wrote friends and kin about their preparation for and anxiety about oral examinations. They understood that such rituals publicly tested not only their oratorical skills but their manhood as well. By displaying their speaking skills, grace, and self-assurance—all traits required of southern gentlemen—students demonstrated their preparedness to join the exclusive ranks of confident, commanding southern men. Even disciplinary matters revealed the power and prominence of this cohort of boys. Boards of trustees typically consisted of leading state or even national figures; during hearings, young men presented themselves to the most important men in their states. Rioters at the University of Virginia, for example, appeared before the school's first board of trustees, which included three former presidents: Thomas Jefferson, James Madison, and James Monroe.[26]

The patterns of class power and self-conscious sectionalism that commenced in the early national era hardened in the antebellum decades. Southern students attending northern colleges grew ever more hostile to their hosts and unapologetically defensive about slavery after the 1820s. Attending Yale in 1834, George McPhail complained, "They seem determined to set our negroes free at all hazard, and raise them to a level with the white population and if possible a little above it."[27] Enthusiasm for southern institutions of higher learning also spiked in the antebellum decades. The University of Mississippi and the University of the South were both created to reduce the flow of southern students to the North and to inculcate pro-southern and proslavery lessons. By the early 1850s, students at the University of Virginia created a Southern Rights Association to defend "the fate of an institution, on which depends, in a great measure, the happiness and the prosperity of the South" and to fend off "the avarice and the lust of power of the North." The organization vowed to boycott northern schools and to employ no northern teachers, and they sought to rally other southern college students to their cause. An initial public letter avowed: "We cannot forget that soon the destinies of the South must be entrusted to our keeping. The present occupants of the arena of action must soon pass away, and we be called upon to fill their places, and to battle in their stead against impending dangers. It becomes therefore our sacred duty to prepare for the contest."[28]

Not surprisingly, South Carolinians led their contemporaries in this strident defense of southern rights, right down to the Civil War. On 8 November 1861, every undergraduate at South Carolina College left school to join the Confederate army. The statesmen of South Carolina who had attended the college in the early national era, meanwhile, designed the plans of secession and war. Alumni also expanded their influence throughout the South, serving as antebellum governors of Georgia, Alabama, Florida, and Mississippi and as congressmen from all those states as well as Texas. This power in southern politics during the 1850s prompted one observer to conclude: "To the College is very largely attributable the influence which has not only made South Carolina the prompt and determined champion of Southern rights and interests, especially state sovereignty, free trade, and the institution of domestic African slavery, but which has also deeply impressed . . . those subjects on the heart and mind of the entire South and Southwest."[29]

In the long term, then, elite efforts to provide a "proper" education for their sons succeeded wildly. In time, this cohort of men learned to aggressively use power to defend family and regional values, ably fulfilling those duties. Many willingly sacrificed their own college-age sons to that cause in the Civil War. In the short term, however, these southern sons of the founding generation seemed anything but dutiful to the professors and administrators attempting to run the universities they attended.

Supervising Southern Collegians

School administrators tried to supervise their southern charges, but their myriad, typically futile efforts revealed how fully these boys embraced their own independence and how reluctantly they submitted to anyone. Restraining southerners proved far more daunting than directing Greek and Latin orations. First of all, university leaders tried to keep students too busy to cause much trouble. The University of North Carolina mandated attendance at morning and evening prayers and church on Sundays; classes filled the hours between nine and noon and between two and five. At 8:00 p.m., after evening prayers and supper, boys were confined to their rooms until the next morning. William Ruffin reported a similarly restrictive schedule at St. Mary's in Maryland. The teenager complained bitterly to his father about being kept busy from dawn to dusk.[30] But no matter how many hours of the day colleges filled, boys found time to engage in forbidden extracurricular activities.

Efforts of professors to keep a close watch over their charges met with similar defiance. Young gentry men bristled under the control of professors who seemed beneath them in status and indifferent to their culture's fixation on manly independence. Cassius Clay, for example, complained to his brother Brutus of far too much supervision at the boarding school he attended in Kentucky: "The prefects are always with us and we don't feel . . . the pleasure of being unrestrained."[31] Classmates protested to relatives and conspired with one another to sabotage what they perceived to be intrusive oversight.

With vigilant professors and hectic schedules failing, university officials passed exhaustively long codes of conduct. University of Georgia administrators created a detailed list of regulations and placed faculty members in dormitories to ensure compliance. The college forbade profanity, fighting, traveling off campus without permission, disrupting study times by talking, singing, or ringing bells, playing billiards and cards, associating with "vile, idle, or dissolute persons," keeping a horse or dog, carrying "any gun, pistol, Dagger, Dirk sword cane or any other offensive weapon," dueling, drunkenness, and assaulting "the President, a Professor, or a Tutor."[32] In addition to mandating attendance at daily prayers, study hall, and class recitations, the University of North Carolina forbade betting on horse races and cockfights, possessing liquor, guns, or dogs, public use of profanity, and public intoxication.[33] As with their schedules, motivated students found plenty of opportunities to flout school restrictions. Clearly, the very existence of regulations forbidding public drunkenness, concealed weapons, and physical attacks on faculty suggests the occurrence of those behaviors.

Money and indulgent parents, officials decided, lay at the heart of their failed management. Curbing the fiscal extravagance that allowed boys to violate so many regulations was paramount in the minds of school officials. Faculty at the University of Georgia articulated the sentiment of many educators when they asserted, "Almost all the misconduct of Students at College, may be traced either directly or indirectly to the imprudent use of money."[34] In 1802, University of North Carolina trustees, having reached the same conclusion, sent a circular letter to each Chapel Hill student's benefactor stipulating every expense a boy could conceivably incur. The trustees did this, in their words, because they were "sensible of the ill consequences produced by Students having more money at their disposal than is sufficient to meet their necessary disbursements during the Session." The authors hoped that "the indulgence of the Parents would not exceed those limits, so far as to furnish a temptation to dissipation, misapplication of time, and a relaxation of morals." In a similar letter sent by the University of Virginia outlining school rules regarding money provided to young men, officials maintained that "the morality and proficiency of the student, as well as the prosperity of this institution, will be alike promoted by imposing this moderation and equality of expenditures." The letter beseeched parents and guardians to refrain from letting "indulgence to the student, defeat this scheme of obvious general benefit." Virginia's plan required students to deposit all funds with a university proctor, forbade boys from spending more than $100 per session on clothes and $40 for "pocket money," and specified that student dress should always be "uniform and plain." Both the Virginia and the North Carolina letters specifically denounced the "indulgence" of young men—which university officials knew to be rife among elite southern families.[35]

Such rules, of course, ran counter to genteel passions for independence, sartorial flair, and generous spending. So despite regulations to the contrary, relatives often subsidized lavish lifestyles that signified family standing and promoted boyish entitlement. That parental indulgence abetted students' lackadaisical compliance with school requirements. And on occasion, parents even helped sons subvert college rules. As Martin Armstrong prepared to graduate from the University of North Carolina in 1819, he wanted to travel to the West rather than stay in Chapel Hill to collect his diploma at graduation. The school, however, required attendance at commencement. So Martin asked his father to write a letter pretending that Martin needed to oversee his father's business in Tennessee and consequently be excused from graduation. Martin even coached his father on the letter's style: "It may also be best to state in it that it is indispensably necessary to have your business attended to either by yourself or me and that your affairs at home will not admit of your absence." Thomas complied with Martin's request, writing a lengthy letter explaining, "I am ignorant of the rules of the college, but I have been flattering myself, that you could perhaps prevail with the Faculty to dispense with the custom of delivering your speech and permit you to go on immediately, after your examination, to Tennessee to attend to my business. . . . I have no other person to whom I can confide that business but yourself and it is most impossible for me to go there myself."[36]

College administrators, then, had to contend with not only willful southern students but also their indulgent, complicit parents. Many felt as if their hands were tied when it came to disciplining the scions of prominent families. At the College of South Carolina, for example, only the trustees could expel students, and they seldom followed the suggestions of professors seeking to dismiss the truculent but wealthy sons of state leaders. Powerless professors, often not much older than their students and substantially poorer, could only try to cajole teenagers into complying with school rules. As one alumni of South Carolina assessed things: "Faculties are compelled to choose between discipline and bread." While not always so transparent, the wealth of students' families undercut efforts at discipline at every southern school. Expulsion meant a loss of tuition, and it antagonized influential state leaders. Feeble administrative responses to elite student misbehavior sometimes worsened rather than remedied problems. When William and Mary students vandalized a church in Williamsburg in 1798, "the Bishop and proffessors [*sic*] talked high of expulsion[.] But the party was so numerous, and many of them so respectable, that, although they had direct proof, nothing was done." When students at Chapel Hill repeatedly harassed President Chapman, the faculty initially "forbore with the young men some time in the hope that this raucous spirit would subside. This though seemed to afford them a course of triumph, and every day furnished new instances of disorder and confusion."[37]

Just as parents employed guilt to influence boys, administrators played on the feelings of parents to try to make them pressure boys to behave. In 1823 the University of North Carolina instituted a new policy of mailing to parents or guardians their students' standing in the class and prayer attendance records. Their stated motivation: the conviction that "parents, for the most part, have but little opportunity of knowing the course which their sons are taking in the university, or the dangers with which their habits are threatened."[38] After suspending William Ruffin, University of North Carolina administrators similarly tried to manipulate his father into correcting the boy. They notified Thomas Ruffin that his boy's readmission hung on an attitude adjustment, which only the father could effect: "I hope he is of a different spirit & that he must feel grieved & mortified at having wounded the feelings of his parents, & interrupted his education."[39] In both instances, rather than charging adults with indifference to or complicity in student wrongdoings, officials tried to ally themselves with what they depicted as wronged or misinformed parents. This approach, administrators apparently hoped, might succeed where outright accusations inevitably failed.

School officials undertook many imaginative approaches to keep students in line. Thomas Jefferson believed that architecture might help. Approached by a group of Tennesseans seeking to found a new college, he advised constructing several smaller buildings instead of one central one: "The large and crowded buildings in which youths are pent up are equally unfriendly to health, to study, to manners, morals & order."[40] Organizers of the University of Georgia planned the location of their school to counter the "evils of town life." Athens lay too far in the country, they wrongly believed, to offer many distractions. At the University of

Virginia, Jefferson initially tried enforcing only modest restraints on students, under the misguided hope that, with fewer rules to follow, students might actually behave. A riot during the first year the school operated, which resulted in the expulsion of a number of students, including one of Jefferson's nephews, put that theory to rest. And in the first decade of the nineteenth century the presidents of nearly all the colleges in the United States participated in an informal network in which they shared the names of boys they expelled, in a largely unsuccessful attempt to stop school-hopping and restrain campus disorder.[41]

Grooming the environment that boys inhabited and playing on their (or their parents') emotions worked no better for school administrators than it did for southern families. Academic conventions, whether intentionally, as with a classical curriculum, or inadvertently, as with unenforced school rules, bolstered southern students' self-importance and their growing conviction that southern men made their own rules.

Even dedicated university leaders sometimes threw up their hands in frustration over the indulged, self-important, and unrestrained teenagers they tried to educate. Controlling southern students, many concluded, was a losing battle. Every year during his tenure as president of South Carolina College, Thomas Cooper grew more and more exasperated with the parade of wild students who beset his campus. Nothing Cooper did seemed to work. Near the end of his administration, he got so disgusted that he quit lecturing in the middle of a term. Thomas Jefferson felt just as appalled by the student body at Virginia. A few months before his death, Jefferson, dismayed at the disorder rife at his beloved university, complained: "I have long been sensible that while I was endeavouring to render my country the greatest of all services, that of regenerating the public education, and placing the rising generation on the level of our sister states . . . I was discharging the odious function of a physician pouring medicine down the throat of a patient insensible of needing it."[42]

Educators and parents dedicated themselves to crafting just the right educational experience for this vital generation of young men. But, like Jefferson and Cooper, they saw only one consistent result: wherever southern students congregated, chaos soon ensued.

CHAPTER FIVE

The (Mis)Behaviors of
Southern Collegians

William Davie, a founder of the University of North Carolina, understood perfectly Thomas Cooper's and Thomas Jefferson's distress, for student rebellions plagued the Chapel Hill campus also. While unsure of a solution, Davie certainly knew where to lay blame: "The real cause may be found in the defects of education in the So. States, the weakness of parental authority, the spirit of the Times, . . . [and] the consequent presumption and loose manners of young men, Boys of 16 or 17 years, without judgment, without experience or almost any kind of knowledge . . . [who] arrogantly affect to judge for themselves, their teachers and their parents." His condemnation of indulgent parents, ineffectual schools, and especially arrogant boys was harsh but accurate. Residing far from the watchful eyes of relatives and operating beyond the control of school authorities, students from wealthy southern families created a raucous peer culture that turned their parents' emphasis on masculine autonomy into justification for mayhem. Extravagance, mischief, and violence ran rampant at every school that large numbers of southern scions attended.[1]

Ironically, the disorder that men such as Davie lamented derived in no small order from boys heeding the lessons their families taught. Like their relatives, most southern sons viewed academic pursuits as ancillary to their experiences at college. And, as their parents desired, boys sought renown as independent, respected men, which they understood came from earning the approval of their classmates. Furthermore, self-mastery required them to resist arbitrary authority, including the sort that schools needed to exercise.

The youthfulness of southern students, as William Davie pointed out, only worsened matters. Boys left home for boarding schools often as young as age ten or twelve and entered universities usually not later than seventeen, hardly an ideal stage of life to exercise judgment and restraint. John Pettigrew started at the University of North Carolina at the age of seventeen, and his brother Ebene-zer, twelve or thirteen at the time, accompanied him. Peter Carr commenced his education at the grammar school at William and Mary at age thirteen. He then attended university there and read law with George Wythe before he turned nineteen.[2] Such precocity was expected of southern gentry sons, who earned the reputation and exercised the prerogatives of manhood while still in their teens. Unfettered by real demands for career proficiency, and expecting to inherit land, slaves, and power upon majority, students felt obliged to assert but not to prove themselves.

As they acted out these southern ethics, young men began to notice and then cultivate their regional distinctiveness. College planted the seeds that turned boys from the South into self-conscious southern men just as these students turned university campuses upside-down.

Handling Parents, Professors, and Peers

Southern students facing this first real test of their manhood found them-selves required to negotiate relationships with three powerful but conflicting groups of people: their families, school officials, and classmates. Before heading off to college, most sons contended primarily with their families' influences in their lives. But attending university shepherded in a very different set of experi-ences. School officials and peers now also weighed in on young men's beliefs and actions, shaping their maturation as well as complicating their relationships with relatives. In addition to sharpening their charges' minds, professors and administrators tried—and usually failed—to redefine students' values. Southern boys stridently resisted university efforts at control, and they typically viewed the men who attempted to educate them with condescension, if not outright dis-dain. Those adversarial relationships taught young southern gentlemen vital les-sons about resisting external authority and defending manly prerogatives. Peers were an equally important, if far more welcome, new part of students' lives. Classmates shared emotionally resonate bonds that helped collegians thwart their professors, manipulate their parents, and affirm their distinctive concep-tions of manliness.

While immersed in this new world of professors and friends, young men continued to feel deeply attached to their families emotionally. Initially after leaving home for distant colleges, most southern boys felt forlorn. "It has been only 10 days since we left Virginia," wrote Arthur Morson, "and it appears to me to be as many weeks." New South Carolina College student Thomas Johnson missed everything about his home, even "the House-the yard-the trees." Sixteen-year-old John Grimball left Charleston for Princeton in 1816, and his grief over parting with his parents, sister, and friends is palpable: "I reflected that I had to be separated from them for such a long time & perhaps *for ever* the thought itself was death, I could hardly support it, however I restrained my feelings as much as I could." And separated from his beloved siblings while attending medical school in Philadelphia, Solomon Mordecai felt his life "deprived of its highest, its only zest."[3] Such professions of longing and devotion demonstrate that the lessons of family affection taught to boys in childhood made leaving home wrenching. But manhood required education and education required travel from home, so southern sons and their parents endured the heartache of separation.

While young men obviously imbibed this ethic of family devotion, their letters home from college reveal that they learned other, less intended lessons about affections from their parents. Boys had understood from childhood that emotions could be powerful tools of manipulation. Their parents used conditional love and the threatened withdrawal of affection to keep them in line as children. At college these sons turned the tables; they became adept at manipulating their families' emotions to duck responsibilities and frustrate oversight. For example, health concerns plagued parents sending their sons away to university, particularly when they studied in the North. Boys used those anxieties to justify lackadaisical performances at college and secure family indulgence. Sickness from excessive study emerged as a recurrent theme in early national student correspondence. Maryland student Richard Hopkins, for instance, informed his mother of his decision to "relax somewhat from hard study" in order to counter the negative effects of school work on his body: "My too close application to a multiplicity of readings . . . has so far weakened my health and constitution, and such constant pouring over Books in a bended posture has brought a pain in the Breast which has produced a spitting of blood which seems to threaten a consumptive tendency."[4] William Ball, sadly, did fall ill during the final months of his medical studies in Europe, and he attributed his poor health to uninterrupted study. Just weeks after securing his degree in 1808, Ball's health deteriorated so much that he left London for Madeira, assuring his father, "I shall soon be my own man again." He died that winter, not from excessive bookishness but from consumption.[5] Family fears about health (whether legitimate or inflamed by their sons) allowed some young men to dither at school but avoid reprisals from kin.

Students understood their parents' ambitions as well as their fears, and they knew that writing reassuring letters about their dutifulness and accomplishments would work in their favor. In a typically calculated letter, Virginian

Charles Lee assured his mother, "I do not think I have much propensity to idleness & dissipation. . . . The rock on which I am in the greatest danger of splitting is a disposition to aim too high, or at too much."[6] A steady flow of letters emphasizing these priorities, boys came to realize, ensured that families continued to dote on them and subsidize their college careers.

Boys also knew that their parents preferred to encourage rather than coerce them, so students caught misbehaving vowed to right their course if only adults would forebear a bit longer. Virginian Francis Gilmer admitted to poor school performance but, like many other southern sons, he fully intended to do better and "bid an everlasting adieu to a habit disgraceful to children, & ignominious to men." Chapel Hill student Thomas Bennehan likewise wrote his mother professing his intention to abandon his dilatory past and "make the days of my dear Parents as happy as possible and try to repay unto them their kindness."[7]

Some of the assertions students made surely struck even the most hopeful of parents as too good to be true. In a transparently disingenuous letter, William Ball praised the educational choices his father made for him: "I can't help admiring the plan You took in sending me here, for by having but few acquaintances, I have very little enticement to pleasure."[8] (And what eighteen-year-old wants friends and pleasure?) In letters to his mother, teenager John Palmer spun an equally implausible tale about his comportment at college. He pledged to study hard and "act conscientiously" when he first arrived at South Carolina College in 1818. He even selected as a roommate a similarly diligent boy: "A better and more studious chum I could not desire." In the years that followed, he swore to his mother that he shunned the company of disreputable young men. John left out the fact that he did not need others to derail his performance in school—he proved quite adept at misbehavior all on his own. A violent confrontation with the school president and an expulsion in 1822 capped off several years of academic mediocrity.[9]

Distance made a great ally to students seeking to manipulate their anxious but indulgent families. Although newspapers and university disciplinary boards reported nearly chronic disorder on campuses, students disavowed any involvement. While admitting that "the follies of youth" and his numerous friends "at times diverted the attention of my studies," William Quynn nonetheless adamantly maintained that the "Venomous tongue" of his father's untrustworthy neighbors exaggerated the young man's waywardness. Edmund Mason assured his brother that he spent all his time at Chapel Hill studying, as did his classmates: "I look around me, and see nothing but study." And Richard Randolph, a William and Mary student, went so far as to insist that he knew little of the dreadful behavior nearly epidemic among his peers in Williamsburg because he was "always in my Room in those hours which are by some taken up in dissipation and debauch."[10]

One issue that students usually did not mislead their families about was their academic records, in part because official reports from campus made those kinds of evasions pointless. As important, however, was the fact that students knew that their parents ranked edification beneath reputation. Students who strategically skewed explanations of their dutifulness, character, and social activities felt comfortable confessing (and some actually boasted about) their scholastic shortcomings. As graduation from Harvard approached, Virginian Edward Marshall admitted, "I expect no honor, my past laziness does not deserve it." And he casually reported, "The honors are generally out of fashion with the southerners." In letters back home, students detailed their academic boredom and apathy. In an 1801 letter to his father, fifteen-year-old Walter Lenoir listed a number of reasons why he disliked school. First, Walter complained, he found "no Company that is worth Calling Company." Furthermore, he explained, "I never Could take no Delight in Learning the Lattin [*sic*] Language."[11] (English, apparently, inspired no more enthusiasm.) James Henry Hammond recalled in his memoir that he "abhorred tasks" as a student, and that during his early years at South Carolina College "I gave myself up to idle associates & neither read nor studied until towards the close of my time." Hammond's roommate, Thomas Jefferson Withers, confessed a similar attitude toward education. Indeed, he believed "I have so long indulged as to lose completely that kind of controll over my mind which enables one to read with attention & with interest."[12] Young southerners would never have given voice to a similar indifference to reputational matters or their duty to family and country, but they understood that their relatives would not be shocked or even terribly concerned about academic apathy.

Not every student, it must be noted, squandered his educational potential. Some dilatory students redoubled their efforts at school when graduation loomed. James Henry Hammond ranked near the bottom of his class after a year of attending (but seldom studying at) South Carolina College. As an upperclassman, he righted his course and graduated fourth in a class of thirty-one.[13] Occasionally, young men faithfully applied themselves to edification. North Carolinian Alfred Mordecai stood out among many of his contemporaries in his devotion to and success at school. Only fifteen when he left home to attend West Point, Alfred graduated at the head of his class at age nineteen. Shortly after arriving at West Point, he wrote his older brother Solomon to express his contrition over having been "ungrateful . . . [and] knowingly inflicting pain on you." Alfred promised

Solomon, "All my exertions shall hereafter tend to make you forget the past & hope the best from the future." Whereas young men regularly delivered such proclamations, Alfred actually made good on his. Two years later, one of the Mordecai sisters proudly reported that "our amiable Alfred . . . surpasses my highest expectations." The location of Alfred's training—at West Point—probably played as influential a role in his good comportment as anything else. West Point imposed far more discipline than did state universities. As Cadet Mordecai explained, "Here, if a Cadet says any thing disrespectful to a Professor or to a Sentinel he is immediately put in prison & no more said about it."[14] While the military academy compelled more rectitude, Alfred Mordecai still stood out among his cohort of southern contemporaries, where disorder and duplicity too often prevailed.

While most young men were not above misleading and manipulating their families, they avoided outright conflict whenever possible. Fighting was a last resort, arrived at only if subtle manipulation, vows of rehabilitation, and obdurate denials failed to satisfy relatives.[15] The premium families placed on affection and reciprocal duties militated against overt discord. Furthermore, the implied if seldom exercised power of the purse kept most boys from challenging their parents too blatantly or casually. While they knew that adults seldom actually disinherited children, few promising southern sons wanted to risk becoming the exception to the rule. Students recognized that money and indulgence could evaporate, and they remained dependent on parents and kin for financial and emotional support.[16] Few saw an advantage in antagonizing kin through direct confrontation, especially when evasion and denials worked so well. Fear of the withdrawal of parental affection, commonly used by fathers to correct disappointing sons, also checked sons' challenges to their fathers. In contrast to the hollow threat of disinheritance, adults could and did withhold love and approval from their sons, often to good effect. Robert Wirt found himself on the receiving end of this distressing tactic as he struggled at West Point in the 1820s. His father's rebukes left the young cadet "very much hurt." During one low point he even "begged for his father's encouragement and approval." But only Robert's mother gave any comfort to her son.[17] Economic dependence and emotional attachments, then, kept collegians from pushing their families too far.

Southern students exhibited no such restraint in their dealings with university officials, who they generally viewed as annoying inferiors. Southern sons acted with far more impudence in their dealings with professors and school officials than with their fathers and kin. They could not finesse or dodge their teachers, and they did not feel affectionate or deferential toward school officials.

Indeed, southern students routinely ignored the authority of academicians and aggressively resisted school rules—attitudes they masked in dealing with their relatives.

Southern boys openly criticized their professors, demonstrating their sense of self-importance and disrespect for university authority. Hugh Grigsby, a Virginian at Yale in the 1820s, complained that "the faculty of Yale are a diminutive and low-minded set." Joseph Watson, a student at William and Mary in the 1790s, criticized his professors as well. One, he charged, administered exams that "ought to have disgraced him" and another knew nearly nothing of the language he pretended to teach. William Ball was cheeky enough to confess his disdain for his teachers to his brother, but savvy enough to keep such criticisms otherwise private: "If the Professors were told that I said they were all a pack of fools, they would no doubt screw me at my examinations." Circulating caricatures and rumors about faculty, even burning effigies of them, was not uncommon in southern circles.[18]

Students appeared no less critical and confrontational in their encounters with faculty than in their writings about them. Their interactions with teachers and administrators confirmed young southerners' sense of entitlement and zeal for independence. If teachers pointed out their misbehavior, southern students acted boldly unapologetic. William Lee Kennedy, for example, was a sophomore at the University of North Carolina in 1828 when a professor caught him carving on a bench on campus. When upbraided, Kennedy asserted "that as he assisted in paying for them he should cut them as he pleased." Called before a disciplinary board of faculty, Kennedy remained defiant: "Through the whole of the interview he continued to express himself with rudeness, and in a spirit of captiousness and altercation."[19] Such willfulness in southern boys started early. John Randolph was only twelve years old when he wrote his mother, unapologetically, of "a violent quarrel" with one of his teachers over whether he could burn a candle in his room. John maintained that the candle belonged to him, and therefore he could use it whenever he wanted, regardless of school rules. In fact, the head of the school sided with young John and against his teacher.[20]

Even formal sanctions did not temper some young men's defiance. John Gaillard, a junior at South Carolina College, was expelled after insulting the entire faculty during a suspension hearing. According to the report filed by President Jonathan Maxcy with the board of trustees, when "repeatedly ordered by the President to desist from abusive & insulting language, he [Gaillard] treated the Faculty in the most rude & indecent manner, accusing them of injustice & oppression, & declaring his determination not to submit to them."[21]

Students considered themselves at least the equal of and often superior to university administrators and professors. And, as John Gaillard publicly avowed, they were not about to reflexively defer to such men, whatever their academic positions. Southern sons knew well the power their backgrounds promised them, and with word and deed they notified school leaders of that status. When Moses Waddel attempted to expel Robert Toomes from the University of Georgia, the student condescendingly chided the school president: "Perhaps you do not know whom you are addressing in such language." The young man informed the esteemed educator that he was not simply a student, "but a citizen of the State of Georgia."[22]

Students felt emboldened to treat their professors with open contempt by their college classmates. To be certain, young southerners had first learned about resisting arbitrary authority and exercising manly autonomy from their families. But the close bonds they formed with like-minded classmates turned those principles into justification for defiance and aggression.

The friendships that students shared mattered deeply to them, as their letters to one another testify. South Carolinian John Grimball captured the emotions of many southern boys when he wrote about what his friendship with William Reid meant to him: "Although a man may be reduced to the extreme of human misery, if he have a friend to sympathize with him, he feels that he has some thing left whereon to rest. On the other hand let a man have everything his heart desires if he have not a friend . . . who will rejoice in his good fortune, his happiness is incomplete."[23] Away from all things familiar and surrounded by young men of similar age and circumstance, university classmates routinely formed close attachments that helped assuage homesickness and fill leisure hours. Some student correspondents, adopting the romantic prose style fashionable in the era, wrote letters to male friends that, to the modern ear, sound not entirely platonic. After arriving at Hampden-Sydney College in 1811, Daniel Baker wrote back home to his dear friend in Georgia about their separation: "I have become acquainted with several I highly esteem, *but they are not Georges.* . . . Oh, my Friend I have indeed learnt how to appreciate your cheerfull company and conversation—I have been so lonesome." A month later, Daniel continued his lamentation over their separation for what he anticipated would be four years: "Must we then be so long separate? shall one sweet interview be allowed us in all that time?—'tis painfull to think of it, will not our former intimacy be forgotten? . . . shall we still be solicitous to see each other? shall we long for a friendly and tender and sweet embrace?!" While some scholars argue friendships between students could become homoerotic and even homosexual, no such evidence exists among southern boys. Instead, this cohort relied on friendships for emotional and social needs, while keeping an eye on the long-term political and reputational benefits of boyhood attachments.[24]

The consequences of friendships formed in college went far beyond companionship. Some boys cooperated together in their studies, while many others competed in peer groups for accomplishments.[25] And college friendships persisted long after graduation. Attachments formed in youth not only shaped a man's early reputation but also provided important business and political contacts throughout his career. Parents understood all of this and they wrote often and extensively, trying to influence their sons' circle of friends. Frances Pinckney even secured a benefactor for her son while he studied in England to ensure he did not "keep the Company of wicked profane boys."[26] Other parents passed along information about specific classmates, hoping to encourage beneficial attachments. After hearing about the waywardness of a fellow Kentuckian attending the same college as his son William, Joel Lyle instructed William to "have no communications with William Binch. His conduct has been too conspicuous heretofore, not to attach an association disagreeable [to] any one and especially to a Kentuckian who would keep his company." John Ball Sr. likewise sent information about local boys to John Jr., advising him which friendships to cultivate and which to avoid.[27] But young men had their own ideas about what friendships to form and what values to embrace in those circles.

Peer groups became the ultimate arbiters of college student behavior. Congregated together with little adult supervision, students relied on their peers, more than their parents and certainly more than professors, to suggest the boundaries of acceptable comportment. Young men operated according to their own set of rules, shunning indiscretions they found deplorable while teaching and concealing others. From one another boys learned what was tolerated in a man, and together they practiced behaving independently while fulfilling obligations to a larger group. Peer groups intensified youthful independence, they exacerbated students' tendency to defy university authorities, and they helped boys evade parental supervision. Friendships, in short, provided the venue for college boys to act out their manhood—and what a show it was.

The Chaos of College

In retrospect, the chaos and violence that ran rife at early American colleges and universities seems entirely predictable. Teenage boys, separated for the first time from families and communities, living together with limited supervision, encouraged by their culture to be independent and assertive, and in control of their own finances and living arrangements: it was a recipe for disaster.[28] Student misbehavior ran the gamut from humorous mischief to organized violence. Boys attending the University of Georgia rolled cannon balls down hallways to disrupt classes, drank excessively, and caroused as much as the small town of Athens would allow. They also committed more serious offenses such as fighting, keeping pistols, and stabbing each other. President Thomas Cooper's annual reports to the South Carolina College Board of Trustees revealed the same pattern of truculence and lawlessness; many of his students simply refused to follow school rules or focus on academic pursuits.[29]

Occasionally and perhaps self-servingly, southern students wrote home about their peers' misconduct while emphatically disavowing any involvement. University of Virginia student Edmund Hubard stated that many of his classmates appeared "to have forgotten what was their intention, in coming to this Institution. . . . Instead of attending to their Books, they are sauntering about from one days end to another in all kind of rascality, and mischief." Thomas Amis reported in 1798 that at Chapel Hill student disorder was so pervasive that "there has been nothing going forward here but expulsions & suspensions." And William Grayson regretted that incoming freshmen at South Carolina College typically made "rapid advances in smoking, chewing, playing billiards, concocting sherry cobblers, gin slings, and mint juleps . . . to say nothing of more questionable matters." Most boys made invidious comparisons between themselves and their disorderly classmates and used their reports to curry favor with kinfolk. After Kentuckian William Barry moved to Virginia to attend William and Mary, for example, he wrote his brother describing the perverted morals of his classmates. Barry swore that only his constant vigilance allowed him to escape this "licentious vortex."[30]

As such letters indicated, college offered myriad opportunities for boys to engage in tomfoolery. South Carolina College president Thomas Cooper described how a group of boys "stole my horse out of the stable shaved its tail & mane, and rode it about in the night till it was nearly exhausted." Students at Chapel Hill also stole the horse of a disliked professor and shaved its tail. This numbered among a host of "depredations on his property" designed, in the words of the school's president, to "render his life as miserable as possible." While attending Hampden-Sydney, Edmund Hubard reported that "some of the Students drove a gang of Turkies in the dn [dining] Hall last week. . . . They were sometimes in the coffee, sometimes in the butter, and very often on the Students."[31]

Between pranks, boys drank and gambled. Despite Chapel Hill's prohibition against students drinking alcohol, one North Carolinian complained, "You will find some trifling, dissipated giddy youths slyly smuggling the forbidden object. . . . What a pity that those who might otherwise be the ornament of the Nation should blindly rush headlong to their own destruction." Beverley Tucker noted that students at William and Mary "enjoyed mint juleps in the morning, gin twists at noon, wine at dinner, and cards afterwards."[32] In addition to (and in some cases instead of) Latin and Greek, students immersed themselves in such youthful indiscretions. Some became notorious gamblers. Edgar Allan Poe's betting addiction at the University of Virginia is infamous. And James Madison's stepson, Payne Todd, gambled away more money than James could bear to admit to Dolley.[33]

Severn Eyre numbered among the few boys willing to discuss the sexual indiscretions that many of his contemporaries committed. When he first arrived in London in 1785 to study medicine, he showed far more interest in the city's prostitutes than academics. Among the things he confessed: "Saturday evening took a walk merely to view the fine girls of the town, as [they] are commonly called. . . . I forbade every temptation 'till induced (more from curiosity than any other motive) by a little creature between ten & twelve years of age to take her in a coach & here I'll end my letter."[34] Most references to sexual experimentation were more veiled. A Carolina student, for example, admitted spending his school break in London with "a few handsome fallen angels of the other Sex." And William Gibbes, Thomas Pinckney, and Jacob Read were arrested after a drunken night in London that Gibbes conceded was "a rendezvous for Bucks and disorderly spirits."[35]

This cohort continually squandered money. The young half brothers of Isaac and John Ball Jr. proved shamelessly incorrigible on that front. Forced to oversee the boys' educations after their father's death, John Jr. and Isaac tried everything to right Alwyn, Hugh Swinton, and Elias. Sent to a boarding school in Vermont in their early teens, the boys unsuccessfully demanded cash from Alden Partridge, the schoolmaster. When their extortion efforts failed, Alwyn and Elias sold their clothes to finance their surreptitious abandonment of the school. Efforts to educate the boys in England proved equally disastrous. Alwyn and Elias dropped out of school within six months and their dreadful reputations traveled so far so fast that John Jr.'s agent could find no private tutor willing take on the boys. Finally, when a tutor was cajoled into teaching them, Alwyn extorted their tuition money from the frightened fellow so that he and Elias could travel throughout Europe with a group of minstrels. Financial straits forced them to return to Charleston seven months after they departed, having spent over $2,600 in that short time.[36]

Hedonism and irresponsibility frequently gave way to acts of violence. University students not only attacked one another but also their professors. Augustus Alston and Leonidas King were expelled from the University of North Carolina in October 1824 after they "committed violence upon the persons of some of the faculty." The previous year one student was dismissed from Chapel Hill "for having a pistol for the purpose of exploding gunpowder" and two others started a fight that resulted in a stabbing.[37]

Fights broke out with great regularity. On the eve of his graduation from Chapel Hill, Martin Armstrong got embroiled in a conflict between rival groups of classmates. Tough talk gave way to a violent clash between Armstrong and William Haywood. According to a university official, Armstrong "struck him [Haywood] on the head with a club, and knocked him down, repeating his blows as he fell, so that he was deprived of sense for the time." Armstrong ran away from Chapel Hill and was later suspended. His friends, however, joked about Haywood's injuries and suggested that Armstrong's "standing was never half so high as it is at this time." Apparently university leaders sympathized with Armstrong on some level, for President Joseph Caldwell wrote him that the faculty would, in time, "confer on you the degree of Bachelor of Arts, should you ever wish it to be done."[38] Although the early South has a reputation for dueling, students seldom engaged in "affairs of honor." They threatened one another with duels, but usually lacked the restraint and organization required to carry them off.[39]

Students did frequently and effectively organize themselves in resistance against school regulations. Friendships at school encouraged boys to act in concert to subvert rules and to defend one another when caught. In some cases, student uprisings appeared partly justifiable. Both at South Carolina College and at the University of North Carolina students rebelled over the food provided by the steward. According to Chapel Hill student John Pettigrew, "The steward provides very sorrily. There is not one in Colledge that does not complain. . . . [I]t is impossible to describe the badness of the tea and coffee, & the meat generally stinks, & has maggots in it."[40] But in most cases, boys collectively violated rules that compromised their autonomy and restricted their fun.

Generally students who organized to subvert college policies simply wanted to have their way; and their tactics often worked. Students at William and Mary successfully organized to thwart the expulsion of a classmate. The student, referred to as Smith, quarreled with the local postmaster and, angered over his treatment and bolstered with several glasses of wine, he went to the post office and "indulged himself, in the most unrestrained and immoderate abuse" of the postmaster. Unbeknownst to Smith, a professor overheard the tirade and reported the boy to campus officials. When questioned, Smith not only acknowledged his behavior but asserted that it was "justifiable on the ground of a previous insult, and desired the professors to proceed." The professors did proceed—to expel him. This only provoked outrage among Smith's classmates, who threatened to attack the homes of the professors and organized a committee to appeal directly to the bishop of the school. The students were relentless, the professors waffled, and the school "at length determined to let the business drop and S[mith] remain a student." In 1801, fifteen students quit Transylvania in a successful bid to force school trustees to fire a professor. And nearly eighty South Carolina College students, bristling at a school policy that mandated campus residence, signed a pact and moved off campus.[41]

Such tactics succeeded because friends and classmates hung together in their resistance of school policies, even if their defiance led to reprimands, suspensions, or expulsions. Paul Carrington reported that at William and Mary students regularly cooperated to protect classmates who violated school rules: "There is an idea of dishonour connected with the name of an informer, which no student will ever be willing to attach to himself." In the winter of 1821–22, seniors at South Carolina College, in open rebellion against the faculty, "forbade any student to approach any professor for information on pain of social ostracism."[42] Students at the University of North Carolina showed the same enthusiasm for individual honor and group solidarity. Despite the threat of expulsion, the overwhelming majority of Chapel Hill students refused to disclose the names of participants in an 1814 uprising. Explaining the situation to one guardian, faculty member Abner Stith wrote, "I need not tell you the motives which activated them in withholding their information; for you having been a member of College, know very well the custom of the students." After the 1827 boycott at South Carolina College, school officials gave the boys who abandoned the school one week to return to campus. Few accepted the offer: "The majority holding themselves bound by their written engagement with each other, have refused to comply." In the end, the college expelled nearly seventy-five students.[43]

An 1822 assessment by South Carolina College's Thomas Cooper captured the student culture that exasperated university officials found themselves up against: "The Senior Class have adopted as their guiding system of morality, that they are under no obligation to obey the Laws of the College, but merely to abide by the punishment inflicted on disobedience *if they should* be discovered." Moreover,

"Every Student in College, holds himself bound to conceal any offence against the Laws of the Land as well as the Laws of the College: the robbing of henroosts, the nightly prowling about to steal Turkies from all the houses in the neighbourhood are constant practices, among a set of young men who would never forgive you, if you doubted their honour, altho' I know this form of declaration is little else than an insolent cover from falsehood among many of them." He reported one particular night in which "they were guilty . . . of every outrage that they had the power to commit. The Professors were threatened, pistols were snapt at them, guns fired near them, . . . [Cooper was] burnt in Effigy; the windows of my bed room have been repeatedly shattered at various hours of the night, & guns fired under my window." Confronting the students only provoked them: "If we were to ask any young man, who did so, he w'd feel insulted at the Question, and deem his honour injured by being asked if he knew the perpetrator of a crime, altho' he stood near the offender at the time."[44]

Although Thomas Cooper knew that misbehaving students disrupted colleges throughout America, he also realized that his students stood apart—in their refusal to submit to authority, their indifference to academics, their fixation on reputation, and particularly their violence. It seemed clear to educators as well as parents and the young men themselves that southern students were in a league of their own.

Becoming Southern

No one seeking to educate adolescent boys in the young nation enjoyed a particularly smooth go of it. The American Revolution promoted an intensified spirit of individual rights and resistance to arbitrary authority, and students imbibing (perhaps distorting) these values rebelled on campuses throughout the young nation. The freedoms afforded college students tempted even upstanding adolescents. Northern universities, then, saw their share of mischief and riots as well. In 1807, some 150 students at Princeton "took to the street" in protest against administrative actions, and the governor of New Jersey was forced to call out the state militia to quell the riot. And at Harvard in 1791, someone laced breakfast with an emetic, "temporarily halting all campus proceedings."[45] Although far more successful than universities at controlling young men's impulses, even West Point was not immune to their willfulness. Kentuckian Charles Thruston confessed to his father that despite the regimented schedule at West Point, the student-faculty ratio undercut authority: "There are so few professors to so many of us that it is impossible to attend to us all every day."[46] For that matter, young men throughout the Western world behaved badly when given the money, time, and peer group influences that university offered. At European schools "coarse expressions and sexual innuendo" were commonplace, and riots sometimes disrupted European universities just as they did in the United States. Generally educators in the Atlantic world believed that boys, congregated together at school, "were a menace to themselves and to society."[47]

Yet within this general climate, raucous southerners clearly stood apart, outpacing the misbehavior of northern boys and refining unruliness to a high art form. Edward Hooker, a Connecticut native who taught at South Carolina College, insisted, "Southern students require a different management from those in the northern colleges. . . . I do not suppose the same rigid discipline of the North can easily be introduced here." Thomas Cooper even suspected that "no collegiate institution could be permanent south of the Potowmack" because of the arrogance of southern students.[48]

Furthermore, when turmoil erupted at prestigious northern schools, southern students often got the blame. Princeton University trustees attributed most of the disorder on their campus to "especially obnoxious" students hailing from wealthy southern plantations. And indeed, a cohort of Virginians, including Edmund Pendleton and brothers Caleb and Robert Breckinridge, stood at the center of an 1802 uprising at the New Jersey school.[49] At Yale, Virginian Hugh Grigsby observed that "so many Southerners have been rather wild in Yale that they set down every Southerner for a rogue." And after yet another student revolt at Princeton, in 1807, even South Carolinian Martha Ramsay concluded that the fault lay with the spoiled sons of southern planters who "carry their idleness, their impatience of control, their extravagance, their self consequence" with them to college.[50]

Things were even worse at southern universities and colleges. Southerners bristled at authority more than northern contemporaries, and southern institutions, populated nearly exclusively by locals, erupted in violence more often than schools in the North. Even avid supporters of southern universities recognized the problem. Considering the University of North Carolina, David Lees lamented that "the term College has become almost synonymous with dissipation, & it is to be regretted that this idea of our Literary institution is generally too replete with truth." As Virginians made plans for their new university, Joseph Cabell, a state senator who played a critical role in securing funding for the school and aided Thomas Jefferson in the endeavor, confessed that he needed "to be informed on the best mode of governing a large mass of students, without the use of the bayonet."[51]

Nervous relatives and disapproving northerners searched for the sources of this character problem. Some concluded the trouble began in early childhood. Thomas Cooper maintained that "parental indulgence" ruined southern boys for college.[52] Northern tutor Davis Thacher experienced this "parental indulgence" firsthand. Thacher moved from Massachusetts to South Carolina in 1816 to teach on a lowcountry plantation, but he lasted only just over a year in the job. He abandoned it because the mother of his pupils "thwarts my attempts in governing the children—she seldom if ever cross'd their inclination by denying improper requests—in this she seem'd to over look their best good, & have regard only to their present gratification."[53] Inferior early education only compounded the problems of training southern sons. Thomas Cooper attributed no small share of the intellectual shortcoming of his students at South Carolina College to the deficient grammar schools in the state. Further, he complained that he knew "of no school in this, or in the neighbouring states, where a sufficiently good foundation is laid for a collegiate education: we are compelled to admit students half prepared, because no others offer to us." A University of Georgia supporter echoed this belief; boys, he said, are "introduced into situations where with half-formed judgments they are but too apt to run into excesses and improprieties of almost any kind."[54]

Other observers pointed out the connection between the general irreligiosity of southern elites and the waywardness of their boys. Charles Pettigrew reluctantly considered removing his son Ebenezer from the University of North Carolina in 1797 and sending him "to the northward" to finish his education, because he feared the boy could not remain at Chapel Hill "without the danger of having all fear of the Almighty eradicated from his mind." When Virginian John Taylor considered sending his son George to Yale, he wrote President Timothy Dwight, who responded with a diatribe against southern students who denigrated religion in New England and disrupted Yale. Northern visitors often criticized southern indifference to religion in training youths. Edward Hooker complained about the illiteracy, indolence, and impiety of his hosts in Columbia, South Carolina. Hooker expressed particular concern about the dearth of churches in the town. This posed a profound problem for South Carolina College: "Eighty rising youths of just the proper age to be forming their moral and religious principles which are to govern them in life and stay them in death—and no stated preaching in town."[55]

What Thomas Jefferson termed the "practiced domination" required of slave masters and the status slave ownership brought young men further inflated their sense of self-importance. Indeed, the wealth and prerogatives that sons of slaveholding families enjoyed explains much of their comportment. David Swain, who later became president of the University of North Carolina, realized that young sons of slaveholders at the school were too wealthy and spoiled to concentrate on academics. He told his father, "Prosperity has in my conception had a pernicious effect on the institution." In Swain's assessment: "The students are generally the sons of wealthy men, & are in search of pleasure & any thing else but mental improvement. Dissipation and badness & profanity too generally prevail, & I am quite certain that few good scholars are made."[56] Slaveholding also fueled the truculence and violence manifested by southern boys. In the 1780s and 1790s, southern patriarchs acknowledged how slaveholding diminished their sons. In 1786, Virginian Robert Carter III sent his two sons to college in Rhode Island expressly to protect them from the insidious effects of slaveholding. This owner of over five hundred slaves understood that slavery was "very destructive both to the morals and Advancement of Youth," and he determined to keep his boys away from Virginia "till each of them arrive at the age of 21 years."[57] By the 1800s such internal criticism occurred less frequently, although some men still quietly conceded the negative consequences of slave mastery for youthful character. George Swain reminded his son, on reading the young man's critique of the University of North Carolina, that "the dissipation you speak of pervades all the States where Slavery abounds. Were you conversant with the habits of So. Carolina or Georgia University you would find darker traces there than at Chapel Hill."[58]

While adults pondered the causes of what they interpreted as these young men's character deficiencies, the students themselves took pride in what they increasingly defined as their southern distinctiveness. Universities became the crucible of sectional loyalty, as this cohort moved from identifying with their locality and their nation to identifying predominately and proudly with being southern.

In the early years of the Republic local allegiances mattered a great deal to southern students. When medical student Severn Eyre needed money while studying in London in the 1780s, he turned to a fellow Virginian, and when he needed counsel he did likewise, "walking three miles thro' ye snow, well knowing . . . the best chance of obtaining satisfactory advice would be from a Virginian." And after six months of studying at William and Mary, Kentuckian William Barry confessed, "The more I see of Virginia, the more I am attached to the Western Country."[59] Young men from southern states attending college in the North exhibited clear local biases, congregating in friendship circles along state lines, rooming together, and traveling with one another during vacations. Edmund Ruffin Jr., for example, kept track of the Virginians coming and going from his Connecticut boarding school and he roomed with two fellow Virginians. John Calhoun roomed at Yale with fellow Carolinian Chris Gadsden, who although "not particularly given to study," made a good companion. Alfred Beckley looked for fellow Kentuckians when he arrived at West Point, but he unhappily reported that "there are but few from Kentucky here—two from Lexington among the number. I wish there was one more from F[rankfort]."[60]

The more these students lived in close contact with northerners, the more they came to comprehend the fundamental similarities that bound boys from the various southern states together. State loyalties continued to matter, but the greater difference appeared not between Virginians and Carolinians but between southerners and Yankees. Students frequently recorded their regional biases. South Carolinian William Martin, in a typical appraisal, found New Englanders "almost invariably homely . . . [and] industrious & parsimoning in the extreme." Some southern boys acknowledged northerners' religiosity and work ethic, but far more criticized their frugality and social awkwardness.[61] Northerners and southerners recognized a host of differences from the mundane (including pronunciation and eating patterns) to the profound, but the most significant centered on slaveholding. Pushed by their parents, especially those from the Deep South, to reject northern critiques of slavery and accused by their professors of carrying slaveholding's violent nature onto college campuses, students began to appreciate how much their manhood depended on racial mastery. By the 1810s, southern students articulated not only regional identification but also sectional tensions. Boys from southern states increasingly defined themselves as proud southerners and disparaged their northern classmates as judgmental, calculating "Yankees."[62]

As they grew more invested in regional loyalties, southern collegians also developed their own peer-based understanding of southern character. The behaviors that adults found upsetting and defined as arrogance, dissipation, and violence, young men found gratifying and interpreted as pride, independence, and the exercise of manly power.

Young southerners saw no reason why expressing those qualities at university should undermine their standing as men—quite the contrary. In the long run, any number of disorderly and indifferent southern students in fact became accomplished, respected men. For example, Paul Cameron served on the board of trustees at the University of North Carolina, was a major contributor to the school, and shepherded its rebuilding after the Civil War. His name remains an important presence on campus. But his first experiences at Chapel Hill hardly predicted such a happy association: he was expelled in 1824 for starting a fistfight during evening prayers over a chair he wanted that another boy occupied. As an adult, Beverley Tucker taught law at his alma mater, William and Mary, but in his youth the Virginian proved an unruly student. Attending grammar school at Williamsburg in the 1790s, he was punished for disruptive behavior and ranked "at the foot of his class" academically.[63] James Henry Hammond was also a terrible student until his senior year, and John Calhoun hardly distinguished himself at Yale—but this did not slow their rise to power in South Carolina.

Men such as Calhoun and Cameron acquired standing as southern patriarchs only after a long, arduous process—college was only their first milestone. As his nephew Phineas Kollock graduated from college, Georgian Edward Campbell reflected on the boy's entry into the next stage of life, in which responsibilities would be greater and failures graver: "The ordeal of College life through which you have passed with so much credit to yourself is a pretty good test of virtuous principle on that miniature ocean of life however . . . you are now, my dear Nephew, about to embark on a more tempestuous and dangerous Voyage."[64] As Campbell's letter revealed, the further a boy moved toward manhood, the less forgiving adults became.

Even the most arrogant of collegians knew that Edward Campbell was right. Leaving school required southern sons to say good-bye to youthful excesses and face additional, more demanding tests of their worthiness as men. Young men felt anxious, even fearful about entering the next stage of life. In the months after he left South Carolina College and his friends, Thomas (Jeff) Withers confessed to his former roommate James Hammond that he feared "the happiest part of my days are o'er, gone forever." Having left behind the youthful frivolities indulged at college, Withers lamented, "The cares of life seem to have commenced their blasts upon me," and he concluded that "it is likely that I am just entering into the feelings of manhood."[65]

The second, more exacting test of a boy's manhood—his ability to command social respect by acting the part of a gentleman—both overlapped with and transcended formal education. Families indifferent to lackadaisical academic performances proved far more vigorous in their efforts to turn awkward sons into refined gentlemen. And in this test, young men shared in rather than simply worsened their parents' "anxiety of mind."

CHAPTER SIX

The Southern Code of Gentlemanly Conduct

Seldom havens of intellectualism or contemplation, universities served a vital social function for southern elites: they were the setting for young men to begin the arduous, protracted process of acquiring the reputation of gentlemen. Early republican southerners evinced a passion (verging on obsession) for social status and believed that a young man's future hung on public perceptions. Adults therefore pushed their charges to closely adhere to the advice literature that proliferated in early national America and laid out a precise, elaborate code of behavior that would allow their sons to earn their manhood. Meeting these standards meant that a successful southern gentleman essentially turned his life into a performance. The first act began in adolescence.[1]

Time worked against fretful southern elites seeking to make their boys into gentlemen. Anxious about their extensive duties and limited time, advisors to these young men repeatedly warned of the imperative of forming a proper reputation in fleeting youth. Thomas Jefferson cautioned his fifteen-year-old nephew Peter Carr, "Time now begins to be precious to you. Every day you lose, will retard a day your entrance on that public stage whereon you may begin to be useful to yourself." John Haywood similarly warned his young sons, "Now is the time for you all to lay up that store of information and knowledge which is to avail you when you become Men—If you apply yourselves diligently at the present time, you will rejoice that you did, when you are grown . . . [and] gone into life, as Men." And Edward Harden explained to his son and namesake, "You have now entered college—it is an important crisis in your life, and from it you may date the commencement of your manhood, when every action will tend to your advancement, or retard the accomplishment of your future."[2] Southern men universally agreed that youth was the only time to develop the traits that would allow for an honorable reputation—and avoid the lifelong consequences of ignominy. Virginian Harmer Gilmer maintained that "the future destiny of the man depends in a great measure on the habits which he contracts during youth, if they are of a vicious nature, he will be totally incapable to shake them off." North Carolinian Thomas Armstrong similarly explained to his teenage son that "the folly of a moment may fix a stigma on the character of a young man which he may not be able through his whole life to wipe away."[3] Southerners filled their letters—their primary teaching tools—with these sorts of desperate calls to wisely use youth to acquire the name of a gentleman.

The Southern Route to Refinement

Although northerners shared this penchant for reputation building with southerners, a number of factors divided the two regions. First, southern slaveholders surpassed northern elites in their disposable income and acquisition of the artifacts of refinement: homes, clothes, amusements, and travel. And from the colonial era, southern elites tended to be more avid readers of conduct books.[4] They thus possessed both greater desire and more opportunities to indulge in reputational affectations than did their northern neighbors. Second, the gentry continued to dominate southern society after Independence, whereas in the northern states the middle class increasingly shaped cultural values. Southern elites emphasized little of the economic restraint that this increasingly powerful northern middle class valued. Southern gentlemen favored more grandiose, ostentatious displays of wealth as markers of social merit. Finally, the South remained a more agrarian and organic society than did the North in the early Republic. As economic transformations leveled the traditional hierarchical order of northern towns, the links between lineage, reputation, and power became more tenuous. In southern society, however, a man's stature in his community continued to shape his success in business and politics. While reputation mattered to middle-class northerners, for them status was more something derived from personal success than something leading to it; self-made manhood increasingly carried the day in their region.[5] In the South, the acquisition and display of gentlemanly reputations remained more elaborate, more elite dominated, and more essential than in the North. As James Fenimore Cooper observed, "in proportion to the population, there are more men who belong to what is termed the class of gentlemen, in the old southern States of America than in any other country in the world."[6]

This North-South divergence of masculine values played a critical role in the formation of regional identities in the late eighteenth and early nineteenth centuries. Northern rejection of traditional standards of gentility inflated elite southerners' sense of superiority. Southerners imagined themselves as more refined and gracious than their coarse northern neighbors. Southern men's exaggerated displays of dress and oratory, meanwhile, met with ridicule by northerners. To a growing number of northerners, schooled in middle-class values of moderation and self-determination, the southern gentry's exaggerated shows of gentility seemed an affected throwback to the colonial past. Southern men dismissed such criticisms by northerners and non-elites as jealous ignorance and encouraged their sons to build reputations through public displays of gentility. After all, the local peer group of like-minded southern elites—not outsiders— decided a man's place in southern society.

Slaveholding played a leading role in the distinctive masculine values of southern gentlemen. Many travelers to the South linked the aristocratic impulses of the reputation-obsessed gentry to their racial order. J. B. Dunlop found South Carolina's societal inequities intimately interwoven with slavery: "Accustomed as they are to Lord universal sway over their Negroes, they can hardly conceal their Sentiments in Society which notwithstanding all their pretensions are strongly tinged with Aristocracy." Elijah Fletcher, a New England native tutoring in the South, similarly condemned the hypocrisy of Virginia elites who "boasted . . . of their liberty and equality" but dominated poor whites: "Their actions give the lie to their professions. Their [*sic*] is no more equality between the rich and poor than their [*sic*] is in the most despotic government." North Carolina fared no better. Yale graduate Henry Bernard found that the residents of Chapel Hill "like most southerners are indolent, and like very much to lounge about and let the slaves do the work." Timothy Ford concurred: for many rich slaveholding southerners, he observed, "life is whil'd away in idleness, or consumed in dissipation."[7] Residents of the South suspected the connections between slaveholding and men's arrogance and idleness, and some worried that witnessing mastery over slaves warped their children's character.[8] Despite these concerns, slaveholding southerners proudly displayed the symbols of refinement that slave profits bought and flaunted the social status they enjoyed as a consequence of being masters.

The behaviors that gentlemen valued—self-confidence, independence, assertiveness—were also oppositional to the actions required of slaves. Elite men even racialized their criticisms of one another. Men who failed to fulfill societal standards, those who abrogated the power and the duties their wealth and whiteness bought them, had, in the common parlance, "blackened" their reputations. For southern men a reputation of refinement thus went hand in hand with dominion over others and formed the core of southern self-consciousness.

Simply holding slaves did not, however, validate a claim of refined manhood in southern society. Only close adherence to social rules made a wealthy master a true gentleman.

Chesterfieldian Graces in the South's Great Houses

From the colonial era through the nineteenth century, southern elites looked to England as the model for their ideas about gentility. Britons seldom accepted their provincial countrymen as legitimate claimants to genteel status, but neither persistent rebuke in the colonial era nor the collapse of the imperial relationship in the 1770s diminished southern gentry affinity for English aristocratic standards. Southerners continued to prize English goods, education, and advice literature throughout the early national period. After Independence, they became their own arbiters of refinement, but they continued to rely on English standards of evaluation, particularly conduct books.[9]

Deeply influenced by advice literature, particularly the English writer Lord Chesterfield, whose *Letters to His Son* swept America in the late eighteenth and early nineteenth centuries, southerners valued a reputation of social refinement over all other attributes.[10] Chesterfield and his compatriots advised readers on rigorously grooming the self for presentation in society. Gentility, they insisted, required public affirmation. Only through unremitting self-regulation could men act out proper behaviors, suppress inappropriate actions, and acquire a gentleman's reputation. By way of example, Chesterfield bragged that forty years had passed since he said or did anything without considering the impact on his reputation.[11] Southern parents mimicked the advice of Chesterfield, coaching sons on how a refined man mastered himself, body and mind.

Neither southern parents nor sons would have equated this self-mastery with present-day notions of restraint or moderation. Rather, the self-mastery they sought focused on a limited range of activities and related exclusively to behavior in genteel society.[12] Moreover, self-mastery was married to the appearance (if seldom the unqualified reality) of autonomy. Young men cultivated the ability to gauge societal perceptions of behavior and then, if they wanted renown as men, behaved accordingly. In a sense, each boy served as his own judge; except boys did so only within the boundaries of acceptability, with the careful counsel of relatives, and under the peril of social ostracism. Southern parents tended to offer more elaborate advice but also tolerate less compliance than northern parents. Boys from the South could engage in activities such as drinking, gambling, and sexual experimentation condemned by middle-class northerners. Unless extreme and the source of public shame, these behaviors, which today imply an absence of self-control, did not compromise a man's reputation of refinement in the early Republic South. Southern elites instead viewed these actions as another manifestation of self-mastery: no one truly controlled a man but himself. Southern sons felt more passionately about this independence than their northern contemporaries. Yet at the same time young men realized that their independence had to conform to socially defined parameters, and that if they veered too far from the prescribed course, they would lose their claim to manhood. Men thus needed to seem autonomous—to make their own choices—but to choose only what their culture deemed manly. Males learned to perform this type of self-mastery in order to be known as men.

Suggestions for copying Chesterfieldian performances pervaded the advisory letters of southern adults. John Ball Sr. owned several copies of the letter book, often paraphrased Chesterfield in letters to John Jr., and pressed the boy to follow Chesterfield's guidance on sociability and style. John Ramsey of North Carolina agreed: "There are so many polite reflections and useful lessons [in Chesterfield's letters] that no man can be well accomplished either in mind or body but with their perusal." Student Noah Jones held Chesterfield up as an exemplar of the successful integration of "learning and manners." Women also endorsed Chesterfield's guidance. Winifred Green, for instance, offered a common reiteration of Chesterfieldian counsel when she directed her son to use the author as a guide "to be at your ease in any company."[13]

Ease in company was the cornerstone of Chesterfield's advice and the trait that southern elites most wanted to see in their sons. Socializing gracefully marked a man's southernness as well as his refinement. Southerners prided themselves on their superior sociability and gracious accommodation of visitors to the region. When New Englander Ebenezer Kellogg visited Georgia in 1817–18, he raved about the hospitality of his hosts. Residing for much of December at the estate of a lowcountry planter, Kellogg explained that "in his amiable family I find much to make me forget I am a stranger. No acts of kindness are omitted to render my situation comfortable and pleasant." Charles Cotton, traveling in the South at the turn of the nineteenth century, informed his relatives in England, "I am credibly informed that hospitality on the most liberal scale prevails from Philadelphia southward." His arrival in Charleston (which he described as "one of the gayest places in America") confirmed that report. Cotton was "met with great civilities wherever I have been." Philadelphian Thomas Palmer praised Virginians for their "hospitality . . . [and] unbounded generosity."[14] Acting gregarious and hospitable allowed men to present themselves as true southern gentlemen, so boys needed to learn to manifest that image.

This relaxed conviviality was externally driven, part of the public performance that refined southern manhood required. It did not matter if a man felt comfortable socializing, only that he appeared so. As one father explaining the power of community perception wrote: "Public Opinion has great influence on the conduct of men & he who is regardless of it, will sooner or later sink into disgrace and contempt or into vice & immorality—It is the standard by which men are generally measured & . . . [must] be sought for & desired."[15]

Southerners made clear to their sons that a public reputation of genteel sociability ranked above all other priorities, including academics. When southern parents sent their sons off to college or university they hoped, first and foremost, to see them adopt proper social behaviors and thereby move from boyhood to refined manhood. Sterling Ruffin typified this priority; he prompted his son Thomas "to be not only attentive to your books, but particularly so to your manners. A man may be better read than his neighbor, & yet not acquire half the respect if the other should be more accommodating." At best, gentlemen recommended balancing books and socializing. Kentuckian William Barry, for example, explained to his brother, "To pass life in an agreeable manner, a man should not devote himself so entirely to pleasure as to neglect or postpone necessary business, nor should he be so much a man of business as to dislike elegant amusements: a proper mixture of both should be observed." Even George Washington did not believe "becoming a mere scholar is a desirable education for a gentleman."[16]

Not surprisingly, teenagers sometimes took this emphasis on Chesterfieldian-style socializing to extremes. While attending school in Paris, young Harry Manigault looked forward to studying under a renowned mathematician because, as he explained, it offered "the pleasure of being some part of my time with a portion of the fairer sex, for he has a tolerable good looking better part, and two handsome daughters to boot." George Izard bragged that his admission to a prestigious military academy ensured him easy access to and "a considerable degree of consequence" in Parisian society; the city's aristocrats, George bragged, "treated me on all occasions as one of their family." As James Strobhart reflected on his South Carolina College days, he captured perfectly the attitude of many southern sons: "I spent the months in Columbia as pleasantly as I ever spent any in my life. I . . . visited the ladies regularly, and went to all the balls and parties.

You may judge by this that I did not injure any matter by hard study."[17] Southern elite boys could afford to focus on the social arts and sidestep the educational demands placed on northerners because their future wealth rested in part on inheriting slaves and land. Whereas middle-class northerners used college to prepare for careers, southern scions crafted reputations, which they understood, from everything their elders said, would decide their destinies.

Guiding Sons toward Respectability

While writers such as Chesterfield provided the road map to refinement, family was the vehicle for forming reputations. Older kin shepherded adolescents from boyhood to genteel manhood, providing exhaustive advice about earning public respect. Kin devoted themselves to this task because they knew that the actions of a boy reflected on his family of origin. As adults, men represented their households and secured the future of their families in society. Therefore, crafting a proper reputation was not only a complex personal task but also a vital family duty—which helps explain why adults viewed reputation formation as such a high-stakes enterprise.

Elites trying to guide young men toward the all-important skill of gracious socializing struggled against adolescent awkwardness. Like many other parents, John and Jane Ball worried about their eldest son's "natural turn," which they described as "too much of the reserve & unsociable," and they repeatedly asked him to overcome those undesirable qualities. Young men on the receiving end of such critiques often felt plagued by their shortcomings. As a student at Yale, John C. Calhoun fretted over his poor social skills, confessing that he found it vexing to "get over the repugnance which I always have to addressing perfect strangers."[18]

One way that established gentlemen corrected these deficiencies was by bringing adolescents into their social worlds and acting as patrons for them. One visitor to Charleston marveled at the bonds between generations: "The young are not only admitted to a familiar intercourse with the older and the most distinguished men, but these latter take a pleasure in cultivating the talents and improving the tastes and manners of the others." A newcomer to Virginia seconded this observation: "There appears to be great familiarity between the youth and aged in these parts. The young and old attend the same diversions and parties and conduct [themselves] in each others company with a seeming equality. This mode of educating children has a salutary operation in destroying bashfulness and making a young person appear with great ease in any company."[19]

Adults worried about the reputational consequences of boys being at "great ease" with the wrong company also tried to manipulate their sons' peer groups. Convinced that a man's social circle defined him, older kin wrote repeatedly about the imperative of making advantageous friendships. In a typical missive, Thomas Armstrong reminded his son Martin, "There is no better nor more common criterion to judge of a man's character and principles than knowing the company he keeps. Great care ought therefore to be exercised by a young man in first setting out, in his choice of company; for by it he must and will be judged." Boys routinely received stern warnings against forming bonds too quickly or injudiciously and divulging too much to even their most trusted friends. Andrew Jackson cautioned his nephew Andrew Jackson Donelson when making friends to "be guarded at all points" and "make confidents of few." Jackson explained that men sometimes masqueraded as friends "the better to deceive, you must therefore be carefull on forming new acquaintances, how & where you repose confidence."[20] While vigilant in offering this sort of advice, adults did not try to compel proper friendships because they prized autonomy in their boys.

Reluctant to issue demands to their sons, southern adults still wanted to make certain that young men understood that the reputations they secured redounded to the credit or detriment of their entire families. While young Albert Lenoir studied at Greenville College in the 1810s, his father William Ballard Lenoir reminded him that his good conduct would help secure the future standing of his younger siblings: "You have a number of young brothers, your conduct will in some measure operate for or against them, as well as sisters. Let them not be the worse for having an elder brother." After her husband died, Harriott Pinckney Horry beseeched her son Daniel to reflect on how his reputation affected his family: "The loss of your Father . . . and your near approach to 17 years of age makes this a proper time for reflection, for forming your manners & establishing such a character as to make you . . . a real blessing to me and your sister in particular as well as to your other near connections in general."[21]

As hard as they tried to inculcate respectability for both their sons' and their families' sake, southerners also understood the necessity of individual effort. In a typical letter, Sterling Ruffin assured his son Thomas that "nothing shall be wanting on my part to promote your future welfare, by puting [*sic*] every advantage in your power." But what Thomas ultimately made of himself lay in his own hands. St. George Tucker likewise wrote his stepsons, students at Princeton in the 1780s, that their lineage afforded them nearly endless opportunities, but that they alone would decide their accomplishments. Ruffin and Tucker, like their contemporaries, wrote about the necessity of personal initiative *and* the opportunities provided by interested relatives; both were needed to ensure a reputation of refined southern manhood.[22] Crafting a boy's reputation thus became a reciprocal process, with family members (replicating their actions regarding formal education) hoping to inspire but reluctant to compel genteel behavior.

Regional Variations

Although elites throughout the region generally shared the same masculine goals, the South was hardly monolithic in the early national era. The ability of local gentry to achieve cultural standards differed, even if their aspirations did not. Charleston reportedly offered the finest displays of gentility in the entire South. Visitors typically agreed that the city's leading families lived in a style even "more polished than the Virginians." Travelers also singled out other cities such as Williamsburg, Savannah, and Raleigh for their graceful accommodation of visitors and fashionable elites. Southerners and regional outsiders typically found the lifestyles of urban dwellers superior to country folk, excepting the plantation district of Virginia.[23]

The most significant regional differences in the early national South divided established elites in the tidewater from up-and-coming gentry in the interior. The early southern frontier states of Kentucky and Tennessee took a different path toward refinement than did their more established tidewater contemporaries. Whereas elites from the seaboard states saw little to gain by moving west, men from the middling ranks were drawn by land and social mobility on the frontier. Once settled in towns such as Knoxville, Lexington, and Louisville, these status-seeking migrants hoped to replicate the lifestyles of the coastal elites. But their economic and physical circumstances complicated those efforts.

During the initial migration of whites across the Appalachians, expressions of manhood diverged from tidewater values. As historian Joan Cashin persuasively demonstrated, patriarchy got a new lease on life on the southern frontier. Men, separated from families and communities in the East, faced fewer barriers to overt displays of masculine power and became more violent in their households and toward their slaves.[24] In the early stages of resettlement of the southern frontier, physical bravery and hunting prowess were the most highly valued masculine characteristics. As one early Kentuckian explained, "I was raised on the frontiers of Kentucky, in the midst of the Indian war, where men were only respected in proportion to their valor and skill in fighting Indians, and killing wild beasts."[25]

The gradual displacement of Indian peoples and the concurrent growth and increasing sophistication of white populations changed these masculine ideals.

Farming replaced hunting as the primary economic base of Tennessee and Kentucky at the close of the eighteenth century, and, as historian Stephen Aron explained, "men graduated to a more mature manhood reserved for those who had achieved 'independence.' "[26] Self-sufficient farming then gave way to plantation agriculture in some regions of the southern frontier, which moved those slaveholders closer to the refined masculine ideals of tidewater gentry. Traveling to Kentucky in the 1810s, Georgia native William Cumming found the Lexington area quite sophisticated and proclaimed that bluegrass Kentuckians, while "not yet [achieving] the refinement of the first circles in the Atlantic States," nevertheless demonstrated "a very desirable stile of manners."[27] By the turn of the century in several Tennessee and Kentucky cities, elites' homes, gardens, and social activities, as well as their attempts to launch the next generation of southern men, duplicated the refined style of seaboard gentry. These new elite men sought to prove their refined masculinity to skeptical gentlemen in established regions of the South. Thomas Todd, for example, challenged his son Charles, a student at William and Mary, to "show the proud Virginian that a child of the forest in the wilds of Kentucky can vie with him in mental acquirements, that Nature is as fond & endows her sons of the *West*, as liberally, as those of the *East*."[28] Despite earlier variations, then, wealthy and powerful fathers from both the coastal and the interior states in the South agreed on the imperative to train sons to act the part of gentlemen so that they could earn their manhood and make a valid claim to power.

Epistolary Practices

Like Lord Chesterfield, southern families used letters as their primary tools to instruct their adolescent kinsmen on the art of genteel manhood.[29] Young boys of the southern gentry often spent long periods during their formative years apart from their relatives. Attendance at boarding schools and then universities kept teenage boys away from home at precisely the time that their kin worried most about their progress toward refined masculinity. Moreover, letters could be preserved—again as Chesterfield did—for frequent consultation and extended consideration. Relatives frequently wrote sons to safeguard their advisory letters and to reread these epistolary lessons again and again.

In addition to their significance in teaching cultural values, letters also physically represented correspondents. Southern elites fairly obsessed over the appearance of letters because readers used them to evaluate writers' refinement or rudeness. Writers might correspond for years without actually seeing one another, so letters provided the only material evidence of their merits. Although attention to correspondence was a national phenomenon, the status-fixated nature of southern society intensified the zeal for fastidious letter writing among the region's elites. To southern gentlemen, every part of a letter, the content, penmanship, even the type of stationary, affirmed or refuted a man's respectability. North Carolinian David Lees likened the outward appearance of a letter—particularly the size and quality of the paper and the manner in which it was folded—to a man's attire. Lees declared properly presenting one's epistles as important "as that a young person should be neatly & fashionably dressed when he appears in the company of strangers."[30]

The surviving private correspondence of the southern gentry in this era bears a remarkably consistent appearance. The penmanship is neat, the lines of the letters straight and evenly spaced, the quality of the paper uniform, the pages generally filled, and the fold lines precise. Even brief notes conformed to this standard, but usually included an apology for not writing more fully. Content, prose, spelling, visual presentation, and tone all met with scrutiny. In a typical critique Tennessean Francis Ramsey inspected every part of his son William's letter: "improve your diction and writing, make your letters large and fair . . . strive to improve with every epistle you write—be particularly attentive to your spelling, to the grammatical construction of your words and to the forming of your letters."[31] Relatives even warned against improperly selecting and folding stationery. David Lees directed his siblings to keep his letter as a model for proper folding. Green Clay criticized people who sloppily folded and sealed their letters and warned his son to avoid such "foolish" errors. And Edmund Ruffin Jr. felt embarrassed about the quality of paper he used to write his father and vowed to secure a better grade before sending another letter home.[32]

Southerners rigorously, even obsessively, scrutinized their sons' letters because they understood that corresponding was neither a private nor an insignificant matter. In early America, recipients often shared their letters with relatives and acquaintances. Consequently, strangers sometimes first came to know young men through personal (but not private) correspondence. In a typical warning, Sterling Ruffin urged his son Thomas to carefully attend to the letters he sent his sister: "You will reflect my Son that Strangers will see your letters to her, which makes it absolutely necessary that you should be extremely attentive not only to diction, but spelling & fair writing—Let it not be said that an elder Brother who has been so long at the best schools . . . should write a letter which would disgrace a plough Boy."[33]

The advice adults gave boys prepared them for a lifetime of writing representations of themselves. Politicians, lawyers, and merchants often transacted their business by correspondence. In the eyes of recipients, letters epitomized the man who authored them, so no detail seemed inconsequential.

When the mediocre talents of boys failed to meet the lofty expectations of adults, kinfolk inundated young men with directives about adopting a suitable epistolary style. Edmund Hubard, a student at Hampden-Sydney in the 1820s, corresponded with his brother Robert Thruston Hubard, who offered repeated and varied advice about writing. First, he instructed Edmund to "fill up the sheet with something and dont scribble off a few lines and say you are in a hurry." Then Robert criticized Edmund's handwriting: "It is miserable . . . a bad hand & a bad composition are intolerable." Peter Guerrant disparaged his brother Charles for writing brief, poorly organized letters to the sibling group. Charles's carelessness set a bad precedent, insisted Peter, who advised him "in all your writings to be particularly attentive to your style. Let it be concise, intelligent and strictly grammatical."[34]

Misspellings conveyed carelessness and ignorance, insisted southern elites, and no gentleman could afford to let others view him in such negative light. An exasperated Ralph Wormeley rebuked his son for confusing "here" and "hear" and "accepted" and "excepted" and reminded the young man of Chesterfield's cautionary tale about spelling: "Lord Chesterfield tells his son, that he knew a nobleman (more shame for him!) who was ridiculed all his life for writing *upon the hole,* instead of *whole.*" Margaret Manigault felt shocked and disappointed when her son Charles sent home from his Philadelphia school letters riddled with misspelled words and other errors. She informed the teenager that she counted nine misspellings on the first page alone. "If you knew how disgraceful such faults are," Margaret lectured, "you would spare no pains to correct them." John Randolph pointed out a number of errors in the letters he received from Theodore Dudley. One letter, only nine lines long, contained errors in four, including subject-verb disagreements, misspellings, and dropped words. And to make matters worse, complained Randolph, the penmanship was "very bad . . . and every part of it betrays negligence and a *carelessness* of *excelling*—a most deplorable symptom in a young man."[35]

As John Randolph indicated, penmanship was an immediately discernible symbol of a boy's refinement, and so it too required close scrutiny. Robert Hubard found his younger brother's handwriting to be "ugly scrawl . . . such as a Monkey would make with a little practice." Francis Ramsey linked his son's poor penmanship directly to his masculine reputation: "You ought not to write so small and so cramp a hand as you do—If you were to accustom your self to write a larger hand, your writing would appear better and more Masculine than it does."[36]

Strict etiquette also governed extended correspondence. Frequent correspondents expected letters to be numbered or otherwise accounted for in subsequent epistles. The spotty reliability of mail delivery in the 1780s and 1790s made such accounting not only courteous but also necessary. Thoughtful writers also acknowledged the receipt of correspondence or money very early in letters. Adults upbraided boys who forgot such courtesies.

To encourage filial compliance with this rigorous code, some fathers vetted their sons' letters. Willie Jones, for example, asked his fourteen-year-old son to begin writing to a family friend. But he instructed the young man to first "send your Letters by post, under Cover, to me, and I will transmit them to Mr. Morgan." Roger Pinckney's benefactor read and corrected the boy's letters to his mother before sending them along to Charleston. Although less insistent, Sterling Ruffin desired the same thing in his offspring. He informed his son Thomas that, when the boy wrote to his sister, "it would give me a great deal of pleasure for your letters to each other to pass thro' my hands."[37]

Once boys learned the basics of writing genteel representations of themselves, families encouraged them to expand their circle of correspondents. Fathers often told sons to write to older relatives or family friends, not simply to show affection but rather to hone their epistolary style and advance themselves in the world. When John Ball Jr.'s letters satisfied his demanding father, the elder Ball suggested that the Harvard student begin writing regularly to his uncle and "as many genteel people . . . as your scholastic employments will admit." Kentuckian Green Clay similarly instructed his son Cassius to correspond with a number of prominent men, including their kinsman Henry Clay. And he asked Cassius to write Henry Clay in French! Thus Cassius gained a threefold benefit: he strengthened his letter writing, his French, and his ties to his powerful relative.[38]

If boys failed to write as graciously or as often as adults expected, ignoring cultural norms and subverting familial oversight, relatives first turned to their favorite tactic: guilt. When student Charles Cochran ignored his duty to write his mother, she doubted his love: "O my Dr Charles have you allmost forgot your Dr Mother? or do you love her less because you are so far off?" Hoping to inspire his son Thomas to write home regularly, Sterling Ruffin similarly invoked the parent-son bond: "Surely," he wrote the young man, "none can, or at least ought to be nearer than a Father and Son."[39] Chronic inattention to epistolary duties led to more aggressive complaints. After Charles Guerrant, a cadet at West Point in the 1810s, ignored corresponding with his brother John, the elder Guerrant expressed his "mortification at not receiving a letter from you for the last two months. . . . I am sorry to find you so negligent, in a matter which whilst it would consume so little of your time would add to the comfort & satisfaction of your friends." Annie Bullitt lambasted her brother William for failing to write home while traveling to Ohio, and tersely informed him, "I do not intend to condescend to write to you any more until you answer one of mine."[40]

When boys did write home, most adopted at least the superficial style adults expected, but few, even those with a graceful hand and properly folded letter, wrote as often as their families wanted. Parents inundated boys with appeals to write more frequently and fully. Some even tried issuing demands. One father insisted that his son "write once a week by Post untill I countermand the order." And another, also requiring weekly letters, set up a schedule for correspondence with his son.[41] But such pressure for prolificacy succeeded only as far as young men agreed, and sons' lack of enthusiasm about writing home often disappointed parents.

Letters were the gateway to other (meticulous and exhaustive) instruction and evaluation. If sons failed to write, adults could not gauge their progress in forming proper reputations. But rather than discouraging relatives, young men's often lackadaisical attitudes toward correspondence intensified their families' efforts to teach them the code of southern gentlemanly comportment, which only commenced with graceful socializing and ritualized letter writing. Being affirmed as reputable men required boys to alter their physical, emotional, and social lives, to put away personal predispositions and always and artfully act the part of gentlemen.

CHAPTER SEVEN

Acting the Part of a Gentleman

Their relatives' unrelenting letter writing campaigns convinced adolescents that their status as gentlemen and prospects as patriarchs depended on the reputation they cultivated in youth. Reputation, South Carolina teenager John Palmer parroted, was "like brittle glass once shattered it can never more be repaired." Boys therefore routinely vowed to vigilantly attend to their public standing. Like scores of his contemporaries, medical student William Quynn assured his father that he knew "my future progress and happiness in life, depends upon the manner, in w'ch I employ these short two or three years." He therefore promised his father, "You may rely on my applying myself, with unremitting ardour."[1]

But the list of behaviors young men were expected to manicure in order to acquire the right reputation ran quite long, and included dress, diet, recreations, friends, emotions, and even facial expressions. Furthermore, following the Chesterfieldian model, that self-scrutiny needed to appear entirely natural. While engaged in this relentless performance, young men could never seem affected. Anyone who failed to appear effortlessly gracious could be dismissed, as one William and Mary student was by his classmates, for being "a complete fop."[2] Even compliant boys—that rarest of characters—could feel overwhelmed by so intimidating a test.

Gentry sons, then, did not always follow through on the promises they made to apprehensive kinfolk. The difficulty of meeting the requirements of gentility was only one problem. Young men also bristled at so many intrusions into their independence. And with their peers they developed their own ideas about what constituted respectability. The frequent disconnect between their rhetoric of dutifulness and the real temperament of southern youths led adults to spend a lot of time and emotional energy worrying about the irreparable damage boys could do to their reputations and their families. Cornelius Ayer bemoaned the fact that his younger brother's excessive "drinking and frollicking" was spoiling his reputation. Instead of trying to salvage it, Cornelius complained, "you still continue to make it blacker and blacker, and I am sorry to say that you are ruined for ever to eternity." Roger Pinckney's benefactor expressed the same concern, warning the willful boy, "If you do not be careful, of the two or three years to come, nothing will make amend during your whole Life."[3] Not every son inspired so bleak an assessment, of course. But most, their families concluded, needed steady oversight and direction, which was the last thing young men wanted.

Gentlemanly Comportment

Southern elites tried their best to teach their sons an exhaustive list of activities required to act the part of gentlemen. While these lessons varied from the superficial, including dress, to the intimate, such as emotional expressions, they shared one thing in common: all these coached behaviors were for public show.

Throughout early America men understood that appearance, most obviously fashionable dress, informed reputation. In eighteenth-century America, color signified rank, with brighter hues reserved for elites. Wealthy men also paid meticulous attention to collars and cuffs, which had to be stark white and of fine linen. Fabric played an even greater role in affirming social status. Elites preferred silk, satin, and velvet; poorer people wore rougher, cheaper fabrics.[4] Throughout America the self-styled "better sort" dressed to reflect their status and impress their peers. Arriving in Philadelphia in the 1780s, Maryland native William Quynn remarked that "the only manner, young Gentlemen have in this place of Introducing themselves into Genteel Company; is from the appearance of a fine Garment; which is the only Criterion, by which they form an opinion of a man's vice or Virtue." Edmund Ruffin Jr. also found that among both his northern and southern classmates "the boys if they have not as good clothes as the rest are never satisfied and are always laughed at."[5]

Wealthy slaveholding southerners took this national interest in fashion to extremes. As clothing styles evolved in the early nineteenth century (for example, pants replaced knee breeches), "the male body carried fewer signs to be read for social status," as Joyce Appleby has explained.[6] If these signs became more subtle, southern gentlemen still placed a premium on manicuring their outward appearances. In the early national era northerners increasingly found southern elites "showy, their clothes ostentatious."[7] But rich southerners continued to see stylish clothing as revelatory of a man's merit. Georgian Mary Ann Harden explained to her son Edward, "You must attend to your dress my son, and have all your clothes done up nicely . . . for a stranger is always judged of by his manner of dress." John Ball Sr. likewise directed his son to always dress in a fashion to "keep way with the first circles at Cambridge." Even if strapped for cash, parents allowed the purchase of new suits and shoes. When his sons attended college in the 1820s, Virginian Richard Brown confessed that "times are bad & money difficult to be procured," but he nevertheless allowed the boys to purchase pantaloons and coats at school and acquired summer clothing for them in his hometown.[8]

Young men fully absorbed their elder kin's predilection for fine fashions. Boys counted clothing expenses as essential as books and boarding and wrote more expansive descriptions of their and their classmates' wardrobes than their studies. Many spent until they could assure themselves that, in the words of one boy, their clothes "are all genteel, [and] I do not want for anything."[9] Indeed, southern boys fairly obsessed over acquiring the proper clothing. Dress mattered so much to Virginian Severn Eyre that he complained upon arriving for school in London of being "confined to the house 'till thursday for want of fashionable cloaths." Shortly after starting St. Mary's College, William Ruffin asked his mother to mail him a ring containing her hair and a breastpin, "as they are a part of the dress among the Students."[10] Other young men requested new shoes, coats, hats, and waistcoats, all to keep up with the styles and expenditures of their peers. These connoisseurs of fashion also learned to use that knowledge to police class lines. Leonidas Polk, for example, made fun of a "backwoodsman" classmate at the University of North Carolina for the boy's ignorance of style: the less sophisticated student hired a tailor and received a coat "in the top of the fashion," but, unaware of shifts in style, he rejected the fashionable jacket and asked for an out-of-date replacement.[11]

Dressing the part of a gentleman required not only wealth and sophistication but restraint as well—and parents found teaching this part of the lesson extremely difficult. Young men who overindulged were maligned as fops, which damaged status in adult society nearly as much as poor attire. Boys who violated the fine distinctions between elegance and excessiveness required strong correction. Martha Ramsay, for example, sent a blistering letter to her son for overspending on "foppish clothes" and charged him with "shameful dissipation."[12] David Ramsay earned such rebuke because he imperiled his reputation and squandered family resources, both unacceptable for a future patriarch.

The expectation of gentility and restraint affected ideals about the physical body as well. Weight mattered significantly, as a lean body conveyed refinement, self-mastery, and virility. Parents feared that overindulgence in food threatened both health and reputation, and they routinely queried college boys about their girth. John Ball Sr. fretted upon hearing that his son had "grown very fat" while attending Harvard and directed the young man to "consider bodily exercise *daily*, as part of your indispensable duty." Many adults concurred, insisting that overeating was base and rude. One father urged his son, while attending dinner parties, to "never give in to excess; nor let the pleasures of the table, or the bottle seduce you to indulge . . . to select properly from the plate at table will shew, whether a man is well educated or not."[13] Many young men reported their exact weight and worried when they gained too much. Thomas Bennehan, for instance, confessed to his sister, "I have fattened a little," while attending the University of North Carolina. Sons echoed their parents' disapproval of heaviness and derided friends who gained too many pounds. Thomas Pinckney Jr. and his cousin Harriott Pinckney mocked a recently married friend who put on significant weight after his nuptials. Being underweight was also problematic, for it implied frailty. Brothers Charles and Robert Harris quizzed one another about their respective weights, particularly after Robert suffered an illness. Charles hoped his brother had "recovered from your emaciation and now weigh full 150 lbs."[14]

Height also informed the masculine status of southern men, although less so than weight, because it lay beyond individual control. Still, young men took pride in getting taller, and relatives worried about short kinsmen. Attending boarding school in Massachusetts, fifteen-year-old Georgian John Wallace Jr. happily reported to his sister that he had grown quite tall: "I am five feet nine inches—and grow proportionably stout." Roger Pinckney's aunt requested that he send her "an exact measurement of your height" after hearing unflattering reports that the teenager "would be very short indeed." Natural physical attributes alone, however, could never make a man. Ralph Wormeley articulated this conviction in a letter to his wayward son Warner: "You are tall, and are in stature, perhaps manly, but I am sorry to say, in understanding you are a child."[15]

Gentry evaluations of the body centered not only on physical attributes but also on how boys used their bodies in public. Regulation of the mouth, for example, worried parents to no end. They counseled sons to be vigilant about proper facial expressions, eating habits, speech patterns, and conversation topics. Dutiful adherents to Chesterfieldian-style advice, they reminded adolescents, avoided laughing and scowling, yawning, singing in public, talking while chewing, discussing indelicate matters, and improperly enunciating words. Posture similarly merited extensive attention. Refined men carried themselves to exhibit their authority in society, and southerners adhered to a nearly exhaustive routine of controlling bodily actions. Adults wrote long letters to young men warning against stilted gestures and carriage and suggesting proper ways of sitting, standing, walking, and gesturing.

Southerners similarly read the male body for signs of vigor and vitality. Kinsmen sought to inculcate a passion for robust outdoor activities in boys from an early age. They encouraged daily physical exercise, even advising students to avoid excessive study, which undercut a healthy lifestyle. Thomas Amis recommended his cousin Thomas Bennehan refrain from letting academics preclude "your taking such exercise as is necessary for the duration of your mind & Body." Thomas Jefferson advised Peter Carr to spend two hours a day exercising: "Health must not be sacrificed to learning. A strong body makes the mind strong." Walking, according to Jefferson, "is the best possible exercise," and he recommended specific times of day and lengths of walks to Carr. And George Jones wrote his son Noble to go horseback riding every day. The exercise "would enable you to return daily to your studies with increased vigor."[16] Most young men appeared to enjoy physical exertion and accepted that activities such as horseback riding and hunting signified their manhood within their communities. Young students took daily walks, went hunting and riding together, and recorded their exercises in their diaries and letters to relatives.[17]

Fathers and sons also agreed about the importance of speech in proving a man's worth in southern society. Artful conversation was vital to genteel status, and it facilitated the political power of southern men. According to historian Kenneth Greenberg, oratory "was the public display of a superior personality" and allowed gentlemen to perform "their superior intelligence and virtue."[18] As was the case with clothing, passion for conversational and oratorical grace increasingly became a southern phenomenon in the early national era. Such attributes allowed elite southern men to publicly separate themselves from nonelite rivals in their own region and to convince themselves of their superiority over northern contemporaries. South Carolina College president Jonathan Maxcy understood why debating skills mattered so much to his students: "Whatever the tests in other lands, here a man must speak and speak well if he expects to acquire and maintain a permanent influence in society."[19]

Fathers paid great attention to their sons' oratorical skills and offered a host of ideas for improvement. Practice made perfect, and many fathers echoed the suggestion Joel Lyle made to his son: "To give you confidence in yourself . . . let your fellow students hear you . . . before you make your grand Debut." John Ball Sr. thought that speaking nightly before a mirror might help his son to overcome his reticence. And John Randolph even provided a written pronunciation guide for Theodore Dudley, and warned him against "vulgarisms" such as pronouncing "mah" instead of "my" and "saying hurrubble, sensubble, indolunce, &c."[20]

Young men typically adopted this passion for oratory, bragging about their successes and going to great lengths to best shortcomings. Virginian Hugh Grigsby studied singing to "improve my voice, not as much in strength . . . but in softness and in richness of tone." And Francis Gilmer studied the law, he admitted, "not so much to learn at the bar as to come of my time and attention to the attainment of a proper mode of speaking."[21]

Adults and adolescents likewise agreed that traveling marked a man's refinement.[22] Women's duties to family and home as well as the social requirement that they be attended by chaperones limited their trips. Though northern men seconded the values of travel, they less often than southern aristocrats enjoyed the time and wealth to indulge in extended forays. Thus well-funded and extended travels distinguished elite southern boys from women, northerners, and non-elites. Moreover, the ability to travel without impediment starkly contrasted with the rigidly circumscribed physical worlds of slaves.

To see and know the world prepared a boy for manhood and leadership. Offering a typical analysis, William Barry explained that as his son traveled "a new world will open to his ardent mind and present new motives for action." Barry took the boy on trips through the southern frontier in order to "let him become acquainted with the world gradually. This I consider a most essential part of education; a knowledge of *books* and *men* must be combined." Young men loved visiting new places and often extended their travels to and from school in order to explore the young nation. When Kentuckian Charles Thruston left home to attend West Point, he stopped over in both Philadelphia and New York. The visits allowed him to attend museums, buy stylish furnishings for his room, and circulate among polite society. This sort of familiarity with other regions and prominent men helped move a boy toward maturity and the assumption of power.[23]

Travel was but one of several leisure activities that southern men treated as serious business. Although typically depicted by contemporary visitors (and historians) as part of a leisured, even idle culture, southern elites actually gave great time and attention to cultivating proper pastimes.[24] Far more than simple distractions, the recreations of southern gentlemen allowed them to show off their genteel status and set themselves apart from other ranks in southern society. Yeoman families enjoyed little spare time and even less disposable income, which limited their ability to hunt for sport, bet on horse races, or entertain their neighbors. The expense of attending plays and traveling likewise exempted all but the elite class. Furthermore, certain leisure activities such as formal dancing required a level of trained proficiency that few laboring men enjoyed. Strategic amusements also separated southern elites from northerners. Visitors to the early national South routinely pointed out southern gentlemen's love of horse racing, cards, sports, and drinking. Philadelphian Thomas Palmer marveled that "these amusements, if they can be so termed, are not even prohibited by the laws."[25] Outsiders also frequently juxtaposed the "industry" of the North with the "idleness" of the southern elite and linked the southern predisposition toward leisure to slavery. One traveler bluntly concluded: "The whites generally speaking, consider it discreditable to work."[26]

Elites pressed young scions to develop recreations conducive to proper manly reputations. Some hobbies, including playing a musical instrument, dancing, fencing, and painting, conveyed gentility. Other activities, such as horse racing and betting, allowed men to publicly display their economic power and self-confidence. Finally, more physically aggressive activities, especially hunting, demonstrated the masculine prowess of these scions. Hunting was, in fact, an ideal recreation for a boy seeking to become a southern man. It bred physical agility and strength, and it allowed boys to showcase their talents before adult men and therefore facilitate public recognition of their manhood. Thomas Jefferson highly recommended hunting. He explained to Peter Carr that it "gives a moderate exercise to the body, it gives boldness, enterprize, and independence to the mind."[27]

Enjoyment of these activities, however, needed to be moderated so that young men did not appear totally undisciplined or imperil their family assets. Southern gentlemen regularly engaged in recreational behaviors, particularly drinking and gambling, that could easily be taken to excess. Southern gentlemen loved to drink, collected wines, and lubricated social functions with alcohol. One visitor to South Carolina found excessive drinking a mark of manhood, observing that "the more wine he can swallow the more accomplished he conceives himself."[28] But southerners shunned alcoholics as vulgar. Negotiating that line proved difficult for impulsive adolescents, particularly when drinking constituted a key component of the masculinity they sought. Some succeeded, but others faltered.

Gambling, another favored leisure pursuit of elite men, was also highly addictive and financially perilous. Like drinking, gambling showed a man's spirit and self-mastery. But it was all too easy for young men's betting habits to slip from amusing to obsessive. James Madison's stepson, the aptly named Payne, became addicted to gambling at a young age, ruined his reputation, humiliated his mother, and squandered the family estate. And after just one year at the University of Virginia, Edgar Allan Poe returned to his guardian John Allan's home having accumulated debts, mostly from gambling, in excess of two thousand dollars.[29]

When young men overindulged, whether with eating, shopping, or betting, their families explained the terrible reputational costs of such excesses. But the youths' self-confidence and the encouragement of their peer groups emboldened sons to challenge their parents' values and trumpet their own ideas about manly comportment.

Whose Respectability? Contesting the Gentleman's Role

Although southerners placed a premium on family harmony, the disjuncture between parents' refined ideals and sons' indulgent behaviors sometimes forced conflict. For example, southern parents asked boys to give the same scrutiny to their emotions as they did their clothes, but young men usually failed in those efforts. According to adults, a dutiful son carefully monitored and molded his feelings in order to earn a reputation of refined manhood. Offering typical parental advice, Joel Lyle explained to his son that mastering one's emotions mattered more than "all your acquirements" at college. Adults frequently counseled sons to repress anger, mirth, and sadness. Roger Pinckney's benefactor, for instance, warned his fourteen-year-old charge and the boy's friends to avoid stretching "your Mouths from Ear to Ear by immoderate laughing." Ralph Wormeley wanted his son to "avoid bad speaking, vehement gestures, and roaring laughter."[30]

In comparison to the advice on dress (which impressed friends) or even letters (which engendered parental approval and ensured the flow of money), boys saw few advantages to exerting this sort of emotional restraint. More typically they acted so out of control that rebuke for emotional excesses pervaded family correspondence. John Eppes castigated his son Francis after learning that the boy angrily accused a classmate of stealing from him. Demanding the teenager "curb and correct your temper," John avowed, "The greatest curse that can be inflicted on a human being is a suspicious temper." A restrained demeanor, conversely, commanded respect and should be the boy's ultimate goal.[31]

Typically rash and brash, young men largely rejected parental appeals to moderate public expression of their feelings. Instead they reveled in peer culture that lauded bravado and often resulted in indecorous, headstrong displays. Their appalling actions demonstrated the perils of parents' inculcating autonomy in childhood and then requesting respectability in the teenage years. Virginian

Warner Wormeley provides an apt case. In spite of repeated appeals and re-criminations from his father, the young Virginian violated every norm for re-fined manhood. In the words of Ralph Wormeley: "My eldest Son is very nearly every thing I wish him not to be—he wants understanding—is deficient in manners—is idle, expensive, and addicted to low company." Warner squandered money prodigiously during his residence in London, and, instead of socializing in respectable company, spent his time "sauntering about the Streets of London" and keeping "bad company."[32] Georgian Benjamin Cater, another reckless young gentleman, began his slide toward dissipation by spending too much money while attending school in New York. Eventually he impregnated a servant in his boarding house, left school, defrauded his benefactors, abruptly quit the count-ing house where he clerked, and fell into "a lazy indolent life." All of this transpired before Benjamin's twentieth birthday and despite the best efforts of friends and mentors to right his path.[33]

Young men also felt entitled to make whatever friendships they desired, despite parental warnings about judiciously selecting close companions. Some boys, to be certain, heeded that counsel. Traveling to Philadelphia in 1782, Marylander William Quynn was greeted by a Mr. Fox, who "offered anything in his power to serve me." Remembering his father's explanation about friendships requiring reciprocity and marking a man's reputation, William declined the offer, "as I would wish not to receive any favours, which would lay me under obligations unanswerable in my present situation, so I have deferred accepting any."[34] More often than not, however, the follies of youth and their sense of autonomy pulled boys toward questionable friendships and disreputable be-havior. The hedonistic attitudes of autonomous young men, then, did not derive from their utter disregard for reputation. Instead, boys cared deeply about what their friends and classmates thought of them and often acted according to the code of conduct that their peers—not their parents—created. Excessive drinking, spending, and carousing could earn a young man respect from his equally self-indulgent peers. Boys defended their right to set these standards as well as the reputations they earned by fulfilling them.

Duels constituted the ultimate defense of reputation and display of status among adult southern gentlemen. The "affair of honor" persisted longer in the South than elsewhere in nineteenth-century America and played a profound role in demarcating gentility among men in the region. According to Bertram Wyatt-Brown, duels publicly divided "respectable gentlemen from the rest of society."[35] Few adolescents fought duels in the early Republic era, however. A number of factors combined to discourage dueling among youths. First, most duels arose over political rather than personal conflicts, and young men lacked the political motivation as well as the fully developed sense of community authority that dueling required. Moreover, dueling, with its elaborately choreographed, ritualistic violence, required more self-control than most adolescents possessed. There were, to be sure, occasional exceptions, including the infamous "trout duel" at South Carolina College. The event, precipitated when two friends reached for the same plate of fish in the dining hall and both refused to relent, left one teenager dead and the other lame and so despondent that he died three years later.[36] But such episodes were exceptional. Boys were far more likely to commit spontaneous acts of violence than to coolly coordinate duels.

While seldom duelists, young men went to great lengths to defend reputations that they probably should have disavowed. John Palmer, a South Carolina College student, provides a perfect example. In the spring of 1822, Palmer, a lackluster but wealthy student, was expelled from the college, a matter he explained in a lengthy, unapologetic letter to his mother. By John's account, a group of students returned to campus from a ball "not altogether sober" and continued their party in student housing. When their drunken revelry awakened the president, Thomas Cooper, he and a faculty member, Lardner Vanuxem, came to inspect the student quarters. The students, including John, barricaded themselves in their rooms. One student stood guard, hidden from view, with a chair he eventually threw at Cooper and Vanuxem. After dodging the chair, Cooper and Vanuxem broke down the door and demanded the names of the offenders. By John's accounting: "Dr. Cooper then advanced and in a great rage enquired of me my name. Upon telling him I did not wish to give it he struck me with his cane. . . . I instantly demanded his motive for attacking my person. He abused me with language that would have disgraced a jockey and said he had had his brains almost knocked out and again asked my name." Throughout the tussle, John refused to disclose his identity, so Vanuxem "forcibly carried" John into the antechamber and found out his name from other students. "Never had my feelings been so severely wounded, struck and then abused without the means of redress," complained the teenager. After appealing to the faculty one by one, and bolstered by his classmates, who signed a petition on his behalf, John eventually secured his reinstatement to the college. But he insisted that his reputation still suffered and that the college president owed him an apology. He leveled a flurry of invectives and legal threats when Cooper refused to comply. As John explained to his mother, "I have demanded satisfaction of Dr. Cooper for striking me, but he refused to give any. I threatened to prosecute him for damages and also to carry him before the trustees. Satisfaction of some kind I must have."[37]

Boys such as John Palmer clearly adopted societal concerns over reputation, but, as his experience also revealed, estimable behavior meant something different in youth culture than it did to southern adults. Certain of their own importance, these bold teenagers responded with defiance and defensiveness at the slightest challenge. Henry Clay Jr., for example, let a minor misunderstanding with a postal clerk at West Point escalate to violence. When ordered out of the post office, the aggrieved cadet struck the clerk with a piece of iron. Unsatisfied, Clay sped to his quarters to arm himself; only the intercession of other cadets kept the disagreement—over payment of a letter—from potentially turning deadly. Clay reported the entire tale to his father, and struck a defiant tone even though his behavior got him suspended from West Point: "Tell my mother, that although her son has acted precipatately he has nevertheless acted honourably." Young men felt entitled to respect and confidently challenged authority figures who failed to give it. When Andrew Jackson Donelson and several of his friends were dismissed from West Point in 1818, they promptly traveled to Washington to seek redress from the secretary of war and the U.S. Congress. And boys felt no qualms about judging powerful men. In addition to regularly and roundly criticizing their schoolmasters, southern scions also showed contempt for political leaders. Ralph Izard Jr., still not seventeen years old, felt sure enough of his own judgment to condemn the secretary of the Treasury, whom he met while dining with the president: "Of all the men I ever saw, I never found one who looked so much like a thief, he cannot even look a man in the face, always looking out of the corner of his eye."[38]

Sons revealed these same attitudes when they and their families disagreed over money, which happened all the time. The wealth of southern gentry families, their affinity for refinement, and their enthusiasm for male independence all encouraged extravagance in adolescents. But parents also wanted to inculcate fiscal responsibility. To early national southern parents, money mattered far beyond the bottom line. If sons expected to acquire a proper reputation, they had to manage money in a socially respectable fashion. On a more practical level, southern sons needed to learn to oversee finances in order to protect the fiscal futures of their families. Boys, however, treated finances as a manifestation of their autonomy. Adolescents spent money wildly to entertain themselves, to impress their peers, and out of youthful imprudence.

Southern parents maintained that refined men earned their reputations in part by controlling their use of money. Boys therefore needed to walk a fine line between excessive frugality (a frequent criticism of northerners) and decadence (associated with Europeans). Parents and guardians advised using money to "keep way" with peers, but warned against excessive spending that would empty family coffers and compromise reputations. Sterling Ruffin, for example, condemned "parsimony or niggardliness" and directed his son to "[steer] a middle course between meanness & extravagance." Andrew Jackson likewise counseled his nephew Andrew Jackson Donelson to "practice oeconomy—but to draw proper distinction, between that and parsimony."[39]

Never eager to antagonize relatives, young men routinely wrote about their *intentions* to follow parental counsel about spending money genteelly. Boys' actions, however, belied their words. Shortly after departing Virginia to attend school in Philadelphia, James Hubard vowed that "the utmost frugality shall be used by me, on every occasion." Well, nearly every occasion. Stopping off in Petersburg, he purchased a new coat, stockings, and "a fashionable Hat." Apparently broke by the time he reached Baltimore, he borrowed money from a family friend. But, James swore, once he actually got to Philadelphia "I shall fall upon the most frugal mode of spending . . . [and] adopt the plan you advised to me."[40]

As James Hubard's letters hinted, few sons followed through on such promises. Instead, improvidence reached epidemic proportions among southern collegians; they simply loved spending money. When Virginian Edward Tayloe attended Harvard in 1819–23, his expenditures showcased the southern predilection for the finer things in life. The teenager paid a servant, a livery stable, and tavern keepers, in addition to his boarding fees. Hats, shoes, clothing, and room furnishings were, apparently, necessities. In his first year, Edward spent over twice as much on clothes as on tuition, and nearly as much on a trip to Washington as on tuition. Every year he meticulously reported his expenditures to his father, down to the cost of postage. Yet the first year, he also reported spending $91.87 on "sundries." The second year, after accounting for tuition, room and board, books, clothes, boots, a hat, curtains, laundry, a visit to a dentist, and postage, Edward still recorded $208.33 for "Pocket Money" and "Sundries." John Tayloe found such lavish spending at least tolerable if not outright desirable, since he continued to pay his son's bills for four years.[41]

Elites encouraged such extravagance by teaching sons to pursue refined, expensive lifestyles and then allowing them to oversee their own funds. Committed to manly autonomy, adults regularly let teenage students manage all the money intended for their education. When George Izard accompanied his nephew Harry Manigault to enroll in Princeton in 1804, he did just that. In a letter to Harry's father, George explained that "much of the youth from the Southward of the same age were entrusted by their Friends with the Money deemed necessary for all their expenses. Your son was desirous to have the same confidence placed in Him, & I judged it was proper to gratify him."[42] While usually requiring a strict accounting of costs after the fact (students mailed parents ledger accounts for each session's expenses), relatives exercised little oversight up front. When this approach (almost inevitably) backfired, adults compounded the trouble by choosing to respond to profligacy with subtlety and suggestions. They hoped these tactics would give young men the opportunity to independently correct any problems, avoid conflict, and build confidence. Robert Hubard tried to flatter his younger brother into more responsible spending: "I was a little surprised on the receipt of your letter, to find that you are in want of money, though I do not attribute it to your want of economy, but to the unavoidable expenses, which you have to incur—I am very glad of one thing that you are not disposed to imitate your companions." George Swain blended guilt with flattery in coaching his son's spending: "You know that it will give me a considerable scuffle to support you through the term, but I have the pleasure of knowing or believing that you will use my hard earnings with all the economy consistent with propriety."[43] One can easily imagine how such impotent speeches stacked up against the allure of shopping, drinking, and gambling with friends.

An exchange between Theodore Dudley and his uncle John Randolph further demonstrates the dynamics between benefactors and young men. In 1806 Randolph inquired whether Dudley had received a bank note he sent, and Theodore bristled at the interference in his financial affairs. Randolph struck an apologetic stance when he explained the difference between asking whether the note arrived and seeking to find out how it was spent. Randolph explained that he inquired only out of fear the note had been lost or stolen, not out of intentional intrusion into the student's finances: "No, my son; whatever cash I send you (unless for some special purpose) is yours: you will spend it as you please, and I have nothing to say to it. . . . To pry into such affairs would not only betray a want of that confidence, and even a suspicion discreditable to us both, but infringe upon your rights and independence."[44]

Excessive or repeated overspending could, of course, prompt recriminations. After John Pettigrew sent an accounting of his expenditures at the University of North Carolina, his father objected to John's spending money in local taverns: "I think it by no means reputable, for Students to be found in public houses." In especially egregious cases, parents used more dramatic language. Roger Pinckney's relatives in South Carolina and his benefactor in Europe swore they would cut off his money supply unless the fifteen-year-old corrected his ways. Exasperated with his son Warner's ceaseless spending, in 1801 Ralph Wormeley also threatened to disinherit the wayward boy and "leave my estate to my daughters, and only so much to you, as may keep you from indigence and want."[45]

Boys usually saw through the hollowness of such threats. And parents spurned the public shame that accompanied disinheritance, for such renunciations of family ties announced parental ineffectiveness and family disharmony. Only chronically dreadful misbehavior provoked the severing of kinship bonds; parents admitted or boys surmised as much.

Moreover, for every parent who bristled at extravagance, many others, eager to bolster the reputations of young men, acceded to filial demands for ever more money. Delighted that his third son, Henry Jr., did not follow the dissipated course taken by his two elder offspring (Thomas became an alcoholic and Theodore a mental patient), Henry Clay wanted to supply the West Point cadet with whatever "comforts" he needed: "Tell me frankly & you know I will supply you with any pecuniary means in my power." George Izard happily remembered that his allowance while studying in Paris "was sufficient to place me on a footing with the wealthiest of those with whom I associated." Some benefactors even apologized for not being able to supply more money. When, for example, an economic downturn delayed North Carolinian Spier Whitaker in sending funds to his brother Matthew, Spier hoped "it will arrive in time to prevent any serious embarrassment on your part."[46]

Given the actions (and inactions) of parents, one can understand why many young men took the continuous flow of family money as an entitlement and struck a belligerent tone with cost-conscious adults. When challenged about his spending habits, Marylander William Quynn flatly informed his father that he needed to "conduct my Studies with reputation" and that "your remittances are too limited." Cornelius Ayer, attending South Carolina College in the 1810s, asserted the superiority of his judgment of fiscal matters over that of his father. Having spent his tuition money on, among other things, laundering his clothes and hiring a servant, Cornelius expected criticism from his father. But, he maintained, "when you know that the money is not spent foolishly, nor carelessly I think you might afford me a little more." Cornelius contended that a servant was a necessity (in ways, apparently, that spelling lessons were not): "No one can live here unless he has some one to weight on him."[47]

Boys simply assumed that they should be allowed money enough to win the favor of their peers and asserted their prerogatives on this score. Joseph Breckinridge argued that he wanted only enough money to "enable me to meet all the demand of College, and dress *as a gentleman*." Boys often pointed out that attending social events that publicly affirmed refinement required the outlay of considerable funds. When his Chapel Hill classmates elected Martin Armstrong to offer a toast at a supper honoring George Washington's birthday, he informed his father, "We according to custom had to treat those from whom we received these distinctions." Peers unwilling to pay risked their popularity. As Charles Lee reported, his classmates dropped friends in straightened circumstance: "If you alledge you are unable to contribute your share . . . you must at the same time say you are unable to keep genteel company, & accordingly sneak off."[48] By playing into their relatives' desires that they act like gentlemen and win the respect of their peers, sons spent as they desired. As a result, in buying the artifacts of refinement they also exercised their power as independent men.

As their sons grew up, many elites must have wished they had followed that old axiom: be careful what you ask for, you just might get it. For better or worse, these early Republic boys were becoming what their relatives wanted: genteel, assertive, and independent. In the process, they redefined respectability according to the ethics of their peers. But they were not yet men until they secured worthy wives. And when boys wooed girls, the stakes escalated, boys' options narrowed, and parents reasserted their power.

PART THREE

PATRIARCHS

CHAPTER EIGHT

Supervising Suitors

Southerners envisioned marriage as essential to the accomplishment of manhood. As Kentuckian William Barry explained, marriage gave a man "stability, as well as a more respectable standing in society. . . . By means of it, a person forms new connections which add to his influence and make his sources of enjoyment more numerous. Young men who do not marry become necessarily dissipated." Because of the high stakes—money, status, pleasure, and manhood—that accrued with marriage, southern elites took courtship very seriously and refused to consign matrimony to the whims of young lovers. Finding a mate was not simply a private, emotional matter; it was intrinsically bound up in considerations of public reputation and calculated power. Families closely supervised romantic and sexual affairs and tried to ensure that youthful passions did not prevail over gentry ambitions.[1]

The Obligation to Love Wisely

Given the great stock elite southerners put in manly independence, one might reasonably conclude that young men married according to their own designs. But gentry sons did not get to make unfettered romantic matches. As in other milestones toward manhood, marital success required young men to honor familial duties, not simply indulge individual desires. Kin determined the timing of a young man's foray into romance, and class and regional interests circumscribed the field of options before young people.[2] Boys could choose who they courted, but only from a small pool of genteel, educated, wealthy southern girls. Furthermore, communities policed romantic and sexual behaviors. While gentry circles tolerated clandestine youthful indiscretions, they would not abide scandal, since widespread knowledge of sexual deviance imperiled family standing. So, in this as in so much else in these young men's lives, the quest for public validation clashed with the promise of autonomy.

Adults found deviations from these strictures about courtship far less tolerable than the transgressions of schoolboys. After all, marriages put money and property at risk. While they still preferred negotiation to coercion, with these higher stakes adults made clear their intention to have sons meet their obligations to choose mates wisely. Parents and sons sometimes struggled to find common ground. The early Republic generation, already raised to assert their independence, also imbibed the national emphasis on romantic expressiveness. Some southern boys criticized their parents' predilection for economically influenced marriages and the persistent communal oversight of romances. William Barry of Kentucky, for example, emphatically declared that, when it came to marriage, "people should always think and judge for themselves."[3] Southern elites, however, refused to abandon the class and kin considerations that had served them so well since the colonial era. Romantic flights of fancy could not be allowed to subvert familial aspirations and ruin their sons' futures.

Adults wanted to make sure that boys understood that a genteel education laid the foundation for fortuitous matches, so marriage always followed schooling. Warnings about completing studies before commencing courtships were standard fare in advisory letters to southern youths. Arthur Lee Campbell wrote his son Matthew: "Let me caution you against being too readily captivated with new acquaintances. . . . Whilst you reasonably indulge in Social intercourse to keep from becoming Melancholy, Morose or boorishly rusty, take especial care to not fall in love with any lady whatever until your Studies be fully compleated." Joel Lyle likewise directed his son William, a Princeton student in the 1820s, to "respect the ladies, but begin not to think yourself a favorite of the fair sex, nor let them steal your heart from your Books."[4] Only once boys completed their education would families support serious courting. While his brother Robert pursued a degree, prominent North Carolinian Charles Wilson Harris advised the young man to "steer a distance from Love & matrimony." After Robert determined to return home and become a planter, however, Charles's opinion changed. With his career commencing, Robert should seek a wife; his brother expected "to hear, soon after, that you have joined yourself to an amiable [woman] who is as much the choice of your friends as of yourself."[5]

Parents argued that a premature match would threaten a young man's future in southern society, for youthful romances distracted from the essential pursuits of refinement and education. Although happy that his son had fallen in love with the daughter of the prominent Middleton family, Edward Rutledge insisted that the young man complete his legal training before marrying. "At the proper time," he avowed, "nothing could be more agreeable to me than the connexion contemplated by my Son." But education must come before any such union. Only after he completed his training, Edward insisted, would his son be able to "maintain a Family in the stile of a Gentleman."[6]

Although they liked flirting more than studying, southern elite boys generally acceded to their elders' decrees about the timing of courtships. John Colhoun Jr. considered it "foolish" for him and his friend William Reid to even discuss serious romances. The teenage student thought himself "too young to think seriously of choosing a partner for life. I therefore at present indulge nothing more than friendship for any female."[7] While flirtations pervaded college life, most young men deferred serious courting until the end of their education. One young University of Georgia student reported that, on a return visit to his Savannah home, he was "on the look out for some one, who in four years, I hope to take unto myself." Although he had his eye on one young woman in particular and felt certain that "she is the only girl that . . . would suit me," the young man understood that he could not even consider marriage for several years. Students assured their nervous kinfolk that they learned this lesson well. Kentuckian and West Point cadet Robert Anderson reported, "As to my courting I can not think of it, as it would interfere too much with my duties." William and Mary student Chapman Johnson seconded Anderson: "I find that an extensive acquaintance would be incompatible with close study."[8]

A number of factors explain the acquiescence of otherwise strong-willed boys to this adult desire. Money played a big part. As Edward Rutledge pointed out, maintaining a wife and home in the fashion required by southern gentry lay beyond the resources of most young men, and sons required familial backing (and thus approval) in order to assume a place of power in society. In some instances, relatives threatened to use economic leverage against boys who forgot these facts. John Lloyd of South Carolina, for instance, vowed he would disinherit his nephew if the young man persisted in his plans to wed an impoverished girl.[9] In most cases, however, no such articulation was necessary. Boys knew what power money exerted, who held the purse strings, and how much disobedience adults would tolerate. And adults took marriage far more seriously than they did education; the indulgences granted college boys were not extended in this more serious test of manhood. Boys shrewdly followed the rules that relatives intended to enforce. They also reveled in the autonomy and irresponsibility of adolescence. While longing to marry at the appropriate time, few wanted to truncate their youthful freedoms. Understanding the myriad responsibilities that lay before them once they assumed their place at the top of the South's patriarchal society, few teenage boys sought a premature entry into manhood. As one young man observed, marriage meant that "boyish trifles are to yield to the scenes of manhood."[10]

Although money and youthful frivolity influenced these young men, their prospective mates probably played the greatest role in their acceptance of adult demands that education and refinement precede courtship. Young women, absorbing the values of their older kin, placed a high value on refinement and education. Elite girls knew that their husband's reputation would dictate their future place in southern society. Consequently, they demanded of suitors all the prerequisites to respectability and power: wealth, family reputation, and education. While courted by Georgian Adam Alexander, Sarah Gilbert bluntly informed him that she was "glad that you study hard as I do not like *lazy men*," and she encouraged him to "exert yourself considerably." Sarah Gibbes conveyed the same message to her teenage son John, a Princeton student in the 1780s. "Most Ladies," the South Carolina mother explained, "admire the man of sense"; consequently, "if you wish success in one [pursuit] you must endeavour to be perfect in the other."[11]

Girls' fears about unwisely choosing a husband made them powerful allies of parents orchestrating the timing of relationships. Adults repeatedly warned girls to select lifelong mates only among a pool of respectable, affluent men and only after rigorous contemplation because, in the words of one mother, "a woman's happiness depends entirely in the Husband she is united to."[12] Considered reason and family guidance—not whimsical infatuation—should underlie the acceptance of any proposal. Divorce was exceedingly rare in southern states; society offered little place for single or separated women, and men retained custody of minor children. There was, in short, little way out of an unhappy match short of the grave.[13] Marrying too young increased all of these risks and, parents reminded their daughters, could result in lifelong misery. Anne Randolph, for example, tried to keep her daughters single until "they were old enough to form a proper judgment of Mankind." When her fifteen-year-old daughter Judith fell in love with eighteen-year-old Richard Randolph, Anne condemned the idea of the teens marrying. Marriage was inherently perilous for women, she insisted, and the danger "is doubled when they marry very young; it is impossible for them to know each others disposition; for at sixteen and nineteen we think everybody perfect that we take a fancy to."[14]

Adults found it more difficult to manipulate *who* a boy pursued than *when* he began courting. Believing proper matches vital to family futures, elites spent a lot of energy trying to circumscribe the range of women men could court. Adults prodded sons to seek out women from respected families holding significant estates and living in the same region or locale. Parents typically frowned on engagements with women outside the South, or even beyond their locality. When, for example, John Ball Jr. attended Harvard, his father directed him to "preserve your heart for some fair lady of Carolina." Indeed, both John's mother and father expected him to marry among the prominent families of the South Carolina lowcountry, and they hinted that a poor marital choice could result in disinheritance. John Jr. got the message. After graduating in 1802, he returned to Charleston and married his first cousin. Although happy when her son gained the esteem of several "worthy" families while studying at Princeton, Sarah Gibbes likewise warned her teenager to avoid falling in love: "Pray My Dear Jack are you not in danger of losing your heart."[15] To be certain, regional biases ran both ways, with anti-southern sentiment coloring northern views of southern women and diminishing their desirability in the minds of some northern men. Warning her son against marrying a Virginian, a Pennsylvania mother declared, "Their manners, habits, nay very ideas are different." And Thomas Larkin, a Massachusetts native working in North Carolina, flatly denounced any idea of marrying southern women: "I never knew a Yankee that took a wife here, and settled in the contry [*sic*], but what became riduced in his business by it. They can not prosper . . . and at the end they become downright Carolinians."[16]

Boys did not obediently follow this part of the plan laid out by their relatives. Young men enjoyed flirting with a wider range of girls than their parents found appropriate. Most eventually honored regional loyalties in their marriages, but the challenges they made during adolescence kept adults vigilant. Courting remained a contested terrain between the generations, even if elders eventually held sway on many matters.

Students and young travelers proudly reported on their active social lives with girls from the cities they visited. South Carolinian Lambert Lance caroused until midnight with attractive girls he met in Princeton. Studying medicine in Philadelphia in the 1820s, North Carolinian Fabius Haywood marveled at the number of beautiful girls in the city: "The ladies dress as gay as butterflies on a summer day, and there seems to be thousands of them a day on Chestnut. I go down often to look at them." And while seldom mentioning academics, South Carolinian John Grimball found plenty of time to attend balls, parties, and dinners, with "the *Beauties*" of Princeton. He bragged in a letter to a friend, "The place abounds with handsome young ladies."[17]

Some boys went even further in their romantic dalliances with regional outsiders. After a few years residing in Massachusetts, South Carolina native John Colhoun Jr. began to prefer the girls of Boston: "I have but lately found out that the Yankee girls are very fine and upon due consideration, think they would make much better wives (if I may be allowed to think at all on the subject) than the southern."[18] In some cases, young folks from different parts of the nation fell in love and married. During the late eighteenth century, elites viewed such far-flung matches as missed opportunities to enhance local status and wealth. But as southern notions of regionalism intensified in the early decades of the nineteenth century, such unions increasingly compromised status in southern society. Colhoun, writing in 1818, feared being labeled a "deserter" for confessing his enchantment with Boston girls. Young men like him knew that their families increasingly viewed serious relationships with girls from the North with disdain. So while boys still pined for and flirted with outsiders, they usually married from within their locale.

Increasingly in the 1810s and 1820s, dutiful sons promised their relatives that they wanted to affirm local loyalties as they entered into serious courtships. When Robert Anderson attended West Point in the 1820s, the teenager assured his sister that the lovely New York girls never distracted him from his devotion to home: "Although surrounded by the most captivating galaxy of beauty that I ever witnessed, although on every side I saw beautiful ladies who were laughing & in the most agreeable manner, and by their winning manners seemed to invite me to become acquainted with them, still I felt as if I was not in my right place." Virginian and Harvard student Charles Carter Lee likewise conveyed in a letter home his determination to withstand the overtures of women in Boston. Charles did, however, concede that "it is with the greatest difficulty I can resist the repeated solicitations of the ladies."[19]

The proximity of local girls and the peer groups in which young people circulated aided adults in their efforts to promote local allegiances through the next generation's marriages. Young men typically returned home after completing their studies. Therefore, when they approached the right stage of life to seek a mate, they tended to be surrounded by neighbors and circulate among local elites.

One issue almost never factored into adults' thinking about appropriate matches: religion. Few elite families even mentioned, much less squabbled over, the religious leanings of young lovers. In fact, religion inspired commentary only in cases of profound differences in beliefs, such as when Christians and Jews fell in love. For example, it merited discussions when Edward Marshall, a Christian, fell in love with a Jewish woman, and when Moses Mordecai, a Jew, wanted to marry a Gentile. But even in these cases, a second factor complicated the unions. Marshall's girlfriend was from the North. As he admitted, "Jew & Gentile, Yankee & Southern cannot be easily united." And Moses's family suspected his intended lacked a proper education.[20] Such discussions were rare exceptions. Typically, families negotiated interfaith unions to a mutually agreeable resolution. For example, before the Stier family consented to their daughter Rosalie's marriage to George Calvert, Calvert signed a premarital contract stipulating that all their children would be raised Catholic. Similarly, families easily overcame concerns about the irreligiosity of a suitor. The Gamble family, devout Presbyterians, accepted their daughter Elizabeth's engagement to William Wirt, despite his impious past.[21] The Calverts and Gambles typified the experience of families in the early national South, whose letters and diaries record a near vacuum of commentary on the religious implications of courtships. Class was another matter entirely.

The Economics of Courting

Southern elites felt most strongly about the necessity of promoting family interests through strategic matches. The pressure parents placed on boys to cement wealth and power through their romances contradicted the growing national trend toward marrying for love. In the nineteenth-century North, the evolution toward first a market economy and then an industrialized, urban society altered family relations in general and mate selection in particular. Coupled with shifts in cultural values that emphasized individualism and sentimentalism, these economic changes eroded the power of extended kin and undercut patriarchal power. Young people in the North, no longer so reliant on relatives for their economic future and encouraged by societal values to seek personal fulfillment, increasingly selected their own partners. Romantic love replaced familial interests (religious, political, financial) as the primary basis for marriage among the increasingly influential middle class.[22]

The South took a more crooked path, both in terms of economics and family values. The lingering agrarianism of the South, the continued influence of the slaveholding gentry over southern society, and the reliance of these powerful elites on slave labor made the South distinctive within the young nation. Economic innovations did not so thoroughly transform southern gentry families as they did the northern middle class. Although southerners embraced the ideals of individualism and affection, they did so in a moderated form. Slavery perpetuated the subordination of white wives, and patriarchalism remained more powerful and more pronounced in southern than in northern marriages. Moreover, among southern elites, economic and political interests continued to sway spousal selection long after northerners, led by the middle class, reordered their priorities.[23]

Although they often lauded the new ideals of romantic love, southern adults also openly disapproved of economically disadvantageous matches. Love was well and good, until it imperiled status. Marrying without respect to financial consequences was, according to William Short, the most dangerous mistake a man could make. William conceded, "There is an infinite world of follies & of various grades that may be committed by young men—They may be wild & dissipated & idle." But marrying down was the worst: "It destroys the prospect in life of him who commits it" and it produced children destined to live in "misery and want." He cautioned his nephew "never to purchase short pleasures at the price of long regrets."[24]

Older kin tried to coax young people toward advantageous matches by warning the early Republic generation against the perils of passion-induced impoverishment. But southern boys, influenced by advice literature touting affectionate individualism and full of youthful passion, sometimes clashed with adults over the basis of an appropriate match. Heady with infatuation, young men complained about adults inserting money into romantic matters and the southern gentry's predisposition to encourage materialism and belittle true love. But when faced with youthful reproach of financially informed marriages, adults held firm. Southern elites refused to abandon the marriage patterns that underlay their wealth and power. If young men persisted in defending their prerogatives in choosing a mate, generational disagreements could produce conflicts. But in these struggles, unlike spats over how students spent money or who they befriended, parents, not sons, usually held sway.

Since adults did not like to dictate to young men, they initially negotiated over questionable matches. In 1827 George Henry Calvert, eldest son of wealthy Maryland planter George Calvert, abandoned his father's home over a dispute regarding George Henry's desire to marry Elizabeth Steuart. The younger Calvert believed his father's sole objection to the match was the young woman's modest means. George Henry, deeply in love with Elizabeth, recoiled from his father's calculated objection. Since even principled men required money, George Henry quizzed an uncle about the prospect of living off proceeds from his mother's estate. In response, his uncle explained that the twenty-four-year-old, who earned no independent income, could expect only a pittance from his mother's trust. The uncle wisely concluded, "It seems to me that the eldest son of Mr. Calvert has a lot to lose if he breaks with his father." Yet even from this dismal position, George Henry arranged a compromise with his father. In exchange for his delaying the marriage for two years and building up his own assets, his father withdrew his objections. Clearly the elder Calvert held the power to thwart his son's desires; he chose instead to bargain with the young man so that his affections and the family's interests could both be fulfilled.[25]

Of course, since parents encouraged and often required economic self-sufficiency before marriage, financially dependent young men saw few alternatives to compliance if parents toed a hard line. George Henry Calvert got his way, but he did so on his father's timetable and by his father's accounting. Likewise, when twenty-three-year-old Beverley Tucker, struggling to launch a legal career and still financially reliant on his father, announced in the summer of 1807 his intentions to marry Mary "Polly" Coalter, his father, St. George Tucker, balked. Although Beverley explained that his half-brother, John Randolph, promised to furnish the couple a house, St. George remained resolute: so long as Beverley depended on him to pay his bills, no wedding would take place. St. George directed his son to "Abandon every Idea of marrying until by Industry and Assiduity you have laid an actual foundation for your mutual support & that of your family, without the aid of your Brother."[26]

Marriage was simply too important and too permanent to squander, so if young people persisted in ignoring the financial ramifications of their selection of a mate, relatives upped the ante. John Lloyd opposed his nephew Richard Champion's choice in a girlfriend, and warned the young man that if a couple lacked "sufficient means to procure ye comforts & conveniences of Life . . . the most ardent love becomes cool." When Richard failed to heed this subtle warning and proceeded to plan an engagement with the impoverished woman, his uncle got more pointed: "The idea which possesses ye mind of too many young persons, that Love will support ye want of fortune is romantick, idle, & ridiculous, &, those who have suffered themselves to be deluded by that, have, when too late discovered their mistake." Warnings then turned into threats. If Richard insisted in wedding this girl, his uncle declared, the "very imprudent matrimonial connexion" would result in Richard's disinheritance. Finally the young man heard his uncle. Richard broke the engagement, and John complimented him on "your prudent determination, & your respectful attention to my sentiment." Richard returned to John's good graces and, presumably, to his will.[27]

When an inopportune marriage threatened the family estate, adults could prove quite uncompromising. Although it was always a last resort, they were willing to follow through on economic threats to coerce youthful compliance. Timothy Ford recounted in his diary the levels to which family contention over marriage could rise. According to Ford, a young member of the South Carolina

Shipping family eloped with a woman his kin found intolerable. His relatives beseeched Shipping to "forget the harlot" and marry another, proper girl, but, proclaiming he could not live without her, the young man refused to relent. The Shippings then issued an ultimatum: either leave the girl or lose his inheritance. Tragically, instead of extracting the young man from the relationship, the demand drove him to suicide.[28]

By the same token, adults who lost the power of the purse could also lose the battle over marriage. Kentuckian Charles Wilkins Short faced a revealing dispute with his uncle over Charles's choice in a wife. When the twenty-year-old wanted to attend medical school in Philadelphia, his uncle William Short footed the bill. William also introduced his young nephew to the influential members of the Philadelphia medical community. When he completed his medical education, facilitated wholly by his uncle, Charles returned to Lexington to open his own practice. Charles also fell in love, and he wrote his uncle about his hopes of wedding soon. William Short responded with a blistering rebuke of Charles's "puppy love" and directed the young man to consider the financial implications of his decision. William predicted heartache and privation after so rash a marriage: "Puppy love . . . when allowed to take body & form, when allowed to change the whole destiny of a man's life & prospects . . . visits this misfortune on generations to come (for there is no couple so prolific as a couple in poverty & incapable of providing for their offspring)." Declaring the idea of a soul mate "a delusion," William Short implored Charles to come to his senses before he squandered his future. Charles, however, remained resolute in his determination to wed the young woman. As he saw things, "To you, my dear Uncle, I owe that knowledge of my profession . . . which will be the main road to my happiness through life, but without this one more addition, that happiness can never be complete."[29] Charles could literally afford to behave in this manner because, thanks to his uncle, he had already secured financial independence in a career that required far less familial support than planting or trading. His uncle could and did invoke family duty, but the elder Short could not financially compel Charles to forgo the marriage.

But these are exceptions. Conflicts seldom reached the acrimonious level of the Short and Shipping families. If a boy hoped to take his place among southern patriarchs, he needed a suitable wife, a sizable fortune, and family support. Only a rare young man was willing to wager his entire future on his feelings. More often, young men sought a compromise, such as the one affected by George Henry Calvert, or assented to family demands, as did Richard Champion.

As much as young people exalted true love, they seldom married out of their ranks. Instead they continued their ancestors' predisposition to use marriage to advance economic and political agendas. As one visitor to the South observed, the elites of the region "plume themselves on rank & fortune, in the making of matches."[30] While never young gentlemen's only concern, a fortune ranked high on the list of qualities they sought in a bride. Marylander Philip Hopkins employed a common phrase among the southern elites when he pondered "seeking my fortune among some one of the fair sex." And Jeff Withers showed similar priorities when he queried James Hammond about a prospect: "Is she smart, respected? handsome, wealthy?" In the end, money mattered greatly in the selection of a wife, at least among those who earned public affirmation as gentlemen. A lot of wealth and power still flowed through family bloodlines in the early national South, and few young women or men sacrificed their patrimony in the name of love.[31]

As they did with the timing of courtships, southern gentry girls abetted the interweaving of marriage and money. Women, even more than men, chose their partners carefully and with a sharp eye toward the assets of their suitors. Young women understood that their future status in southern society and the ease of their adult life would depend on the wealth of their husbands. Virginian Rebecca Beverley condemned marrying solely for money—but she also conceded that she would not marry a poor man, for such a life would be "next to death."[32] Women like Rebecca sought out suitors who would love them, ably provide for them, and promote family stability. Encouraged from an early age to place family duty over personal desire and trained to be more deferential to parents than boys, girls also proved more malleable in courting disputes. Elite women who married against family wishes or to men of questionable assets risked even more than young men. South Carolinian Jane Bruce provides an instructive, sad example of how long families could hold a grudge against an imprudent daughter. In the early 1780s, Jane fell in love with Connecticut native Samuel Jones, but her family refused to accept him. Letters written on his behalf, the appeals of Jane and her friends, and the clear love the couple shared all failed to move the Bruce family. Encouraged by Samuel, Jane came to believe that she could run away with him, and that her family would forgive them. She could not have been more wrong. A decade after the elopement, she and her family remained estranged. Even the birth of their grandchildren did not erase the Bruce family's resentment.[33] For the vast majority of women, the fleeting passions of youth hardly seemed worth a life of familial estrangement, not to mention social irrelevance and impoverishment.

Because adults encouraged and most young people accepted (if sometimes reluctantly) economic influences in courtship matters, the wealthier the man, the greater his choices in a bride. The South Carolina Manigaults ranked among the richest families in the early United States. No wonder, then, that Gabriel Manigault enjoyed his pick of women—or that he asked the daughter of the wealthy lowcountry planter and prominent politician Ralph Izard to be his bride. Similarly, John Ball Jr.'s parents, economic peers of the Manigaults, bluntly assured him that the Ball family fortune "will entitle you to any lady in America."[34] He chose a rich first cousin from Charleston. As these cases indicate, young men who respected the parameters set by their families could expect to freely pursue the (prominent, rich, local) girl of their choosing. They enjoyed romantic independence of a sort, but it was sharply circumscribed by family ambitions.

Overseeing Sexuality

Community appraisals of manly reputations not only influenced marriage decisions; they also extended into the most intimate aspect of men's lives: their sexual experiences. Although southerners were far from loquacious on the subject, their discussions of sexual standards paralleled their thinking about other facets of refined manhood; they carried their fixation on reputation and self-mastery into the bedroom. Kin, friends, and neighbors, not courts and magistrates, policed sexual behavior and distinguished between what could be indulged and what had to be condemned. Southern adults, like their contemporaries throughout the nation, believed that a man's sexual impulses should be channeled into marriage or otherwise controlled by the individual. They expected men to be sexual creatures and to father children, but condemned excessive overt sexual expressions and masturbation. Those who openly violated societal standards imperiled their claims on refined manhood as well as their families' good names.[35] In general, mastering the self—or at least the public appearance of self-mastery— helped distinguish a man from a boy. Thus sexual self-control did not differ appreciably from developing oratorical skills and restraining emotions in polite society. As with these signs of refined manhood, what others thought mattered most.

Public reputation governed southern sexual values and defined sexual deviancy. Southern elites refused to tolerate certain behaviors, including homosexuality and incest, once they came to light and threatened reputations. Other conduct, such as frequenting prostitutes, fathering out-of-wedlock children, or molesting slave women, met with tacit acceptance unless and until it generated public scandal. When reputations were at risk, families could be merciless.

Shame, not incarceration, was the penalty for violating mores, and shame proved an ideal tool in the reputation-obsessed South. Young men learned to moderate their sexual desires as needed to uphold community values or they suffered humiliation and even ostracism. On the other hand, as long as no negative public implications resulted from their behaviors, young men generally did as they pleased.[36]

The most common sexual controversy facing early national slaveholding families centered on the violation of African American bondswomen. From the farm house to the great house—and apparently even to the White House—slaveholding men carried on a range of often violent and inherently exploitative sexual relationships with women they held in captivity. White southerners, visitors from other regions, and slaves themselves all testified to the pervasiveness of interracial sex and rape in the slave South. No laws protected the bodies of slave women. In many locales, the only statutes regarding the sexual violation of bondswomen protected the slave owner against illegal "trespass" on his property.[37] Southern whites denied marriage rights to enslaved men and women, legally reasoning that slaves lacked the ability to voluntarily consent to marriage and that slaves' duties to owners were incompatible with marital vows. This rationalization linked marriage and sexual purity to whiteness and particularly to white southern womanhood. Moreover, the laws defining black children according to the status of their mothers financially encouraged rape. Slaveholders profited from holding their children and half-siblings in bondage. Finally, sexual mastery over slave women provided a powerful source of intimidation for slaveholders. Legally protected and economically and practically beneficial, sexual exploitation of slave women proliferated in the South. Slaveholding men elliptically referred to their "gander months"—the late months of their wives' pregnancies when they sought sex outside marriage, in the slave quarters. Visitors to the region routinely gossiped about miscegenation among slave owners and their property. One guest at Monticello reported seeing "slaves who neither in color nor in features showed any trace of their origin, but their mothers are slaves, so they are slaves too."[38]

Southern men seldom directly discussed their predations on slaves (despite the pervasive presence of interracial children), but the scant evidence available indicates that they wanted to keep any relationships between white men and black women unequal. Gentry men marrying or cohabiting with slave women offended elites and often violated laws. Southern elites reserved their strongest taboo for interracial sex between white women and black men, for it destroyed the fantasy of pure white womanhood and symbolized the ultimate insult to white manhood. Sex between white men and black women, conversely, upheld rather than upended the social order—so long as it was not romantic.[39] Only when interracial relationships between white men and black women appeared affectionate or equal did they raise the ire of southerners. William Ball felt comfortable suggesting to his brother Isaac that he "ought now to get a play thing ... to amuse you at a leisure hour when sitting by a fireside on an evening." But Ball's fellow South Carolinian Samuel DuBose shunned a friend who cohabited with an African American woman. DuBose reported that Charles Sinkler, on receiving his inheritance, "purchased a wench at an enormous price" and "formed a connection with her . . . by whom he has a family"; DuBose consequently pronounced Sinkler "totally lost to society." Once the scion of a prominent family and respected by his peers, Sinkler now provided parents with a cautionary tale, "as one who is traveling that road which they earnestly pray one of them may never enter upon." Such exceptional cases underscore the rule of exploitation in sexual relationships between elite white men and enslaved black women in the South. And they highlight the power of communities to govern sexual behaviors and check male prerogatives, even in masters' sexual use of slaves.[40]

Community values governed other sexual controversies, including illegitimacy, incest, and prostitution. With captive black women at their disposal, elite southern boys apparently frequented prostitutes less often than did their neighbors in the North. When traveling north or abroad, however, desire sometimes met opportunity. Attending medical school in London in the 1780s, Severn Eyre seemed more interested in the "fine girls of the town" than his studies. As his experimentation with prostitutes became routine, Eyre even curtailed other expenses in order to satiate his sexual desires. Without a hint of shame, he discussed the frequency and price of his dalliances, and he even claimed a medicinal benefit from them: "Speaking physically [I] think nature has clearly pointed out their advantages in clearing the head & stomach . . . for I declare positively that Dr. Saunder's lecture is more easily comprehended after such an indiscression." He did, however, beg his brother Littleton never to share his writings (a diary kept in the form of letters to Littleton). But the style of his letters—not his sexual indiscretions—prompted Eyre's concern. The letters, he explained "are wrote in a cursory manner just as thoughts present themselves, without any attention to diction or the usual forms of letter writing." Eyre saw his solicitation of prostitutes as such a forgivable youthful indiscretion that he decided his epistolary carelessness posed a greater threat to his reputation in

Virginia. He expected his brother (and presumably anyone else who knew of his actions) to ignore or forgive his "dalliances."[41]

Benjamin Cater appeared equally blasé about fathering an out-of-wedlock child with a maid in his boarding house. Cater attended schools in New York and New Jersey through the support of his guardian, William Page. In 1814, the dissolute seventeen-year-old Georgian wrote Page to disclose that a servant living in his boarding house "has swore herself to be with child by me." Without a hint of embarrassment or contrition, Cater insisted that "almost every young man in Town had connections with her," and pronounced himself offended by the "scandal scrutinizing eye" of townspeople. Cater's protests apparently carried no weight in New Jersey; a local court required him to pay the township for birthing expenses and childcare or face imprisonment.[42]

Both Eyre's and Cater's actions took place outside their neighborhood and region, and neither faced irreparable social disgrace because the improprieties did not become widely known in their hometowns. Since neither young man threatened the future viability or present reputation of his family, their relatives in essence looked the other way.

Kin and neighbors did not tolerate sexual misconduct that became public knowledge and compromised family standing. In 1820, Henry Lee IV, scion of the prominent Virginia dynasty, commenced an illicit relationship with Betsy McCarty, the nineteen-year-old sister of his wife and a ward in his household. When Betsy suspected a pregnancy (which never reached fruition), she fled to another relative's home and the entire sordid affair became public knowledge. After Lee's actions produced a scandal, local courts interceded, placing Betsy under the care of another relative and finding that "Henry Lee hath been guilty of a flagrant abuse of his trust in the guardianship of his ward Betsy McCarty." According to Virginia statutes at the time, he had committed incest. A less than contrite Lee blamed his public disgrace on this legal technicality and on a lawsuit that a relative filed to recover from Lee the share of Betsy's inheritance that he spent while serving as her guardian. Hoping to remedy what he euphemistically termed "our recent domestic calamity," Lee coaxed a friend into courting Betsy McCarty. In exchange for helping redeem her in the public eye, Robert Mayo stood to control the orphaned girl's extensive fortune. Lee's efforts to cover up his offense backfired, exacerbating community contempt for him. His betrayal of family duty, the involvement of first his relatives and then the courts, and his failed attempts to conceal the matter made him a public disgrace.[43] The Henry Lee scandal reverberated through Chesapeake society for years. A decade later, when Eugenia Calvert fell in love with one of Lee's nephews, Charles Henry Carter, her father objected to the couple's engagement, fearing that the lingering controversy surrounding Carter's uncle might damage Eugenia's reputation.[44]

Homosexuality was the most scandalous sexual activity in the minds of southern elites and the most elusive to recover in sources. References to homosexuality are exceedingly rare in the private papers of early southern elites.[45] In one exception, John C. Calhoun surreptitiously described his conversations with a young friend, Wentworth Boisseau, charged, apparently, with engaging in homosexual relations. Outrage and shame suffused the letters in which Calhoun confided the incident to his cousin and future mother-in-law, Floride Colhoun. Calhoun never expressly articulated the nature of Wentworth's "misconduct"; instead, he used elliptical phrases. When he first heard the news, Calhoun "was shocked beyond measure." He concluded that the young man "is blasted forever in this country. A whole life of virtue could not restore his character." Calhoun speculated that Boisseau "contracted the odious habit . . . while a sailor to the West Indies." Boisseau sought Calhoun's advice, first in a letter and then, secretly, in person. Although Calhoun gave Wentworth Boisseau some money to flee Carolina, he also advised the young man "to give up all ideas of happiness in this life, and, by a life of contrition, to make his peace with heaven."[46]

James Henry Hammond offers a second and far more ambiguous discussion of homosexuality in the early national South. Shortly after Hammond left South Carolina College, he began to correspond with his former roommate, Thomas Jefferson (Jeff) Withers. Jeff wrote unusually sexually graphic letters, sometimes referring to the erections he got in the company of young women. (In one letter, for example, he informed Hammond that "southeasterly breezes doth make my cock stand as furious as a Stud's.") Jeff Withers's letters differed profoundly from those of most of his contemporaries, who edited their correspondence for public consumption. Most young men were far too fearful of community disgrace to use the kind of explicit, even vulgar language that Withers employed. His sexual teasing of Hammond is even more unusual. A few months after Hammond's graduation and the friends' consequent parting, Withers wondered "whether you yet sleep in your shirt-tail, and whether you yet have the extravagant delight of poking and punching a writhing Bedfellow with your long fleshen pole—the exquisite touches of which I have often had the honor of feeling?" Other comments either hinting at or joking about sexual encounters followed. For example, he teased Hammond by suggesting that "your *elongated protuberance*—your *fleshy pole* . . . has acquired complete mastery over you" and imagined him, beastlike, chasing "every she-male you can discover."[47] It seems unlikely, however, that if Hammond and Withers were lovers they would have written so openly about it or that Hammond would have kept the writings. If boys felt that comfortable about public knowledge of such relationships, at least a few more would exist in the historical record. The unspeakable "misconduct" of Boisseau offers a more credible and revealing example of southern perceptions of homosexuality than the crude jokes of Withers.

Although scarce and often veiled, the sexual indiscretions described in the private papers of southern elites all point toward the same set of conclusions. First, families and communities more than legal authorities defined and policed the boundaries of sexual acceptability. Second, those community values circumscribed men's sexual liberties. Young men were required to develop sexual self-restraint and shun behaviors that compromised their public reputations if they wanted to be known as men. Finally, southern sexual values revolved around reputation, not morality or health. Young men who indulged sexual desires that violated these values paid a heavy price for their indiscretions. They were, in the words Samuel DuBose used to describe his disgraced former friend, "totally lost to society."[48]

Most of this cohort knew better than to make the reputation-destroying mistakes committed by Charles Sinkler, Henry Lee, and Wentworth Boisseau. They tried to appease their families and remain sexually discrete so that they could marry well and be known as masterful men.

CHAPTER NINE

Winning a Wife

As they faced the test of winning a suitable wife, young men often found themselves beset with apprehension and self-doubt. Their kinfolk's expectations left a myriad of fears weighing on their minds. Would their relatives' calls to pursue wealthy, prominent women leave them with a cold, unloving wife? Would they succumb to fleeting passion and make a foolish match? How could they be true to their own hearts but respectful of family duties? Pressure from prospective mates compounded these uncertainties. Young women required their suitors to measure up to their high expectations—of refinement, confidence, accomplishment, and manliness—or face the shame of rejection. Successful courting also demanded that young gentlemen master yet more ritualized performances. Suitors needed to act out their affections under the judging gaze of the gentry community in order to wed a desirable bride and continue the transition from boyhood to southern manhood. Nervous young men could not help but wonder: would they be able to confidently perform the elaborate routines that successful courting required, or would they appear clumsy and publicly humiliate themselves?

Those who married well, who attracted brides they loved and who descended from respected gentry families, left behind such anxieties and grew more confident and masterful. By adeptly performing as suitors, controlling their emotions and actions, and reconciling their desires with family duties, they moved closer to proving themselves worthy of being known as men.

Marrying Makes the Man

Southern sons understood that marriage and leadership of an independent household were crucial for the full affirmation of their manhood. National, regional, and class values all combined to push elites toward this perception. Throughout early national America marriage afforded the fullest expression of manhood. As historian Nancy Cott has argued, after Independence marital imagery (in which mates voluntarily consented to a covenant of reciprocal rights and duties) replaced the parent-child metaphor (of hierarchy and patriarchal prerogative) as the dominant symbol of American political culture. Marriage also became the proving ground for republican citizenship. Leading a family gave a husband experience with consensual governance and made him politically relevant. While not strictly speaking a prerequisite for office holding, marriage nonetheless played an elemental role in demonstrating a man's preparedness for civic participation.[1] Heading a household mattered even more among southern gentry men. Marriage typically marked the beginning of independent mastery of slaves. In many cases, fathers gave slaves to newlywed sons. Others acquired slaves through fortuitous marriages. In either scenario, marriage enabled men to command not only independent households but bondspersons as well.[2] And, since slaveholding planter elites dominated civic life in the South, marriage also paved the way to political power. Mastery over wives, children, and slaves marked a man's worthiness for public service and reinforced the southern social order. Moreover, a wife raised a man's children, tended his home, and maintained the artifacts (social activities, gardens, dress, household furnishings) that symbolized his family's gentility. His relationship with her was fundamental to his status as a southern gentleman.

More than any other event, marriage marked the passage from youth to manhood. Southern sons usually married earlier than northern men, because they generally finished their educations sooner and sped toward careers and plantation management. Age, however, mattered far less than accomplishments in determining the appropriateness of marriage and the assumption of manhood. Some married in their late teens, while others waited until their late twenties; it depended on their ability to provide for and lead households. Education and financial independence, not a particular birthday, readied a man to take a wife and be a gentleman. In his memoirs James Henry Hammond described how marriage enabled him to become a southern patriarch. After finishing college, he taught for a time before being admitted to the bar at age twenty-one. Shortly thereafter, the single Hammond began to publish a newspaper, the *Southern Times*. Marriage brought an end to his career search. With a fortuitous union to Catherine Fitzsimons, whom he blatantly pursued for her wealth and prominence, Hammond quit the law and his paper in favor of running the plantation he acquired by their marriage. Extensive slave ownership and a career in politics soon followed. Ralph Izard Jr. likewise looked to marriage to establish his place at the head of southern society. In 1806 the recently engaged twenty-one-year-old left a career in the navy to return home and oversee a Carolina plantation. As did many other young men, Izard saw marriage as a watershed moment in his young life.[3]

Young southern men also sentimentalized marriage, seeing it as an irreplaceable source of fulfillment. John C. Calhoun extolled the benefits of a loving marriage: "To be united in mutual virtuous love," he wrote his fiancée, "is the first and best bliss that God has permitted to our natures." Conversely, men without wives seemed sad and pitiful. As Joseph Hamilton wrote: "What a poor animal would man be without a wife."[4]

Aware of the perceived social and emotional necessity of marriage, young men dreaded the thought of remaining lifelong bachelors. The term *bachelor* bore a negative connotation in early national America. Critics north and south condemned bachelors as "selfish, artful, hypocritical, and treacherous." Single men subverted the social order and, in one man's words, were "injurious to every civilized country."[5] Whenever they used the word *bachelor*, southern boys linked it to failure and unhappiness. For example, one lonesome South Carolinian worried "that I shall drag out in some obscure, mean . . . corner of the world—the monotonous, unhappy and beastly existence of a Bachelor." North Carolinian Solomon Mordecai similarly feared he might "lead the life, or more properly drag on the snail paced existence of a Bachelor." And Carter Harrison queried his former William and Mary classmate David Watson about his romantic life: "In short, do you live, or do you drag out an existence, worse even than Death itself?" If they reached their twenties without becoming engaged, young men worried that diminishing romantic prospects might doom them to the ignominy of bachelorhood. William Ball urged his twenty-one-year-old brother Isaac to make a match soon: "Remember that you are growing older every day and that life is short; therefore get married as soon as You can."[6]

The Art and Anxiety of Courting

Boys carried these convictions about the imperative to get married to the balls, plays, and dinner parties where they tried (often ineptly) to court desirable young women. The elaborate rituals of courtship further crowded their minds. Young women expected to be addressed in a particular fashion; they and their parents closely studied potential suitors for outward manifestations of refinement. And since the larger community watched these performances, incompetence and particularly rejection meant not merely private heartache but also public humiliation. Boys therefore worried about courting as much as they prized it.

Conventions and public judgments shaped every part of a courtship, from flirtations to engagements. Young men initially met girls at social functions attended by large numbers of youths and adults. Church socials, plays, and parties allowed young men to parade themselves before the opposite sex as well as girls' relatives. Far from carefree affairs, these first forays into social life allowed adults to scrutinize a young man's manners and evaluate his merits as a prospective husband. Courtship remained this kind of public, ritualized affair among southern elites for far longer than in northern circles. While northern parents increasingly left romantic matters to the inclinations of their children, southerners clung to their courting traditions. If first encounters suited the affections of the couple and the preferences of their kin, a formal visit to the young woman's home would follow. Such social calls raised the stakes of an affair. Visiting a woman required parental knowledge and carried a more serious air. As one young man explained, meeting a girlfriend at her house was equivalent to "declaring openly my intentions." Calling on a woman at her home also intensified family scrutiny of a young man's refinement and his lineage.[7]

As romances progressed, gifts and trinkets conveyed the seriousness of suitors. Like many other men in the early Republic, Marylander George Calvert wooed Rosalie Stier with jewelry made from locks of his hair. This common fashion in the early nineteenth century intimated permanence of affections. At one point, George presented to Rosalie a pendant consisting of a miniature portrait of himself surrounded by gold and inlaid with his hair. Her mother complained: "I had to place it around her neck. The scamp!—he looked as if he enjoyed seeing it placed there."[8] Other young men commissioned portraits or silhouettes of their beloved. Gifts of this sort displayed both the wealth and the sincerity of the suitor. But a young man also needed to be very careful that he did not prematurely expose his vulnerability. If he acted too eager, he might embarrass himself. Self-restraint was vital, as was self-assurance. Every visit, conversation, and presentation of a gift needed to affirm the confidence and worthiness of the suitor.

Adherence to these rigorous rituals militated against the very casual gracefulness that genteel suitors needed to project. Most of these understandably nervous young men faltered in their early romancing attempts and then lambasted themselves for their failures. Like so many other young men, Virginian Edward Marshall struggled to overcome his timidity: "I am always so sheep-faced in company where I am not familiar, that I have felt great backwardness in pushing myself into her society." Jeff Withers similarly confessed to James Hammond that, at a party in Columbia, "I could not muster courage enough to say one word to any Lady, & really felt in so awkward a predicament that I soon left the establishment." Even successful courting sometimes did not necessarily abate youthful ineptness. Margaret Izard confessed in a letter to a friend that she and Gabriel Manigault fumbled their way through his proposal of marriage: "I believe two poor people were never so embarrassed as we were."[9] Manigault, grandson and heir to the richest man in South Carolina, could afford some blundering. But most girls were less forgiving than Margaret Izard. Young women expected to be pursued by confident, graceful suitors, not tongue-tied boys.

A gulf separated the demands made on young suitors and the romantic competence of most of them. The private correspondence of adolescent boys and girls details a litany of missteps, confusion, and embarrassments. Joseph Manigault, Gabriel's younger brother, reported how a social call on a group of low-country girls devolved into a comedy of errors. Two young sisters, eager to impress the wealthy and available Manigault, humiliated themselves instead. One, while recounting a tale about a cow, "mistook the Gender and told that *he* . . . gave most excellent milk."[10] Like many other young men in similar situations, Thomas Pinckney found himself gripped by fear when he tried to woo Elizabeth Izard. After numerous failed efforts to discern Elizabeth's feelings, Thomas "determined to avail myself of the first fair opportunity of speaking to her, as I find a state of suspense more intolerable, than any certainty." His big chance came when he attended a play with her family. Seated beside Elizabeth, Thomas could not "for the life of me" overcome his reticence. He sat mute through the entire play, silenced by his fear of rejection. He thought after the play would be the best opportunity to talk to Elizabeth, but Mrs. Izard thwarted his chance when she sent him to retrieve the family carriage. Upon his return, the family quickly departed. "You can have no conception of my feelings," Thomas confided to his cousin Harriott, "to see the fairest opportunity that ever presented itself, thus slipping away, perhaps never to recur, gave me a pang I cannot describe."[11]

Ineptitude in these rituals could occasionally escalate beyond humiliation. Courtships were serious, public business in the early South, and misunderstandings about marital intentions could ruin reputations and prompt violence. In his memoirs South Carolinian George Izard recounted his troubled courtship with a young woman and the subsequent duels he scheduled with her brother in 1800 and 1802. Izard insisted that he made it clear to the young women, referred to only as "Miss P.," that his age and financial dependence on his parents precluded marriage. He conceded that, despite this understanding, "our intimacy . . . proceeded and an act of unpardonable imprudence betrayed our mutual affection." Izard never disclosed the nature of this "imprudence," but the woman's brother felt so aggrieved that he demanded that Izard marry her under threat of a duel. Authorities arrested the two before they could commence the duel, however. Izard agreed to a charade engagement: Miss P. promised never to make him marry her if he would publicly announce their engagement and thus save her reputation. Two years later, the brother demanded a resolution of the affair, and another duel was scheduled. This time, the two young men did shoot each other, but both survived.[12] They carried all of this out in front of Charleston's leading families; in acrimonious cases such as this one, community members scrutinized the behaviors of lovers and judged the character of young men based on their reactions to bungled romances.

Courtship letters provide convincing evidence of the ritualistic nature of southern romances. As with all correspondence, young men obsessed over the tone, appearance, and style of their courtship letters—after all, they provided the means of evaluating a man's appeal as a mate. Letter writers made sure to respect custom. Epistolary courtship conventions required young men, who would wield great legal, economic, and physical power once married, to be extremely deferential to women. Men wrote longer, more expressive letters than the women they pursued. In response to lengthy emotional missives from men, women tended to craft brief, guarded replies. A number of factors shaped this disjuncture in length and tone. Advice literature urged young people toward this pattern. Educational disparities reinforced male confidence and female reticence. Moreover, suitors tended to be slightly older, and therefore more experienced and self-assured, than the girls they pursued. Finally, and most importantly, men were supposed to initiate courtships; women responded cautiously to romantic overtures. For all of these reasons, young men took the lead—in self-revelation, expansiveness, and frequency of correspondence.

Successful suitors needed to express their feelings according to conventions. Love letters reflected form and custom more than spontaneous emotions. Louis Goldsborough typified this epistolary ritual when he wooed Elizabeth Wirt. Deferential toward Elizabeth and emotionally effusive, he regularly professed his abiding love for her while declaring that she deserved better than him. The lover's game continued for many months. He wrote long affectionate letters, declaring that his "soul is wrap'd up in yourself" and insisting that no "other being on earth in my imagination, could contribute as much to my happiness &

goodness as yourself." He also maintained, "The great and lasting desire of my life is to prove myself worthy of you, and to claim you as the co-partner of my existence." Georgian Felix Gilbert employed similar language when he courted Sarah Hillhouse. He insisted that Sarah awoke in him feelings he had previously only read about: "I tho't the extacies of Lovers, as I have seen them painted, were all fiction, but I defy the most extravagant of them all to have exceeded me." He followed a consistent pattern in his courtship letters: profuse proclamations of devotion, excessively deferential language, and feigned apologies for perceived slights. Gilbert referred to Sarah as the "best and dearest of women" who filled his nightly dreams. When Sarah entertained another suitor, Gilbert wrote that he knew he was "undeserving the esteem and confidence you have shown me," but swore that his "insinuating and accomplished rival" could never "love more than I do."[13]

Women too played their part, acting circumspect and evasive. Young men understood this ritual of ambivalence and played along. James Lyons, for example, wrote lengthy odes of affection to Henrietta Watkins, reread her letters scores of times, and begged for more frequent correspondence. Henrietta sent short and restrained replies. As marriage loomed, Henrietta hesitated, which left James, in his words, "upon a bed of Torture."[14] Practicality and ritual combined to encourage women to delay marriage as long as men would tolerate. Adults and advice writers directed girls to avoid succumbing to flattery and warned of the perils that befell indiscriminate women. Procrastination allowed women to more objectively evaluate the character of their suitors. Moreover, women understood that their greatest influence in romantic affairs came during courtship: marriage meant subordination to patriarchal demands. And since so much of a wife's identity and status hung on her husband, wise girls made judicious, considered choices.[15]

This custom put suitors in a precarious position. Suitors could not always easily distinguish a coy woman from an uninterested one. Required to repeatedly declare their love to circumspect women, they ran the risk of rejection and public humiliation if they misinterpreted a response. Women, who made the ultimate determination to marry or reject men, exercised significant sway over their suitors' reputations. Young men rightly feared losing their social status as well as the object of their affection.

The ordeal of courting understandably left boys feeling under siege, and many wrote about matchmaking using military metaphors. For example, while away from his Frankfort home attending West Point, Alfred Beckley wanted his friend George Love to keep an eye on his girlfriend: "I asked you to reconnoitre the ground and inform what enemy threatened to lay siege, who had the fairest chance of success, who the fortress seemed inclined to surrender to." Beckley continued his military analogy when giving romantic advice to his friend: "I would advise you to reconnoitre well the ground, seize on all advantageous positions, open your trenches, and lay regular siege but first of all consider whether the fortress is worth your trouble—if so proceed. After commencing run up batteries every where, show a formidable and determined face. Let the enemy see you are fixed on having her. Commence a severe cannonade of compliments, flatteries, sweet and loving glances. . . . Do not accept any conditions. The Capitulation you must insist to be unconditional."[16] It was not only cadets such as Beckley who used the language of military struggles and manly valor. William Ball wrote his brother Isaac about Isaac's efforts at "laying a close siege to Miss Conny." William later corresponded about his brother's romantic "excursion" and of Isaac's "delay in attacking Miss Conny." John C. Calhoun portrayed himself as the powerless "subject" of his beloved Floride Colhoun and assured her that her "sovereignty is established" and he lived "in willing servitude" to her. And Isaac Coles insisted that the woman he pursued was so desirable that "a single glance of her eyes did more mischief among the students [of William and Mary] than the powerful arm of Achilles among the Trojans during the ten Years War."[17]

Regardless of their apprehensions and ineptitude, boys wanted to marry and knew that they needed to in order to become publicly affirmed as men. So they worked hard to master these relentless rituals, well understanding the high cost of failure.

Moving toward Matrimony and Mastery

So how, practically speaking, did one move from the awkwardness of youth, through the maze of societal demands, toward mastery and matrimony? First, young men turned back to the collective identity of kin and class. They heeded the counsel about making strategic matches, sought out courting help from kin and friends, and practiced their skills on older southern women. Further, they struggled to master their own emotions, to moderate expressions of love in order to show themselves capable of mastering households. Accomplishing these requirements emboldened young suitors, and helped turn them from nervous boys into commanding patriarchs. This change is transparent in courting letters. As boys won girls, they cast off the epistolary rhetoric about their powerlessness and devotion, and began to write the reality of their power as white men.

Wise and dutiful sons making this transition sought the attention of girls whose training and lineage validated their reputations for refinement. A thoughtful son looked for a bride with whom he shared a mutual attraction *and* whose education, reputation, and assets would enhance his standing in society. John C. Calhoun enjoyed such a match with Floride Colhoun, the daughter of his cousin and sometimes surrogate mother, also named Floride Colhoun. His intended not only won his heart but also bound him closer to his relatives and provided a handsome inheritance. Describing his relationship, Calhoun wrote, "I am not only happy in the love and esteem of [Floride] . . . but in the concurring assent of all our mutual friends. This swells the cup of bliss to the full."[18] By pleasing himself, cementing family ties, and lining his pockets, Calhoun became a happy husband and respected patriarch.

Conversely, smart young men learned to subvert their passion for women without proper status, education, or assets. Martin Armstrong abandoned his relationship with a young woman after deciding that she lacked a suitable education. Although deeply attracted to her, Armstrong decided that her deficiencies posed "an insuperable obstacle to our union in as much as I cannot think of connecting myself with a woman that has not had . . . any opportunity of cultivating her mind." Echoing Armstrong's values, Daniel Edwards informed his friend William Reid that, while Columbia girls looked just as pretty as those from their hometown of Charleston, "for the want of a good education they are not near so agreeable." Men, then, selected mates not for the passion they inspired in their suitors so much as for their reputation and intellect. Georgian Felix Gilbert assured his fiancée, Sarah Hillhouse, that "much as I love and dote on you, my respect, my esteem and veneration for your mind and character equal my Love—are in fact its basis—its best foundation and surety of its unabating fervor and continuance."[19]

In order to attract well-heeled, respected brides, suitors practiced their skills on older women. Both southerners and visitors touted the superior social graces of elite southern women and understood them to be central to family standing. Sons learned from an early age that misbehaving around a genteel, influential woman scarred a young man's reputation. As Thomas Jefferson explained to Peter Carr, "Nothing can be more unmanly than to treat a lady supercilious[ly]." Sterling Ruffin likewise warned his son Thomas against "not respect[ing] the female sex."[20] Ably engaging with esteemed women, on the other hand, encouraged social graces and enhanced a boy's reputation. Kin and friends often instructed young men to cultivate sociability by attending to the older women they encountered. Andrew Jackson urged Andrew Jackson Donelson to cultivate connections with "virtuous females" whose company "ennobles the mind, cultivates your manners, & prepares the mind for the achievement of every thing great, virtuous, & honourable." And John Haywood looked forward to his brother Stephen's upcoming visit to New Bern, for it offered the young man the opportunity to circulate among worthy, esteemed women: "If my Brother should have the good fortune of becoming acquainted with them, I can but indulge the hope that his mind as well as manners will be thereby much improved."[21]

Encouragement of the sort offered by John Haywood to his brother further aided young men's efforts to become confident suitors. Friendship circles of siblings, kin, classmates, and neighbors provided a refuge from the rigors of romance as well as advice about courting. Intragenerational kin encouraged more youthful autonomy (so long as the choice met the basic class requirement) than did parents, and they acted less judgmentally. Friends and siblings concentrated on comforting one another, not on second-guessing every romantic move. When his amorous efforts foundered, for example, Georgian James Strobhart turned to his trusted cousin John Kirk: "When I think of these things, I wish to God that you were here."[22]

Such support was not incidental to successful courting—it underlay it. Groups of siblings and friends often conducted extensive correspondence detailing the ins and outs of romances. The Ball brothers, William, John Jr., and Isaac, provide a typical example. While he studied in Edinburgh, William relied on the eldest brother, John Jr., to keep him updated on "how Master Isaac comes on with his courtship of Miss Hannah, and whether he is likely to make a match of it." When Isaac's efforts to woo Hannah stalled, William and John feared he might become "an Old Bachelor" and puzzled over what might be undermining his efforts. After a second unsuccessful courtship a few months later, William wondered if the fault lay in Isaac's tentativeness: "I am inclined to think that our Brother has not engaged in these two lost Courtships with all his heart." In addition to analyzing the situation with his brother John, William comforted and urged on Isaac: "Come cheer up for if Miss Conny is determined to die an old maid it is no fault of yours." William counseled Isaac to look to the future and "for some other pretty girl, who has not such an aversion to be wedded."[23]

College friends complemented intragenerational family efforts to aid young suitors. David Watson belonged to a close-knit group of Virginia friends who met at William and Mary and used their friendships to succeed in affairs of the heart. Watson, James Morris, Isaac Coles, and Garrett Minor shared news of their own efforts to woo women and romantic updates about their other college friends. Isaac Coles and James Morris each kept an eye on David's beloved Elizabeth

"Betsy" Maupin, a popular belle David left behind in Williamsburg.[24] South Carolina friends John Grimball and William Reid similarly discussed their courtship efforts, encouraging one another and conspiring together although school kept them hundreds of miles apart. Both suffered from shyness around women, and they used their friendship to offset their insecurities. Grimball reminded Reid that "timid lover never won fair lady," and prompted Reid to "discard your diffidence." In the same letter, Grimball conceded his own inadequacies on this front: "I cant get rid of my *bashfulness,* and consequently have not a very intimate acquaintance with the young ladies of this place." Bolstered by his correspondence with Reid, he resolved to "rub off some of my rusticity" at an upcoming ball.[25]

Female relatives actively participated in these support networks for young suitors. Acting more like equals than subordinates, sisters, cousins, and other kinswomen aided and encouraged their relatives' romantic endeavors. Thomas Pinckney turned to his cousin Harriott Pinckney to aid in his courtship of Elizabeth Izard. Harriott became his confidante and counselor throughout the affair. She even corresponded with Elizabeth's sister in an effort to secretly uncover Elizabeth's feelings for Thomas and bring the two together.[26]

When young men pined for women they left behind in order to attend school, travel, or serve in the military, this reliance on siblings and friends proved quite practical. Peers could, for example, keep watch over fickle girlfriends. Studying in Edinburgh, William Ball feared that his girlfriend would lose interest in him before he could return home. So he asked his brother Isaac to "find out by any means . . . whether there exists in her any affection towards me or not." When the girl Jeff Withers courted asked him to craft a poem for her, he confessed to James Hammond, "I cannot write a word of Poetry more than a Horse," and he begged Hammond to ghostwrite it for him.[27]

Boys also sought out proxy suitors—trusted friends who would continue an amorous pursuit during an absence. Proxy courting both affirmed the emotional power of peer groups and gave young men the means to successfully pursue socially desirable women. Kentuckian and West Point cadet Alfred Beckley got George Love to try to patch up a failed romance for him by conveying his abiding love. When Richard Stockett left Annapolis to study medicine in Philadelphia in 1795, John Leigh continued Richard's courtship of Margaret Hall. Stockett explained to Leigh: "You are the only one whom I can trust . . . it is on you I must depend." Female relatives could also serve in this capacity. When teenager John Wallace Jr. left his Savannah home, he asked his sister Sarah to "Give my sweetheart, H.N. a thousand kisses for me, tell her how much I love her, and all the pretty things you can think of for me."[28]

As suitors made headway with women, they also began, really for the first time, to show genuine interest in self-restraint. Romances marked a turning point. Finally, this advice, long preached by parents (along with the contradictory and more appealing call for youthful autonomy), significantly altered young men's behaviors. Hints of this appear in boys' willingness to hew closely to courting and epistolary rituals. But it becomes even clearer in their efforts to avoid falling victim to unrestrained passion.

Loving one's wife was certainly a heralded ideal. Voicing the opinions of many, William Barry avowed that "the grand object of matrimonial connection, is happiness." A good, loving marriage made a man happier, more fulfilled, more alive. John Palmer interpreted his affection for his future wife, Esther Simons, as an epiphany: "A brighter and more glorious prospect has been unfolding to my view by the enchanting influence of love. . . . [B]y its ennobling power I have experienced an elevation in the scale of existence far above what I ever supposed any contingency of human life could effect." John Calhoun deeply loved his (wealthy, prominent) girlfriend, Floride Colhoun, confessing that he felt as if "my happiness depends on her good opinion." George Izard expressed similar devotion to his future wife. He believed that "if domestic happiness was to be my lot it could only be my sharing it with her."[29]

At the same time, young men learned that passion, if taken to extreme, could engulf them and imperil the self-control that manhood required. Boys in love for the first time often hinted at their fear of losing control. James Lyons, for example, revealingly likened his love for Henrietta Watkins to "that feeling with which a child ventures upon ice."[30] This childlike fear would have to be overcome in order to woo a proper wife.

Men who triumphed in the game of strategic love (including Palmer, Calhoun, and Izard) praised the myriad positive influences that came from their deep but rational and considered affections. Successful suitors sought love without succumbing to passion, and they learned to exercise control over their romantic feelings in order to meet societal expectations of manhood. Engaged men often contrasted the mature, manly affection they professed to feel with the immature, erratic "puppy love" they disparaged as inadequate and irrational. North Carolinian David Swain distinguished the sincere affection he felt for his fiancée Eleanor White with the capriciousness of immature passion. Youthful infatuation, he explained, tended to "blaze for an instant and expire." David's love for Eleanor, conversely, was "constant and stable . . . tempered and tried." William Barry similarly insisted that his feelings for his fiancée were "not the momentary impulse of sudden passion, or the offspring of a blind and enthusiastic attachment, but the result of serious consideration and an attachment founded upon a long and intimate acquaintance."[31]

Worthy suitors also learned the importance of evading Cupid's arrows, symbolic of unthinking passion, which, while enticing, was ultimately a dangerous folly. Men successfully dodged the metaphorical arrows of Cupid and the real perils of humiliating courting failures by restraining themselves. Samuel Hinton, a student at North Carolina in the 1790s, evoked Cupid when describing his emotionally perilous encounters with "the amiable young damsels" at a dancing school he attended. Hinton imagined "the poisonous Arrows of Cupid (that irresistible God) flying reciprocally from breast to breast, and finding myself in a dangerous Situation, . . . I sumed [*sic*] up all my Fortitude, and faced him with his pointed arrows like Hero, and am very glad to tell you Sam is invulnerable."[32]

As importantly, young men learned to hide their emotions if rejected by a lover. This often proved the most difficult part of the self-restraint that manhood required. Relatives and friends routinely counseled spurned suitors to hide their emotions and maintain an outward demeanor of confident indifference. Thomas Todd, for example, encouraged his twenty-year-old son Charles to hide his pain over a rejection: "Altho you may feel *contempt* it should not be shown or discovered—her connexions & friends with whom you are in habits of intimacy will feel hurt at it & in the end destroy all social intercourse between you & them." Fellow Kentuckian Alfred Beckley also urged his recently rejected friend George Love to keep his head held high: "Have proper pride. . . . [and although] she did not respect you still you have a proper respect of yourself not to entirely be overcome by her unkindness."[33]

But with love lost and pride wounded, some struggled mightily to project a public image of indifference. J. W. Johnstone felt miserable when Kentucky belle Mary Ann Bullitt dropped him: "I . . . am sunk into nothing—the hopes of life that warmed my Heart are fled, and the gloomy prospect of disappointment is all that is left to me." Marylander Joseph Richardson felt the same when his girlfriend lost interest in him. Finding himself in "the bottomles abys [*sic*] of misery," he insisted, "My bed is a bed of thorns . . . hellish demons haunt my troubled rest . . . I know no pleasure." Richardson's anguish was palpable: "All hell's before my face. . . . What wretchedness—all despondency."[34]

Such confessions of powerlessness undermined the self-confidence that men needed to embody, and failed suitors knew as much. When Joseph Richardson explained his resolve to never again frantically respond to heartache, his reasoning was unambiguous: "It is unmanly to complain."[35] Young men unable to restrain themselves often lost the women they loved. On the other hand, those who won over desirable brides knew how to overcome rejections and avoid excessive shows of emotion that imperiled masculinity. Suitors understood that unchecked passion endangered their romantic prospects and the status of families. Love, most concluded, should be tempered by reason, adult counsel, and due attention to the wealth and lineage of the prospective bride.

For southern sons romantic love was an important element in, but not the sole basis for, pursuing a wife. Like their northern contemporaries, southern suitors wrote lengthy, affectionate letters that insisted on the supremacy of love in courtship. But like their parents, they married within their own rank and region, with the careful oversight of their relatives, and to enhance their public reputations.

Letters written between lovers in the closing days of courtships reveal the mastery men felt upon becoming affianced and they foreshadowed the masculine dominion in married life. After months of indulging the whims of belles, suitors' solicitous façade began to slip. For instance, tired of the lover's game he played with Elizabeth Wirt, Louis Goldsborough began to suggest the power that he would fully exercise after marriage and the priorities he would honor as a husband. Once engaged, his political ambitions began to interfere with his romancing of Wirt. When Elizabeth complained about his short, infrequent trips to her home, Louis explained that his work in Washington precluded anything more: "When you come to be acquainted with the nature of my duties you will not think, I am sure, that I c'd have done otherwise than to have restrained my desire of visiting you." He also tellingly stated that he would never "place myself, in the sense of duty, in the power of any person . . . in the sense of an inattention to my public duty."[36]

The weddings that concluded courtships similarly bore all the markings of southern gentry values and testified to the manhood that grooms earned. Southerners threw ornate weddings that attracted the attention of both near and farflung neighbors, who formed the audience for gentlemen and their brides to perform their refinement. (Northern weddings typically remained smaller and far more informal in this era.) These spectacles displayed the prominence of the couple and their families, affirming their distinctiveness from their less cultured, poorer neighbors. And the vows that closed the ceremonies, pronouncing the couple "man and wife," articulated the continuation of the groom's individuality but the submission of the bride's self to the new patriarch their match had helped make. In fact, by the time they reached the altar most young men, like Louis Goldsborough, had already turned their attention from private to public matters and begun to prepare themselves to meet their destinies as leaders of their communities, the South, and the Republic.

CHAPTER TEN

Professions and the "Circle about Every Man"

The high-stakes, anxiety-producing mission of shepherding boys toward manhood culminated in families' readying sons for public affirmation as worthy leaders of society. Young men educated and refined themselves and they married desirable, genteel wives in order to most advantageously enter the larger world. As this cohort came of age, they took control of their region's plantations and professions, political institutions, and racial order, and they carried the lessons they learned during their maturation into public life.

For this cohort, leading was not simply their prerogative—it was their responsibility. Refined, reputable southern men served their kin and their communities by administering the economy and political systems. Such leadership obligations could not be casually rejected. Personal predilections had to give way to duty. For all the independence adults encouraged in southern boys, a southern man ultimately lived for others, or he was no man at all.

This requisite leadership commenced with a well-chosen career, which ensured personal fulfillment and social respectability. It was vital that a man select his profession wisely, for that decision above all others determined the power he would assume in society. Historians usually associate the concept of spheres with women's range of roles in early American society (sometimes defined as confining, sometimes as ambiguous, sometimes as empowering), but men often spoke of their sphere as well. In particular, elites prompted young men to use their career choices to expand their circles of influence and thereby acquire more wealth, prestige, and power. In a letter to his young stepsons, St. George Tucker eloquently depicted the hierarchy of careers using a metaphor of spheres:

> The world is a circle about every man, exactly of such a size as his Abilities make it.—It is very well known five miles about Petersburg that Mr. Booker is a good

Chair-maker—that Alexander Taylor is a very tollerable Cabinet-maker. . . . but it is known all over the civilized World that General Washington is a great General— that Doctor Franklin is a great Philosopher & Politician, and that Mr. Rittenhouse is a great mathematical Genius. It is your election at present whether you will have a world like Mr. Booker's & Alexander Taylor's worlds, or a world like General Washington's, Doctor Franklin's and Mr. Rittenhouse's.[1]

John C. Calhoun employed similar, albeit less evocative language when he encouraged a young kinsman, just elected to the South Carolina legislature, to next set his sights on the U.S. Congress. Such a move would "extend the sphere of your usefulness, improvement, and enjoyment." Edward Rutledge likewise urged his son Henry to always seek to broaden the parameters of his authority: "The wider the sphere of action, the greater will be your delight, and the easier your labors." Poor professional choices, conversely, circumscribed a man's world. Charles Harris warned his brother against modest ambitions in general and a proposed move to a small community in particular because it "would, at best, be confining your exertions to a very small sphere." And Thomas Grimké avowed that every gentleman had an obligation "not to devote himself exclusively to a pursuit whose sphere is contracted and whose tendency is to confine him within it." He maintained that an unambitious career eroded a gentleman's circle of influence and compromised his claim on refined manhood: "We shall find that he becomes every day less fitted to fill a larger sphere of usefulness, that his habits of thought & practice become local and peculiar."[2]

When young men considered professions that circumscribed their potential, families interceded more quickly and forcefully than in other matters. Thomas Grimké's strong objections to inauspicious careers came in response to his brother's flirting with a reputationally devastating choice. The Grimkés, in fact, provide a revealing example of how passionately gentry families felt about the connection between careers and manhood. In 1818 Henry Grimké was suspended from South Carolina College, and then he compounded his disgrace by announcing to his family that he intended to become a simple farmer in the upcountry. Henry's father, state supreme court justice John Grimké, had just traveled to Columbia to personally appeal for Henry's readmission to college. He forgave that indiscretion, but when Henry followed up that debacle by announcing his new life plan, John changed tone and tactics. John and his favorite son, Thomas, both wrote lengthy critiques of Henry's idea, stressing the inappropriateness of menial work for a gentleman and the abrogation of family duties his idea represented. Thomas warned his brother to prepare himself for a lifetime spent among "vulgar" men who would always resent him because he was *"a Gentleman and a Gentleman's son . . . in fact above all around you."* Thomas further condemned the plan because, by turning his back on his gentry roots, Henry dishonored his family. Thomas reminded his younger brother that as gentlemen "we are bound to mould our pursuits in life as to fit us for rendering important services to our friends & family."[3] Henry could not in this instance expect the indulgences granted him regarding his studies—the ante had been raised considerably.

As Henry Grimké learned, if a boy wanted to become recognized as a man, he simply had to excel professionally. On the most basic level, achieving financial success through a lucrative career allowed a young man to stop depending on his elder kin and start enjoying his full independence. Since wealth and political power went hand in hand in the early South, boys who chose work wisely and produced profits could expect public office to follow. When career choices brought renown, boys achieved affirmation of their manhood and realized their families' highest ambition. Expressing typical sentiment, Andrew Jackson wrote Andrew Jackson Donelson, "I have but one wish & that is to live untill I see you fairly in life as a professional man."[4]

Southern Ways to Work

Southerners shared with northerners the belief that pursuing a profession that produced economic autonomy and social respectability moved a boy into manhood, but their understanding diverged from that of northerners in a number of ways. To begin with, southern gentry boys entered careers at an earlier age than their northern counterparts. Family wealth and status, as well as the elite emphasis on precocity in boys, pushed southern sons into careers at surprisingly early ages. Young men concluded their medical training and commenced practicing as physicians as young as age eighteen, served as judges and congressmen in their early twenties, and assumed control of vast inheritances of land and slaves as early as age eighteen. Ralph Izard Jr. commanded a frigate in the navy at age seventeen. Micah Taul became a Kentucky county clerk two months shy of his sixteenth birthday. By age twenty-five, he ran for U.S. Congress. At the age of twenty-five, Charles Wilson Harris served as president of the University of North Carolina. James Henry Hammond briefly taught school after graduating from South Carolina College, then studied law and was admitted to the bar at age twenty-one. By age twenty-four he had started a newspaper, practiced law, married, and moved on to planting. At age twenty-seven, he became a U.S. congressman. Henry Clay became Speaker of the U.S. House of Representatives at age thirty-three.[5] Family encouragement of such precocity commenced early in a boy's life, when relatives looked for signs of manly talents even in toddlers. Speeding teenagers to college intensified the expectation of early professional accomplishments.

Elite southerners also expected their sons to be not simply productive in their work lives, but exceptional and distinguished. Here again, idealized traits introduced in boyhood persisted through this final passage to manhood. Good was never enough; greatness was expected of these scions. George Swain, for example, wanted each of his sons "to be a little extraordinary in his own profession." Anne Deas hoped that her brother's entry into the navy would lead to great accomplishments and personal fulfillment. Anne's mother, Alice Izard, although not particularly enthusiastic about her son's decision to enter the navy at age sixteen, nevertheless determined to help "make him perfect in his profession." Since careers commenced early in boys' lives, so too did such prompting about professional distinction. One of Roger Pinckney's benefactors wrote the boy, only a few months past his fourteenth birthday, "I am very anxious that whatever occupation you may in future pursue . . . you shine in the Undertaking."[6]

As with much else in southern gentry culture, perceptions of a man's profession mattered most. As young southerners prepared themselves for their careers, they understood that their exact proficiencies mattered less than their reputation. This made men of the gentry distinctive from the middling or lower ranks in both the North and South, wherein skill in a trade was both an economic necessity and a key marker of manly status. As one southern patriarch explained, a young gentleman should "prepare himself for *general* rather than particular usefulness."[7] For a gentleman, whose livelihood did not depend exclusively on his professional abilities, work life was, in a sense, another ritual of masculine expectations.

In fact, southern men often thought of their public lives as performances. And careers provided an obvious venue for acting out the authority and self-confidence required of men. One Virginian observed in a letter to a young friend, "While you are consulting about the proper *steps* to be used in dancing the *Gig* of Life upon the *Stage* of *Business,* I have been delving in the way that my exit out of the play will most probably find me." And as Green Clay explained to his son Sidney, "When you travel or enter upon the great theatre of the world, you have to act your part . . . and act it well." Young men were imbued with this link between manhood and performance. As Martin Armstrong, newly immersed in a legal career, put it, he intended to "give to the wind all my feminine timidity

. . . [and] perform on my new theatre in a manner at least creditable to such youthful and unexercised talents as mine." Acting the part of men required sons to set aside their own inclinations and embody societal expectations.[8]

One of the trickiest performances called on men to distinguish and enrich themselves through their professional accomplishments while also appearing to be leisured. Southern men needed to succeed in their careers enough to enjoy financial independence and genteel lifestyles, but always appear unconcerned about the drudgery of work. This value system led many southern patriarchs, despite their own region's long history of participation in international markets, to criticize the commercial-mindedness and acquisitiveness of northerners.[9] A profession, they thought, should be prestigious and personally gratifying, lucrative but never pursued solely for money. John Randolph, for example, warned a young kinsman that the "blind pursuit of wealth, for the sake of hoarding, is a species of insanity." And Sterling Ruffin prompted his son to pursue the career "best suited to your taste & talents. . . . It is clearly my opinion that our avocations should be suited to our gifts, or what could be pleasurable, will be laborious & irksome."[10] Northerners who encountered these attitudes often concluded that southern gentlemen did not work at all. Timothy Ford, for one, criticized the "dronish ease & torpid inactivity" of southern planters who, he insisted, seldom if ever worked: "The great majority . . . will not even take the trouble of directing their own business. There are many who call themselves planters who know little about the process. . . . All are committed to overseers & drivers." "Pleasure," he concluded near the end of his stay in the South, "becomes in a great measure their study."[11]

Ford and other visitors accurately perceived patriarchs' disdain for working with their hands. Southern gentlemen also shunned jobs that appeared even tangentially servile. Farming and teaching (as opposed to planting and heading universities), therefore, were not acceptable careers for the scions of the South's leading families. Throughout the early national era, in fact down through the 1850s, northern tutors continued to travel south to teach children of wealthy planters. Qualified southern tutors could seldom be found, since young men possessing the knowledge to do the job neither wanted nor needed to take such relatively low-paying positions.[12] Farming was similarly distasteful. Thomas Grimké warned his brother that farming precluded "intercourse with intelligent men" as well as "the prospect of acquiring some celebrity and of being useful within a larger circle than your immediate neighborhood." Farmers spent their leisure hours not in intellectual or social pursuits but "wasted in idleness" and surrounded by "narrow minded" neighbors.[13] Young men imbibed this derision of certain professions. Charles Harris yearned to be freed from his obligations at the University of North Carolina and "engaged in some professional business in the world." John Brown complained that while temporarily teaching he "was bound to consult the wish and the advantage of my employers." And James Strobhart lamented that declining family fortunes imperiled his future, and he feared that "I shall dwindle down into a humble, Cain like tiller of the soil."[14] Sons learned to shun such labors because they violated the high expectations that elites held for leading men. Instead, southern sons took up professions that promoted their claim to manhood and power over southern society.

Careers "That Make the Man"

What could young men do in order to acquire renown and expand their "circle of influence" without violating societal expectations? Unlike their professionally diversified northern counterparts, they chose from a short list of careers deemed reputable in elite circles. The mastery of a large estate and slave population ranked highest among southern gentry. A planter enjoyed autonomy in his life and full authority over his charges (the black and white members of his "household").[15] Reading law was well regarded and served as a launching pad for political service, considered an indispensable duty by regional elites. In tidewater towns, some gentry boys began business careers under the tutelage of established merchants. Some opted for military careers, and the War of 1812 provided a few with chances to replicate the military heroism of their revolutionary forefathers. Other southern families sent their sons to study medicine, a burgeoning and recently respectable profession. But medicine, like law and the military, often served as a way station to planting and politics, the apex of gentlemanly pursuits.

Planting was by far the most respected profession among southern men. It promised independence, mastery over others, and honor in gentry circles. Henry Izard dreamed of becoming a planter: "What pursuit [is] more worthy, what more innocent, more independent, what carries its own enjoyment more effectively with it, contributes more to health of body & sincerity of mind—for me it is the most certain road to content & happiness." Plantation ownership, elites believed, also held the greatest potential for wealth. And it made a man totally independent. Studying at Yale, John C. Calhoun longed for the freedom his cousin, planter Andrew Pickens Jr., enjoyed: "You are now your own master. You are now free to the enjoyment of life. The temple of fame is now open to you." John Randolph's mother had advised him as a boy, "Keep your land and your land will keep you," and he followed that counsel throughout his life by expanding his land holdings. Planting and slave ownership, which always went hand in hand in the early South, made elite males into southern men and made the southern states a distinctive and self-conscious region.[16]

Since plantation instruction generally took place at home, less written evidence exists regarding preparation for this career than for the training of future merchants, lawyers, or physicians. Some fathers did write to sons away at college preparing them for the plantation life that awaited them. John Ball Sr. kept John Jr. abreast of agricultural news in South Carolina. He wrote the Harvard student about the shift from rice to cotton production and chronicled the demands of managing his five lowcountry plantations. John Sr. also urged his son to spend vacations away from Boston observing agricultural methods. And he informed the teenager about trading partnerships in Charleston, fluctuations in international commodities markets, the effects of weather on particular crops, the difficulties of hiring competent overseers, and soil experiments he conducted. Thus the father shared his world with the son while simultaneously grooming him for the time when those duties would fall to him.[17] But advisory letters to young men beginning careers in law, medicine, or business—professions that required education or mentoring beyond college—were far more commonplace. Those writings affirm the importance of professional distinction to publicly validated manhood, as John Brown succinctly articulated regarding his legal education: he remained diligent in his studies because "it is this that makes the man."[18]

Many of the patterns evident in the collegiate education of young men reappeared in their professional training. Individual initiative was imperative. Typical of the counsel provided to young professionals, Cary Whitaker reminded his cousin Matthew, who planned to study medicine, that "the main thing on which your future eminence and usefulness will depend, rests within yourself." At the same time, young men depended on their kin to launch them in their careers. Benjamin Cater asked his guardian William Page to "procure me a place in a Counting house or whole sail store, without a further procrastination." And he reminded Page, "I am near the years of manhood, and . . . to be a Merchant of any importance requires an early commencement of the business." As with college education, relatives discouraged excessive bookishness at this level. John Randolph counseled Theodore Dudley, who intended to study medicine, to pursue not only academic knowledge but also the practical application of that information. "A man," he warned, "may possess great theoretic knowledge on any subject, and yet be a poor practitioner."[19] And some men in professional training (although far fewer than in college) debauched themselves. Medical students were often singled out for their misconduct. One medical professor accused his students of "vicious dissipation," and a student admitted that many of his classmates "never attend a single lecture, but stick to the billiard table all day and to the whore house all night."[20]

The most pervasive theme in the career advice offered to young gentlemen was the quest for eminence. These young merchants, lawyers, and doctors and their kin and friends wanted public renown more than anything else. Young men seeking medical careers, for example, were encouraged not simply to succeed in their practices but to emulate the excellence of Benjamin Rush. Planters needed to be the most productive in their locales; merchants aspired to the most lucrative contacts. Politicians were Jeffersons and Madisons in the making.

The law brought particular renown in the early South because it offered entrée to office holding. As one parent explained to his son, the "profession of the Law opens the way in America, to the most important offices in the Union" and provides "the scaffold on which you are to rise into public life." So many men linked the law to politics and the Republic, in fact, that bar membership increased nearly four times the rate of population after the Revolution. And legal careers were infused with masculine ideals, including masterful oratory and public prominence. As one mother succinctly explained, law "is by far the genteelist profession."[21]

Elites also respected business and medicine. They largely monopolized those vocations since the training, money, and contacts they required excluded most men outside the elite class. Succeeding in these careers reinforced gentry power as the wealth and prestige that accomplished lawyers, doctors, and merchants accrued set them even further apart from the middling and lower ranks.

Physicians and men who ran mercantile houses often did so as a prelude to or in addition to owning plantations, as did many lawyers. Taught that planting surpassed all other vocations in status and manliness, many young professionals found their first careers disappointing and used those jobs to propel themselves into plantation ownership. Many yearned to become planter-patriarchs. While at Yale, John C. Calhoun could not wait to commence his legal career. But once he began working as a lawyer, his perceptions changed dramatically: "I feel myself now and while I continue in the practice of the law almost as a slave chained down to a particular place and course of life." Despite success, Calhoun confessed, "I still feel a strong aversion to the law; and am determined to forsake it as soon as I can make a decent independence." Calhoun left the law for planting and a political career, first in the South Carolina legislature and, in 1810, in the U.S. Congress. Like Calhoun, John Palmer initially took up a professional career, as a physician. But, also like Calhoun, he did not long practice this line of work and abandoned it for planting. Then he too took his place in public life, serving in the South Carolina legislature and signing the secession resolution in 1860.[22]

Southern men who served in the military expected their sacrifices to validate their manhood and earn the esteem of their contemporaries. John Floyd, a major general in the Georgia militia during the War of 1812, believed that "by discharging the duties of an American patriot" he would elevate his and his family's standing. Convinced that "the honor, character, and vital interests of the State depends upon the fate of the campaign committed to my care," he dedicated himself to succeeding.[23] For some men, military service did bring fame, but others fell short. Brothers Henry and Beverley Tucker both served during the War of 1812, but while Henry won renown in the battle for Washington, Beverley never saw action. Failure in battle represented the gravest compromise of a soldier's manly character. Georgia native William Cumming, who served in the War of 1812, recounted his shame at his company's forced retreat: the episode "wound[ed] my feelings, as a man, a soldier, & an American. . . . It was scandalous."[24]

The War of 1812 offered the post-Revolutionary generation a special opportunity to prove themselves as men and as worthy heirs of the founders. As Steven Watts has shown, the war was a watershed for the young nation, validating American values and the character of the rising generation of leaders.[25] Henry Clay, a chief advocate of the war, believed that the young nation faced a critical test, and that "it is by open and manly war that we can get through it." John Floyd certainly concurred; he believed that the second war with England would "strengthen our independence, and raise the American character to an exalted station among the nations of the earth." Serving in the war repaid a debt this generation owed to the Revolutionary founders, and it gave some up-and-coming southern men, none more than Andrew Jackson, national prestige.[26]

Being a war hero like Jackson or even a dashingly uniformed officer in the local militia could promote a man's standing in gentry society. But most established southern gentlemen did not consider a long-term career in the military as prestigious as one in business, medicine, or the law. The military more often provided a path for boys of the lower and middle ranks, such as Andrew Jackson, to distinguish themselves and rise to the status of gentlemen. A number of factors made aristocrats see other professions as more conducive to their ambition for prestige. Some found the military insufficiently exclusive. Unlike law or medicine, it did not require an expensive education; lineage and wealth mattered little in a military career. While a cadet at West Point, Henry Clay Jr. pointed out the lower status that military service, as opposed to civic leadership, brought to young men: "I know very well that the fame of the warrior is far inferior to that of the Statesman; he only acting the secondary execution."[27] Future patriarchs wanted to exercise primary authority, not carry out orders. Moreover, the military required a level of discipline and submission to authority that ran counter to the culture of southern men. Those southern scions who joined the military rarely made it a lifelong career. Ralph Izard Jr., for example, served five years in the navy, but at age twenty-one he decided to return to South Carolina, where he shortly married and became a prominent plantation owner.[28] So while military service raised the stature of some men, it was not as desirable a long-term occupation as business, law, medicine, or planting.

Wisely chosen careers set men on a course toward political power, the highest expression of affirmed southern manhood and, patriarchs believed, their most sacred duty. Political service was, in the minds of Americans both North and South, vital to the Republic. George Jones wrote his young son Noble about this inviolable responsibility. When tapped for a public office, the elder Jones felt "obliged to discharge the duties of the office" even though "in doing so I sacrifice my private interest and much of my domestic happiness." George went on to explain that "in a Republican government every citizen ought to make these sacrifices when they become necessary; if there be not virtue enough to do so, the government must soon degenerate."[29]

Southern leaders shared with northerners this conviction that men owed their country political service. Each man met that obligation, no matter his inclinations; responsible men bent their own desires to fulfill the call for public service. When Charles Cotesworth Pinckney was offered an appointment as minister to France in 1796, he determined that "all private considerations, were to yield to public good, [and] the present hour required that he should not view himself in the light of an individual." He then sought to carry to Europe his twenty-one-year-old nephew, Henry Rutledge, to serve as his secretary. Henry's father, Edward Rutledge, wrote his son of the news and explained that there really was no choice to make. The circumstances of his lineage, wealth, and education "forbid the idea of private Life." Citizenship in the American Republic required no less of this rising generation. Expressing the feelings of many Americans, an essayist observed that this cohort's fathers had "done enough hitherto in preserving our liberties and nurturing us to manhood; let their sons now resume their stations, and ease them of their toils." Edward Rutledge put those same ideas in personal terms for his young son: "It will be incumbent on the descendants of those, to whom America is indebted for her Independence to vindicate the rights of their Country and maintain them with as sacred a piety, as they would the reputation of their ancestors."[30] Ironically, only autonomous men could fulfill these duties. Independence was the prerequisite for civic service.

Dutifulness and Independence in the World of Work

The central struggle that gentry sons faced first in childhood—between autonomy and responsibility—thus reappeared in this last test of manhood. Young men could choose their own careers, but only from a very short list deemed acceptable by their relatives. Individual distinction was vital, but usually was accomplished only with family counsel and training. Men needed the talent and initiative to stand alone, but they also lived for their larger families.[31]

On the surface, southern families encouraged a good deal of autonomy in career choices. Adults stood ready to assist in any way, but decisions regarding future work devolved to young men—or so it seemed. George Swain, for example, assured his son David that whatever profession he chose, he would "do all in [my] power to gratify your wishes." When David decided to leave college to read law in Raleigh, George seemed disappointed, but he deferred to David's choice, reassuring him that he wished only for David's success and happiness. Kentuckian William Short, learning that his nephew Charles wanted to pursue training as a physician, urged him to "consult yourself & judge soundly as to your real disposition & pursuits—If you find yourself still wishing to pursue this profession . . . you will do well to proceed—but if not . . . it will be best to change now, & adopt the law or any other line that you prefer. For in order to pursue with ardor & with success, any profession we ought to have a decided preference for it." Some southerners even grew impatient when boys failed to make independent choices. Writing his younger brother in 1797, Charles Harris complained, "In the letter which I have received from you, there is a uniform silence respecting your plan for life." He reminded Robert, "You are now seventeen years of age and must know that much depends upon your own exertions and your own plans. . . . Whatever that [career] choice may be, you ought to make it known, that your friends may assist you in bringing it into operation."[32]

And yet there were rigid limitations to the choices available and clear expectations of what careers would provide for men and their families. Henry Clay ostensibly allowed his son, Henry Jr., to determine his own career path: "you may enter on any career you prefer." But Clay listed only two choices: law and the military. Men needed to pursue professions that would enable them to live as gentlemen, head genteel households, and fulfill their duties to country and family. In a typical piece of advice, Thomas Jefferson urged Peter Carr to ready himself "to pursue the interests of your country, the interests of your friends, and your own interests."[33]

While stressing this trio of duties, relatives simultaneously called on young men to use their careers to achieve independence. Southerners expected sons to prove their abilities as professionals, not just rely on inheritances. Because simply inheriting wealth no longer guaranteed manly status in the minds of many Americans, southerners included, boys needed to prove themselves, through individual success, worthy of assuming power over society. William Ball descended from one of South Carolina's (and the nation's) wealthiest families, but even he appreciated that he needed to be self-sufficient. The young medical student reassured his father, "You have always given Me to understand that I have to depend on my profession & my own industry for a livelihood." Frances Pinckney informed her son Roger that even boys with the richest of fathers had to pursue professions that would provide economic independence rather than counting on inheritances, for "no one can tell what misfortunes may attend them in this life." And Charles Harris explained to his brother, "I conceive it highly necessary that every young man should learn some business or some trade which would be attached to his person, and give him an intrinsical worth, independent of his circumstances as to property or family."[34]

Yet teaching fiscal self-sufficiency and work discipline to this generation did not come easy. Parents tried to stress that independent career success required sacrifice. Ralph Wormeley informed his son that "it is impossible in any line of life or profession to be what we wish without pains and labour, nay, we must toil by day and not sleep by night if we ever wish through our own exertions to acquire reputation, or to gain wealth." Adults repeatedly reminded their young kinsmen that career success, just like the earlier tests of manhood, required diligence and confidence. As his son and namesake prepared to commence his legal training, James McDowell prompted the young man to "prepare yourself and resolve to encounter the first difficulties . . . [and] don't let the fear of remark and observation from others intimidate you." Thomas Jefferson similarly counseled Peter Carr to face adversity fearlessly: "Never fear the want of business. A man who qualifies himself well for his calling never fails of employment in it. . . . Go on then with courage, and you will be sure of success."[35]

When initially prodded by their kinfolk, many boys made light of the idea of actually working for a living. William Ball may have assured his father of his intention to be economically self-sufficient, but he also counseled his brother

Isaac: "Never mind disappointment & ill treatment. . . . [I]f we never got crossed a little sometimes, why we would not enjoy the pleasures of life with half the relish we do—so begin a new career & if you are kicked again don't let it grieve you—the more a Man's life is checquired the greater amusement will he have in his old days." William, a medical student, viewed his own career prospects in the same light, joking about the glut of doctors in Charleston without any concern about how that might affect his future. Boys often responded to parental pleas to work hard with derision or disbelief. Raised in wealthy, indulgent homes, many found it hard to accept that their seemingly lenient, accommodating parents were serious. Margaretta Brown had to rebuke her son Orlando for his indifference to career plans: "I am sorry, my dear Orlando, to find you treat the subject of choosing a Profession with so much levity—It is certainly one which deserves serious consideration, and upon which you will soon be called to decide." She notified him that he should not plan on coasting through life on a generous inheritance, for none would be forthcoming.[36]

Economic reality succeeded in adjusting boys' attitudes when parental counsel failed. The year after his mother's reproach, Orlando Brown had settled down into serious medical studies: "He is now ardently engaged in the study of Medicine. . . . You will perhaps think the word 'Ardently' misapplied in relation to any of Orlando's occupations, as you know his indolent habits but . . . he has lately made a *very important discovery*—which is, that no man can attain to eminence in any pursuit, with[out] application!" Ralph Wormeley had a similar experience with his erratic son Warner. He sent Warner to Europe for his education and to make good contacts for a future career in the mercantile business. Warner, however, pursued a life of luxury, confident that little exertion was necessary since he would inherit his father's money, land, and slaves. Ralph warned him to drop this misguided hope and reiterated the need for individual initiative in professional life: "I wish therefore to disabuse you, if you are in error; and to excite you to industry, that you may, by this means, raise yourself to independence, and have no reliance on the labour of our slaves for your future subsistence." Moving from the abstract to the concrete, Ralph informed his indolent son that he intended to divide his property equally among all his children; no one, therefore, could count on guaranteed affluence and leisure.[37] Eventually most boys, even those as hard-headed as Orlando Brown and Warner Wormeley, faced the facts that society demanded that they work independently and succeed at their professions.

Once they fully understood the necessity of their own accomplishments, many southern youths grew apprehensive about their prospects. After his first day working at law, Martin Armstrong confessed in a letter to his father that the court dockets "seemed more abstruse than the greatest intricacy I ever met with in Algebra." Peter Carr similarly found that, on attending a session of the district court in Charlottesville, the law operated in a way fundamentally different from what he had learned in his books. Carr also felt anxious over the competition he could expect in Virginia legal circles, confessing to his uncle, "The prospect of the law is at present rather a disheartening one."[38] As he faced the reality of post-college adulthood, Jeff Withers lamented the passage of one stage of life and feared the commencement of the next: "The gay and flattering shadows of ideal life are fast giving place to the sober realities of existence—and now since we owe to society a grave responsibility . . . we are thrown upon the performance of the solemn duties and *thinking* & *acting* for ourselves." In a subsequent letter, he reiterated his dread: "As the awful period approaches which is to attach to me a *responsibility* not to be evaded, my unhappiness increases & my confidence is weakened." Withers knew full well "the vast importance of *manly perseverance*" but remained unable to work hard. He confessed to his friend James Hammond, "I despise the sight of a Law Book and cannot by any of my puny efforts bring myself to set my shoulder to the wheel." Acknowledging his myriad shortcomings, he doubted "if I shall ever be in any tolerable degree qualified for public duty."[39] Withers wrote unusually melodramatic letters but he was not alone in pining for the college friends and carefree days he left behind as he commenced a career. Using more typically restrained language, Marylander John Howard Jr. admitted that he felt much the same about adjusting to life after college: "It has taken some time to reconcile me to this new mode of life—Indeed I should not say I am reconciled even as yet . . . when I am compelled to remember that those days of youthful friendship, happiness and peace are never to return, regret and sorrow embitter the recollection even of the most happiest moments."[40]

Regardless of their regrets and anxieties, boys simply had to move toward the appearance of self-sufficiency—but they could depend on relatives and friends to speed their progress. Although individual effort was vital and economic self-sufficiency prized among elites, southern sons were not expected to be truly self-made men. Family members and friends provided the connections, counsel, money, and education that launched a man into a respectable profession. For boys following the correct path, kin sought to alleviate their fears and facilitate their achievements. Charles Wilson Harris relied on his uncle, physician Charles Harris, to supervise his medical education. And when Robert Harris considered a career as a merchant, his brother Charles began passing along information about established merchants and likely locations for a new business. Thomas Jefferson made sure that Peter Carr knew the most prominent men in Virginia. Peter read law with George Wythe, and James Madison and James Monroe wrote Jefferson about his progress. William Short provided key connections as well as financial and moral support when his nephew, Charles Short, left Kentucky to study medicine in Philadelphia. Alice Izard's efforts to secure a mentor for her son Ralph, a new naval midshipman, worked marvelously: William Burrows took Ralph Jr. under his wing, moved the teenager into his home for a time, and introduced him to the secretary of the navy and the president. Ralph Jr. maintained that Burrows "could not have treated his son with more affection than he has myself." Young men so expected this kind of support that they felt shocked and betrayed in rare cases when kin ignored them.[41]

Beginning career men also relied on their own networks of friend and business connections to promote professional distinctions. Young law students in Virginia, including Francis Gilmer and John Tyler, created a debating society to hone the oratorical skills required in successful legal careers. They also worked in the offices of established lawyers, observed court proceedings together, and socialized with one another. Older, established men shepherded their young friends toward career respectability, just as they had groomed their social skills. Influential Virginians including Thomas Jefferson, Edmund Randolph, Edmund Pendleton, Robert Carter Nicholas, and William Wirt all supervised the legal education and social connections of young kin and friends. A similar pattern emerged in South Carolina, where one observer noted, "All the attorneys centre in Charleston, [and] are acquainted with one another."[42]

In addition to supplying advice and business connections, older kin provided emotional support for young men apprehensively entering their professions. Relatives praised nervous novice lawyers, physicians, and politicians, encouraging self-confidence and fortitude. Thomas Jefferson meticulously oversaw the legal training of Peter Carr, and, having devoted much energy to the enterprise, was delighted to hear of the young lawyer's early successes. Jefferson congratulated Carr when "your debut in Albemarle was flattering to you" and, more generally, for achieving the self-determination that Jefferson had long encouraged: "I think you have your fortune in your own power, and that nothing is necessary but the will to make it what you please." Thomas Todd similarly praised his son Charles's initial appearance in court, pointing out how the young man's "attention, assiduity, & perseverance . . . are the sure conductors to respectability, imminence & fame." William Burrows, Ralph Izard Jr.'s mentor, assured Ralph's mother, "He will do honor to the service. He is manly and appears to have a laudable ambition."[43]

Successful sons wisely followed the counsel of their kinfolk and adeptly balanced independence and responsibility. Charles Short, for one, chose a career, in medicine, that he believed "appeared to be as much my own inclination as the wish of my relations." Samuel DuBose's recounting of the career prospects of several of his former college classmates underscores the dutifulness of southern boys in their professional lives: one had "commence[d] business under favorable auspices," another was traveling to Europe to study medicine, a third was "an industrious planter," and a fourth had just entered the firm of "one of the first merchants of Charleston."[44] Young men such as these learned to select a career that pleased their families, ensured their economic independence, and promoted social distinction. Their unwise contemporaries who ignored family directives paid a high price for their decisions.

Passing Judgment on a Man's Professional Worth

Young men who faltered in their professional lives found their relatives quick to intercede and reluctant to compromise. As with courtships, families held veto power over professions, and while they much preferred to inspire or shame boys into acting right, they readily condemned bad choices. Sometimes, if decisions were acceptable but not ideal, kin simply announced their resigned disappointment. William Quynn's desire to study medicine, for example, was not entirely pleasing to his father. William, however, maintained that becoming a physician was respectable and he intended to therefore follow "my own choice."[45] Allen Quynn did not prohibit the choice, tacitly acknowledging the validity of William's position regarding both the career and the prerogative of boys. But sons heading down unacceptable career paths did provoke family intervention, for here—unlike cases of disobedience in school or shortcomings in genteel comportment—the stakes were too high to do otherwise. Again, the South Carolina Grimkés provide a revealing example, this time of the tactics of intercession. Both Thomas and his father, John, began their responses to Henry Grimké's proposal that he become a farmer by indicating their respect for his right to choose a career. Thomas maintained that his lengthy epistolary critique was not intended "to dissuade you from pursuing your present plan" but simply to "set before you as forcibly as possible the disadvantages attending" that decision. John Grimké similarly claimed in his letter, "I should wish to indulge the bent of your inclination." But both made plain their disgust with Henry's ill-advised plan. John rhetorically asked his son whether his decision "does not proceed from a culpable indolence, a total indifference to study, amounting to disgust to any sober rational improvement of the mind." And he condemned the character flaws he suspected lay behind Henry's choice: "You know nothing yet of farming, & if you should prove as fond of your bed in the morning . . . I am sure you cannot succeed."[46]

While they received some latitude in stumbling toward proper professions, young men who repeatedly failed to take the proper course frustrated their kin and lost their standing as men in southern society. The Kentucky Clays provide a case in point. Henry Clay sent his erratic son Thomas to read law with a prominent attorney, John Boyle. In mid-January 1825, Boyle wrote Henry Clay that Thomas had "gone to Lexington to spend his Christmas & he has not yet got home." In a subsequent letter, he informed Clay that Thomas failed to devote sufficient time to reading law, preferring novels and plays. Boyle regretted that the young man seemed unwilling to concentrate on more serious pursuits, and reluctantly concluded Thomas "has some defects in his character." Boyle underestimated the problem. By 1827, Henry Clay confessed that the sight of this chronically debauched son brought tears to his eyes: "He begins to shew, at his early age, the effects of a dissipated life—swollen face &c &c."[47] In subsequent letters, Henry Clay stated that Thomas was entirely lost to him, and he redoubled his efforts to groom another son, Henry Jr., to fill the void.

The equally prominent South Carolina Pinckney family watched as their boy, Daniel Horry Jr., also squandered his potential. Daniel's uncles, mother, and grandmother tried to correct him, but the young man resisted all efforts. At one point, after exhausting a number of tactics, his eminent grandmother Eliza Lucas Pinckney demanded that he consider "how mortifying it must be [for the family] to think all of our expectations may be disappointed by a want of resolution and cheerful acquiescence we expected from your good Sence." And she pointed out that "an Idle man is a burthen to Society and himself. . . . Let nothing be wanting on your part to render you a blessing and ornament to your family and Country." But the appeals and rebukes went unanswered, and Horry closed out his dissolute life essentially in exile in Europe.[48]

A third example of undermined respectability comes from Georgia. William Page, already exasperated with his charge Benjamin Cater's disgraceful behavior (the teenager had failed at school and gotten a girl pregnant), nevertheless decided to try once more and got him a job in the mercantile firm of a friend in New York. But only a short while after Benjamin began the clerkship, Page learned that he had disappeared during a break from work and failed to return. William Page's New York contact offered a scathing assessment of the eighteen-year-old ne'er-do-well: "He has been so long accustomed to a lazy indolent life that the least exertion is irksome to him—the mere idea of being obliged to attend at a place of business seems oppressive to him." And the friend refused to help further, "not simply to avoid trouble; but from a conviction that I cannot do a Young Man any good, who considers himself at liberty to act without advice or control in important cases."[49] Page essentially gave up on Cater after this episode. Like Henry Clay and Eliza Pinckney, he bowed to the reality that he could not turn this boy into a southern man.

These three cases reveal both the latitude given to young men (after all, each family worked for years to correct their son's waywardness) and the limits of family indulgence. When they repeatedly failed to follow the path toward respectability and self-sufficiency charted by their benefactors, Clay, Horry, and Page abdicated their claims on southern manhood.

Conversely, young men who chose wisely began to be treated as the peers of their elder kin and former benefactors; all parties came to recognize the manliness of these former boys. Epistolary conversations confirmed this shift. The counseling and cajoling that marked benefactor-charge relations disappeared, replaced by egalitarian friendship. John Ball Sr. and Thomas Jefferson wrote extensive advisory letters to John Ball Jr. and Peter Carr, respectively. But as the young men grew up and became independently established in their careers, the correspondence—literary representations of their relationships—transformed. Jefferson and Carr as well as the Ball father and son adopted epistolary styles that read like discussions between friends. Jefferson quit addressing his letters to "Dear Peter" and began writing to "Dear Sir." John Ball Sr. stopped counseling and starting sharing with and listening to his new partner in the family's enterprises.[50]

Equally importantly, as this generation of sons assumed the full benefits and responsibilities of manhood, they saw themselves as independent, masterful men. One young lawyer, having launched himself into a successful career that his family approved of and that assured his social standing, expressed the self-confident, empowered attitude of this generation of, now, southern men: "I am now my own master and attend to my own business only according to my own inclinations."[51] Being one's "own master" was, of course, a telling phrase to employ in a gentry culture that increasingly understood slaveholding as central to earning manhood.

CHAPTER ELEVEN

Slaveholding and the Destiny of the Republic's Southern Sons

In the summer of 1787, when tensions over the future of slavery emerged during the Constitutional Convention, James Madison, the father of our nation's foundational law and a Virginia slaveholder, chose conciliation. "Great as the evil [of slavery] is," he avowed, "a dismemberment of the union would be worse." Madison's words affirmed not only his (and the founding generation's) ambivalent relationship with racial slavery but also his unwavering commitment to the American Republic. By the 1820s, Madison's ideas about slavery and nationalism no longer carried the day in the South. A new generation of leaders, none more passionate and gifted than John Calhoun, replaced Madison's vision with their own. In Calhoun's estimation, the South's destiny was inextricably and happily tied to slaveholding. Renouncing any thought about slavery's immorality, he insisted, "I hold it to be a good." And nothing mattered more than preserving that bond between slavery and the South. Slavery, he explained, "has grown up with our society and institutions, and is so interwoven with them that to destroy it would be to destroy us as a people."[1] How could so much have changed in one generation?

The independence and mastery prized in southern white men had long stood in direct opposition to the slaves on whom patriarchs built their wealth and power. But in the early national era, slavery became southern, and, from the point of view of a growing number of northerners, objectionable. Awareness of northern suspicions about this uniquely southern institution made the region's elites appreciate how much of their identity depended on the South's racial order. For young patriarchs, the connection between slaveholding and southern manhood, long powerful, became self-conscious—made that way by northerners more than anything else. Their new understanding made this cohort distinct from not only their parents' generation but also their northern contemporaries.

At the same time that they were charged with preserving the Republic their fathers built, these sons also faced the task of defending the increasingly southern institution of slavery. As adults, these men linked their manhood, their class identity, and the destiny of their region to an anachronistic, often disparaged institution. By 1860, no price seemed too great to protect these values.[2]

Slavery Becomes Southern and the South Unites

Although scholars correctly point to the 1820s and 1830s as the foundational decades for politicized sectionalism, private correspondence, particularly regarding southern sons, reveals a social dimension to regional defensiveness that predated the national political discourse of the antebellum decades.[3] The shift in values occurred as the founding generation guided their sons toward manhood. In the 1770s and 1780s, views about slaveholding were far more amorphous and the link between slavery and region far more tenuous than they would become in the early nineteenth century. Politicians argued about the efficacy and morality of slavery, but for a decade or so after Independence these debates did not fall along sectional lines. Rather, in the late eighteenth century southerners as well as northerners condemned slavery; at the same time, northerners gave voice to racial animosities and warned against emancipatory programs just like their neighbors to the south. Upper South leaders in particular recognized how slavery contradicted revolutionary principles and considered emancipatory programs to remedy this problem. Men like John Adams, meanwhile, warned against immediate abolition in the South, for he feared that blacks "turned loose on a world [in] which they had no capacity to procure a subsistence" would rely on "violence, theft or fraud." Although northern politicians moved to gradually end slavery, they often coupled emancipation with disfranchisement of black men and encouragement of emigration out of their states.[4]

While distinctions between South and North, between proslavery and antislavery positions, remained fluid in the late eighteenth century, an undercurrent of sectional self-consciousness, rooted in defending slavery, emerged in the wake of Independence and hardened over time. After the 1820s, this evolution in thinking culminated in the South's politicized defensiveness about slavery. Likewise, by 1830, white northerners identified their region with the inverse of slavery: equality and free labor. Led by New Englanders, free-state whites over the course of the early national era increasingly imagined their society as fundamentally different from and superior to the invidiously compared southern "slave power." Southerners became the "other" for self-styled liberty-loving northerners.[5]

As northerners gradually crafted this self-image, southerners embraced a more consistent regional consciousness built around a reactionary defense of slavery. Hints of this appear in the 1770s and grow more frequent and intense over time. Southerners' suspicions of northerners had been roused after coming in contact with them during the Revolutionary War and in the creation of new state governments, particularly those adopting emancipatory legislation. After the 1780s southerners, aware of northern movements toward eradicating slavery, for the first time needed to defend it, and they grew suspicious of the men who forced them to do so. Virginian John Taylor, for example, voiced qualms about "interested, chicaning" northerners. In the first Congress under the Constitution, South Carolina and Georgia delegates condemned Pennsylvania antislavery activists for "meddling in a business with which they had no concern." And in 1790 a South Carolina congressman complained that a southerner could scarcely visit New York or Pennsylvania "without having his servants induced to flee." During these early struggles, men from southern states perceived men from the North (or, as they sometimes referred to it, "the east") as distinct from themselves and somehow bound together across state lines.[6]

Although not nearly as entrenched and politicized as it would become after the 1820s, tension over slavery could run deep in the early days of the Republic. Marylander Ezekiel Haynie, a medical student, recounted attending a dinner party in Philadelphia in 1788 in which the host needed to quell the "violent passion" which arose as a consequence of a heated conversation about slavery. When one guest defended the institution, another condemned the position, "declaring a person of his sentiments was not fit to live &c &c."[7] In 1803 northerner Oliver Wolcott characterized Virginia society as sick because slave labor supplanted free white labor and denigrated poor whites. Thomas Boysten Adams likewise rooted his antipathy toward the South in slaveholding, and complained, "There is a spirit of domination engrafted on the character of the southern people." Political rancor between Federalists and Republicans as well as events such as the Haitian Revolution, the invention of the cotton gin, and the Virginia domination of the executive branch, sparked tensions between the two regions at the turn of the nineteenth century. As early as 1805, John Adams maintained, "The Southern Men have been actuated by an absolute hatred of New England."[8]

These occasional articulations of sectional tension grew louder and more vitriolic as our cohort became men. Slavery was a controversial southern institution and the source of social and personal tensions in the early national era, long before it defined antebellum politics. And it seemed increasingly clear to northerners in this period that slavery made southerners different, and that southern men planned on defending slavery, regardless of the turn the rest of the Republic took.

The complexity of American attitudes toward slavery in the late eighteenth century and the intensifying bond between defending slavery and southern manhood in the early nineteenth century find full expression in the household of Virginian St. George Tucker. Tucker anticipated the eradication of slavery in the wake of the American Revolution, and he supported the Pennsylvania Abolition Society. Many northern contemporaries rejected Tucker's vision. When in the 1790s he queried Massachusetts friends about the prospect of gradually abolishing slavery in Virginia, they discouraged his efforts. Tucker's correspondents cited financial fears, both for slaveholding Virginians and for northerners invested in slavery-related shipping and manufacturing, as well as political concerns. Despite his antislavery stance, St. George nonetheless bore the mark of the racial values of his age. Concerned about the prohibitive costs of colonization and the perceived danger of free blacks, he proposed that Virginians deny freed slaves political and most civil rights and wait for them to voluntarily (and at their own expense) abandon the state. Thus, Tucker advocated gradual emancipation coupled with ethnic cleansing of a sort. This attitude placed St. George squarely within the mainstream of late-eighteenth-century antislavery thought, and he cooperated with like-minded men throughout the young nation.[9]

The next generation of Tuckers differed sharply in attitude and identity. St. George's sons Beverley and Henry and his stepson John Randolph grew up to become unapologetic defenders of slavery. Beverley, the longest-lived, defended secession at the 1850 Nashville convention. Whereas St. George sought to be reasoned and compromising, his heirs often acted impetuous and defiant. In his biography of Beverley Tucker, historian Robert Brugger linked his character to the South's peculiar institution, and reasoned that "as the youngest boy in an indulgent family [he developed] . . . a smug assurance of superiority" and remained unwilling to submit to authority throughout his life. Beverley's actions, Brugger concluded, "only mirrored a broader issue in Southern society, the tension between the need slaveholders had to exercise nearly absolute power within their realms and the contrary need . . . [to be] suspicious of power."[10] The Tucker family serves as a microcosm of southern elite thinking about slavery between the 1770s and the 1850s: complexity gave way to rigidity, nationalism yielded to sectionalism.

The South's move toward defending slavery and the growing recognition of the centrality of slaveholding to southern manhood proceeded concurrently. As the generation after the revolutionary cohort came of age, so did the perception that defending slavery was both an obligation and a sign of manhood. Schooled in gentry values of personal autonomy and entitlement to social power, young men of Beverley Tucker's generation saw mastering slaves as vital to their manhood. Determined to preserve slaveholding, they failed to privilege nationalism as had their predecessors. Instead, as they took the reins of leadership in the antebellum era, they adopted a strident, slave-centered sectionalism that superseded national as well as local allegiances.

As lines between North and South hardened in the early Republic, divisions within the South over slavery also began to erode. This cohort grew up to identify themselves as southerners more than as Virginians or Kentuckians or Americans. As was the case with defending slavery, this sectional identification gradually evolved over the course of the early national era. Although northerners often imagined southerners to be a distinctive and monolithic lot as early as the Constitutional Convention, in fact southerners disagreed over slave issues well into the early nineteenth century. Yeomen and artisans, for example, cared far less about preserving slavery than did their gentry contemporaries. And gentry planters held different values than did those men who owned fewer slaves.[11]

Within the southern gentry, region played the greatest role in shaping slavery sentiments. Local needs for slaves underlay those varying attitudes. In places such as Virginia antislavery seemed far more reasonable than in South Carolina. In the decades after Independence, a clear divide emerged between upper South leaders, especially Virginians, who intensely debated the economics, morality, and political implications of slaveholding, and lower South leaders, primarily South Carolinians, who early on became vocal and unrelenting defenders of slavery.[12]

Thomas Jefferson's oft-quoted observation about holding the "wolf by the ears" reflected the thinking of many Virginians. Jefferson and his contemporaries in the Chesapeake worried incessantly (but acted only occasionally) over what they perceived to be the unsolvable problem of slavery. In a long advisory letter to his children written in 1803, Virginian Robert Carter confessed both his antipathy toward slavery and his sense of resignation about it: "From the earliest point of time when I began to think of *right* and *wrong*, I conceived a *strong disgust* to the *slave trade* and all its *barbarous* consequences. This aversion was not likely to be *diminished* by becoming a slave-holder and witnessing many cruelties, even at this enlightened day, when the *rights* of man are so *ascer-*

tained." But Carter insisted that a number of factors compromised his ability to extricate himself from slaveholding. Emancipating slaves was "too unpopular a subject" and, when attempted, "has certainly been attended with inconveniences to society." Carter calculated that he lacked the wherewithal to train and fund his slaves without compromising the future of his own children. He thus concluded that widespread emancipation would not "soon prevail in Virginia, or any State to the Southward of it" and that his children would "inherit this *misfortune.*"[13]

Residents from the early southern frontier states of Kentucky and Tennessee were even more outspoken critics. Allen Trimble, a native of Virginia transplanted to Kentucky in childhood, turned against slavery following his slaveholding father's conversion. Trimble and his father felt that "slavery was a great evil" and regretted "the results of the system upon the moral, intellectual and political interests of the country." Kentuckian Daniel Drake also disavowed slavery and praised his father's rejection of the institution. Drake enumerated the ways in which slaveholding damaged white society: "In a Slave state, new investments are constantly made in land and negroes, and hence the soil is constantly passing from the many to the few; slaves take the place of freemen, 'negro quarters' replace the humble habitations of happy families; he who had a stirring and laborious father rides over the augmented plantations as a lord, and the hired man . . . is replaced by the overseer."[14]

The story changed dramatically in the antebellum era as southern men expanded into the Old Southwest, including such states as Alabama, Mississippi, and Texas. By the 1830s and 1840s young men from the tidewater region were flooding onto the cotton frontier, bringing thousands of slaves with them. Land and slaves were their obsessions. Out for a quick profit, they presided over a particularly brutal and disruptive slave regime. Internal debates over slavery were muted and efforts to preserve and expand slavery intensified. Tennessee and Kentucky underwent similar transformations in the early nineteenth century. Slaveholding became firmly entrenched in Kentucky, and Henry Clay, the powerful, genteel slaveholder, replaced Daniel Boone, the rugged frontiersman, as the pinnacle of manhood in the state. The link between being southern men and owning slaves was, then, consistently obvious by the antebellum era, when proslavery expansion overwhelmed the complexity of thought in the early national era.[15]

While opinions about the morality and future viability of slavery varied by locale before the antebellum era, early national southern leaders agreed on two fundamental things. First, slaves could not be immediately released into white society. Gradualism was the agreed upon approach. Southerners manumitting slaves in the late eighteenth and early nineteenth centuries generally followed the model laid down by George Washington: slaves were freed only after suitable education and training for self-sufficiency. One Virginia minister, writing in the 1790s, provided a litany of moral and political objections to slavery. Slavery was, he concluded, "inconsistent with the Law of Nature, with Reason, & the Gospel of Christ. . . . [I]t originated in Error & Iniquity, & has ever been attended with grievous Wrongs." But even given these myriad reasons, he understood that "it is not to be removed without some Difficulty," and so concluded, "it ought to be gradually abolished."[16]

Second, discussions about slavery in the early Republic South emphasized how the institution warped whites rather than how it wronged blacks. Kentuckian Allen Trimble offers an illustrative judgment. Trimble scorned slavery's "evils" but his condemnation stressed the harm it did to masters, arguing that "the negro was not the only sufferer wherever it existed but that its tendency was to enervate the white race and that it would not only produce idle, dissolute men, but that it would be unfavorable to moral and intellectual progress, and prove a curse wherever it existed, especially to the rising generation." The dissipation of Virginia's young men in particular shocked him, and he insisted that he saw "unmistakable evidences of a decline in mental vigor and aspirations among the youth of this great and renowned commonwealth."[17]

The Effects of Slavery on Southern Sons

As slavery became a distinctly and central southern institution, even defenders of the South's racial order worried about the corrupting influence of slave ownership on white youths. Slaveholding adults fretted over the consequences to their sons of witnessing slave domination. Yet they simultaneously taught boys the lessons of mastery required to perpetuate racial bondage and tried to structure coming-of-age experiences to militate against antislavery attitudes. Most importantly, in the early Republic era, they pushed sons to defend an institution that they themselves often defined as insidious.

Regardless of their misgivings, elites viewed slavery and the next generation's education in slaveholding as matters of vital concern. Between the 1790s and the 1820s, fears about perceived northern antislavery sentiments increasingly outweighed apprehensions about white boys being tainted by bondage. Gentry condemnations of slaveholding in general and its effects on young men in particular waned as the nineteenth century progressed. By the 1810s, most southerners were promoting slavery and teaching their sons to do the same.

In the earliest years of the Republic, however, many southerners recognized that mastery imperiled youthful character. Thomas Jefferson, for example, regretted that slavery taught white children "perpetual exercise of the most boisterous passions," and he insisted that only a rare boy could hope to "retain his manners and morals undepraved by such circumstances." Virginians, who led the southern debates over slavery at the turn of the century, proved to be the most vocal critics of slavery's negative influence on young boys.[18]

Some Virginia fathers went so far as to remove their adolescent sons from the South in an effort to keep slaveholding from corrupting them. Robert Carter III, for example, sent his sons to Rhode Island for their education specifically to protect them from slavery. This owner of five hundred slaves became convinced in the 1780s that slavery was "very destructive both to the morals and Advancement of Youth," and he vowed to forbid his sons' return to Virginia until they reached the age of twenty-one.[19] Like Carter, Ralph Wormeley sought to distance his son from the negative effects of and economic reliance on slavery. Ralph explained to Warner: "I sent you to London to try to make you a man of mercantile business, that you may be enabled to live by your own exertions independent of land and Negroes, forseeing that this latter property is becoming less valuable by becoming daily more precarious." Wormeley committed himself to protecting the teen from the corruptive consequences of slaveholding: "[I] wish to keep you out of Virginia; if you come here you are ruined forever." Jefferson concurred with Wormeley's appraisal of the connection between slave mastery and youthful waywardness. In his oft-quoted condemnation of children absorbing their fathers' "lineaments of wrath," Jefferson insisted that the sons of slave masters grew dissipated, licentious, and despotic. Echoing Jefferson's famous warning that children of slave masters "daily exercised in tyranny, cannot but be stamped but by its odious peculiarities," George Mason observed, "Every Master is born a petty tyrant."[20]

Such concerns reverberated beyond Virginia. In a common charge against southern boys, friends of South Carolinian William Heyward reported in 1808 that, owing to the wealth and ease provided him by slavery, the young man was "lounging away his mornings . . . [and] drinking away his afternoons." Martha Ramsay also criticized the effect of slaveholding on the youth of South Carolina, insisting that slavery heightened violence and sapped initiative. She expected her son David to transcend the negative perceptions of southern youth that their involvement with slavery promoted. These commentaries from planter families differed in no significant way from the more voluminous northern observations about slaveholding debasing white children. New Englander Josiah Quincy, for example, maintained that "the brutality used towards the slaves has a very bad tendency with reference to the manners of the people, but a much worse with regard to the youth. . . . By reason of this slavery, the children are early impressed with infamous and destructive ideas, and become extremely vitiated in their manners."[21] Northerners pointed out and southerners admitted that experiences with the region's racial order fueled the dissipation and indulgence rife among wealthy southern youths.

While northerner visitors to the South condemned the indulgent lifestyles that slaveholding southerners led and resented how slavery thwarted the opportunities of middling rank families, the most common northern criticism of slavery in the early Republic centered on how holding others in bondage warped white men.[22] First and foremost, it rendered them tyrannical and violent. Touring the South in the late 1770s, Ebenezer Hazard found the effects of slaveholding on white men to be devastating: "Accustomed to tyrannize from their infancy, they carry with them a disposition to treat all mankind in the same manner they have been used to treat their Negroes." Hazard duplicated the above condemnations of South Carolinians in his travel journal when visiting Georgia the following month.[23]

Moreover, northerners charged that slaveholding made men lazy. As Timothy Ford put it, "Accustomed to have every thing done for them they cannot or will not do anything for themselves." South Carolinians appeared to be the most dissipated, perhaps owing to their deeper immersion in slaveholding and their tremendous wealth. Slaveholding left South Carolina men, according to visitor J. B. Dunlop, dissipated and self-indulgent: "The men are of an Idle disposition, fond of pleasures that lead them into a system of dissipation."[24] But such criticisms certainly transcended the boundaries of South Carolina. Yale graduate Henry Barnard, for example, reported that the residents of Chapel Hill, North Carolina, "like most southerners are indolent, and like very much to lounge about and let the slaves do the work." Traveling through North Carolina in the 1820s, another visitor found that "all mankind appeared comparatively idle. The whites, generally speaking, consider it discreditable to work, and the blacks, as a matter of course, work as little as they can." Visiting Virginia's Shenandoah Valley in 1827, Pennsylvania Henry Gilpin regretted that the residents "have contracted some of the indolence of a slave state, and do not display the same prosperity that you see in Pennsylvania." Living in the South for several years, Thomas Larkin was struck by how infrequently white men labored: "To see a white person do a mean or common job was a strange sight." Northerners also worried about the effects of slaveholding on southern girls, although this was far less commonly discussed than the consequences for boys. Courting a southern girl, one northern man sought to reassure his family of her character by asserting that she "has none of the habits of a Southern woman—& I understand from those who know the family at home that they are utterly free from that indolent helplessness & languid carelessness which is usually the Characteristic of women bred up among slaves."[25]

Finally, outsiders noted how southern slaveholders felt entitled to lavish attention. During his visit to Charleston in 1817, Ebenezer Kellogg found slaveholding residents served constantly by a host of slaves: slaves accompanied carriages, prepared meals, cleaned homes, and indulged the whims of owners.[26] Elite Charlestonians were so over-attended—because slaves affirmed owners' status as well as performed work—that Kellogg saw "great numbers [of slaves] lounging about at almost any hour of the day." Massachusetts native Abiel Abbot reached a similar conclusion about indulged slaveholders in Charleston: "Negroes are so numerous & make so large a part of every domestic establishment that they are obliged to exercise their wits to devise a sufficient variety to keep them employed."[27] And Timothy Ford leveled the same criticism: "From the highest to the lowest class they must have more or less attendance—I have seen tradesmen go through the city followed by a negro carrying their tools. . . . In the higher classes every body must have a vast deal of waiting upon from the oldest to the youngest." Reading Timothy Ford's appraisal of the constant attention given to slaveholding children, it is easy to imagine the entitlement and tyranny that men like Jefferson feared would arise in southern youth: "Every child must be attended, & whenever the whim takes it the servant is dispatched on its service." Indeed, Ford concluded after a few weeks in South Carolina that "in this Country a person can no more act or move without an attending servant than a planet without its sattellites [*sic*]."[28] The chorus of northern condemnations of slavery's effect on southern gentlemen's character swelled at the same time that the North moved toward a free labor self-consciousness cast in opposition to southern slaveholding and as northern politicians complained that "slave power" exaggerated southern influence in the national government.

While they might have concurred with these assessments, southern elites, particularly after the turn of the century, bristled at northerners criticizing their sons and their now peculiar institution of slavery. It was one thing for southern parents to point out sons' shortcomings; to have northerners denounce slaveholding and southern youths was another matter entirely. Concern about the future of slavery and this generation of men led southern parents to question sending their sons to prestigious universities in the northeast and to found state colleges in the South, where future patriarchs could be more appropriately educated. By the 1820s, southerners including Thomas Jefferson flatly insisted that southern boys who attended northern schools imperiled their region: "These seminaries are no longer proper for Southern or Western students. The signs of the times admonish us to call them home."[29] The destiny of southern sons and chattel slavery seemed, even to the architect of the Declaration of Independence, inextricably bound together, regardless of the cost to manly character.

Teaching Slave Mastery

Despite worries about how slavery corrupted sons, southern elites revealed in their writings a determination to preserve slavery and teach their sons to do the same. Driven largely by reactions to domestic and international events in general and the rise of antislavery attitudes in the northeast in particular, elite southerners encouraged young men to make defending slavery a centerpiece of their preparation for leadership. Southerners developed two main fears about the future of slavery. First, they worried that whites—particularly future patriarchs —would lose their will to support slavery. Second, they feared slave insurrections. The Haitian Revolution, which successfully overthrew white domination and created a black republic, threw fuel on the fires of elite anxieties about black rebellions. Catherine Read confided to a friend that "fear & dread" over the prospect of a similar insurrection in South Carolina left her sleepless and "almost frightened me out of my senses."[30] The Haitian Revolution, along with the aborted Denmark Vesey plot in Charleston, petrified southerners, especially those from the black-majority South Carolina lowcountry, and helped escalate proslavery activism throughout the South.

Discussions of defending slavery against external threats, especially northern antislavery attitudes, surfaced in parental letters to young men as early as the 1790s. For instance, as John Ball Jr. studied at Harvard in 1799, his father, one of South Carolina's wealthiest slaveholders, warned him that while living in Massachusetts he would hear "revolutionary principles" that threatened "the destruction of Southern property," and he called on John Jr. to dismiss such sentiments "no matter how liberal those ideas may appear." The patriarch charged the teenager to never forget that the abolition of slavery would spell the end of the Ball dynasty. Even adults who questioned the future viability of slavery warned boys to reject northern antislavery. When his son Thomas attended Princeton in 1803–5, Virginian Sterling Ruffin anticipated that the boy might begin to question slaveholding. And he was right: "I am not surpris'd," Sterling wrote in 1804, "at reading your sentiments on Slavery, as I was well aware of the impressions which a different mode of treatment than those pursued in Virginia, would make on a Heart." He nonetheless cautioned the teenager against simplistic criticisms that ran the risk of "endangering the political safety of the State, & perhaps jeopardising the lives, property, & every thing sacred & dear to the whites." Southerners who adopted antislavery attitudes were increasingly held in disdain in the early nineteenth century as well. North Carolina native Charles Harris, for example, blamed Gabriel's Rebellion, an aborted slave uprising in 1800, partly on equivocating whites: "Our republican neighbors, the Virginians, have lately almost experienced the same blessed effects of their outrageous democratic whims. The negroes of Richmond and its neighbourhood had combined to make a great slaughter of all the white males and elderly women. The younger were to be preserved for their wives."[31]

As they warned young men against being duped by antislavery activism, southern planters also taught sons how to master slaves. Exercising power would, it was hoped, shore up sons' support for slavery and cut down on slaves' rebelliousness. Training sons to effectively dominate slaves could thus alleviate adult concerns about internal apathy and about external violence. The first lesson parents taught centered on undermining rebellions in the slave quarters. Personal advice and published manuals directed swift, public punishment for every infraction. Wise owners also strictly enforced prohibitions against slaves' reading, preaching, and traveling alone. According to patriarchs, the sheer number of slaves in the South required great vigilance. When Thomas Ruffin commented on the liberties enjoyed by free blacks in the North, his father reminded him that the South faced a fundamentally different demographic reality: "The fewer there are of this discreption [*sic*] intermix'd with the whites, the more they are under our immediate eye, & the more they partake of the manners & habits of the whites, & thereby require less rigidity of treatment."[32] In the slave South "rigidity of treatment" carried the day.

Southerners maintained that owner leniency encouraged slave resistance, and men cautioned sons to avoid that mistake or suffer grave consequences. Fathers warned sons that gentleness with slaves undermined order and threatened white lives. John Ball Sr., for example, explained to his teenage son how a kinswoman's laxity had fostered fights in the slave quarters, an attempted poisoning of her, and the murder of a bondsman. Charles Pettigrew of North Carolina, an Episcopal priest and a slaveholding planter, put things more bluntly in a letter to his teenage son Ebenezer: "Slavery & Tyranny must go together—and there is no such thing as having an obedient & useful Slave, without the powerful exercise of undue & tyrannical Authority."[33]

But patriarchs did not want to see themselves as simply "tyrannical authorities"; they aspired to appear benevolent, if firm, in their exercise of power. Fathers therefore schooled their sons, through examples as well as directives, on cultivating paternalistic attitudes. Caring for slaves clearly had a dual purpose: humanitarian and financial. John Ball Sr. taught his son about paternalist ideals: "Always have in mind that our first charitable attentions are due to our slaves." On the other hand, he directed John Jr. to sell a house slave away as "a common field negro" if he ever misbehaved. Writing to her teenage son John, Sarah Gibbes voiced both the crassness and the paternalism of southern slaveholders. In one letter, she insisted that her slaves "surround me when they know I am going to write, to request I would remember them to their Young Master." But just a month later, she worried about a recent measles outbreak on three of their family plantations—not because of the devastating physical effects on her slaves but because "this no doubt will be a real hurt to the Crop."[34]

Young men absorbed this ethic of duty, condescension, and exploitation. They came to believe that their families, black and white, benefited from bondage. Traveling through the Scottish highlands in 1806, William Ball complained in a letter to his brother of "the wretched situation of the highland peasantry" and asserted that "saving the name of Liberty I think my Father's & Uncle's Negroes are much better off."[35] Such expressions showed young men's allegiance to their families and belief in racial slavery. Having embraced that ideal, they stood ready to meet their destiny as mastering men.

Manhood and Mastery Fulfilled

Southern sons answered the call to mastery, taking as a point of pride their ability to control slaves. When thirteen-year-old John Wallace Jr. left his Savannah home to attend a Massachusetts boarding school, he kept in close contact with his sister and mother. On learning from his mother that "the Negroes behave so badly," he assured her, "When I return they will be as obedient and brisk as possible." Boys also often manifested the violence and tyranny that critics predicted. Twelve-year-old Thomas Clay and his brother Theodore are good examples. Their tutor, New Englander Amos Kendall, recorded in his journal how in May 1814 "Thomas got into a mighty rage with some of the negroes, and threatened and exerted all his little power to kill them." That

August, Kendall found Theodore in the kitchen "in a great rage" and holding a slave at knifepoint. He attributed the violence of the Clay brothers to their association with slaveholding.[36]

The practiced domination that slaveholding required, the tremendous wealth it created, and the sense of self-importance it encouraged in slave masters propelled their actions as political leaders in the antebellum era. Beginning with the Missouri crisis, sectional tension over the future of slavery in the expanding Republic took center stage in national politics. The rise of immediate abolitionism in the 1830s made fears about the collapse of slaveholding paramount in southern elites' minds; most united around aggressive proslavery politics. In the years after Missouri a growing number of northern politicians resented the exaggerated power that slaveholders exercised in the federal government because of the three-fifths clause in the Constitution. Southerners, meanwhile, decided that obstacles to the expansion of slaveholding in the territories jeopardized the very existence of the South. Writing in the late 1820s, Massachusetts native Thomas Larkin, who spent several years in North Carolina, pointed out the mutual suspicions that divided northerners and southerners and predicted a bleak future: "The Southern States look with a haughty and suspicious eye on the North. They appear to think the Northern States look out for only themselfs. Those of the North look on the South as a proud over bearing jealous people who want more [than] they ought to have. . . . One day or other there will be a great misunderstanding between the different states." Thomas Jefferson, writing in the spring of 1820, voiced similar dread: "I regret that I am now to die in the belief that the useless sacrifice of themselves by the generation of 1776, to acquire self-government and happiness to their country, is to be thrown away by the unwise and unworthy passions of their sons."[37]

The post-revolutionary generation assumed the mantle of leadership as national political struggles over the expansion of slavery into the West intensified. Protecting slavery, and with it the future of their families, became a rallying cry for this cohort of regional leaders. Whereas their fathers had struggled to support the young nation while honoring local allegiances and had worried about the morality of slaveholding in a democratic Republic, these sons of the South saw things in much starker terms. The South claimed their loyalty. Defending slavery became their greatest mission.

This generation grew up hearing the debates over the future viability of slavery; as men, they silenced those questions. John C. Calhoun spoke for his generation, and there was no equivocation in his message: "Be it good or bad, it has grown up with our society and institutions, and is so interwoven with them that to destroy it would be to destroy us as a people. But let me not be understood as admitting, even by implication, that the existing relation between the two races in the slaveholding States is an evil—far otherwise. I hold it to be a good, as it has thus far proved itself to be, to both, and will continue to prove so if not disturbed by the fell spirit of abolition."[38] James Henry Hammond assumed an even bolder proslavery stance: "There is not a happier, more contented race upon the face of the earth [than slaves]. . . .Their lives and persons [are] . . . protected by the law, all their sufferings alleviated by the kindest and most interested care, and their domestic affections cherished and maintained." Proslavery southern leaders insisted that blacks benefited from bondage and that biology sealed their fate as bondspersons. Race and slavery became immutable in the minds of the new generation of leaders. William and Mary professor Thomas Dew articulated southern elite thinking about race and abolition in an 1832 essay. Abandoning any reluctance about slaveholding, Dew insisted, "The emancipated black carries a mark which no time can erase, he forever wears the indelible symbol of his inferior condition." As with a leopard's spots, blacks were irrevocably marked as inferior, and their inclusion in southern society in any way other than as slaves was inconceivable.[39]

These boys of the early Republic entered manhood and the antebellum era committed to exercising personal autonomy and public authority, convinced of their own importance and of the necessity of defending family status, and dependent on slaveholding for wealth and power. Their claim on southern elite manhood required them to counter every challenge to their families, class, and region. Despite all the anxieties about the shortcomings of this generation, they proved dedicated guardians of this legacy. Their uncompromising, relentless performance of the duties of manhood set their region on a course apart from the Republic and toward a violent confrontation over the values and institutions that made them southern men.

Epilogue

John Palmer was not quite fifteen years old when he left home to attend South Carolina College in 1818. Although insistent that he planned to fulfill his family's call for dutifulness and refinement, four years of college did not exactly bring those vows to fruition. Expelled after his violent confrontation with President Thomas Cooper, he manifested the willfulness and entitlement that marked his cohort by demanding—and getting—a public apology from Cooper. After that ignominious escapade, Palmer studied medicine, a respectable career for a young gentleman, and then returned home to the family estate outside Charleston. He settled down and married well (to a cousin, Esther Simons), started his own family, and with his brother Samuel turned his professional sights from medicine to planting. Palmer eventually acquired 9,300 acres of land (his brother owned 18,600 acres). Some four hundred slaves worked on the brothers' properties. Political power followed: Palmer served for forty-one years in various public offices, including as a magistrate, justice of the peace, state representative, and state senator. While never as prominent as John Calhoun or James Hammond, John Palmer had passed all the tests of manhood and so rightly claimed a place among the leading men of his state. And he and his family, which eventually included sixteen children (half of whom were nieces and nephews he took in when Samuel died in the 1850s) lived in the style that a gentleman's name required. Palmer wore finely tailored clothes and loved racing horses. His wife hosted elegant parties and maintained a genteel household. They hired private tutors for their children and sent the boys to university when they reached adolescence. Palmer struggled with the same problems in his boys as his mother had a generation earlier. His sons and nephews overspent, abandoned schools, got expelled, acted irresponsibly—as students they became their father's sons. And John Palmer, planter, politician, slave master, and patriarch, became a southern man.[1]

Palmer's story is typical of this generation—he earned his manhood by acting well the part. Throughout the entire early national era, the demand for performing manhood was unrelenting. Success in the part required males to live out the gender values prescribed by their society. That role, while differing from feminine expectations, shared in common with the far more frequently studied "bonds of womanhood" both rigidity and specificity. Men's gender called for power and mastery, but it was no less exacting than the expectation of female deference. Southern men were uniformly and absolutely required to be assertive, self-confident, independent, and gracious. Boys hid any contradictory character traits if they wanted to be known as men.

While the requirements for earning manhood were consistent throughout this era, little else remained unchanged. The economy, political culture, geography, and racial composition of the Republic underwent fundamental transformations between the 1790s and the 1820s, each change pushing the leading men from southern states toward a stronger self-identification as southerners. The cotton boom, first fueled by the development of the gin in the 1790s, beckoned southerners to Alabama and Mississippi and later Texas and California. The War of 1812 secured the interior claims of the young United States and convinced citizens of their destined power over an ever-expanding West. As plantations grew in the Deep South, so did slaveholders' conviction that slavery must expand or the South would die. The spread of cotton culture into the Southwest on the heels of the closing of the international slave trade in 1808 also drove a massive, and for African Americans devastating, internal slave trade into the black belt regions of Alabama, Mississippi, and Louisiana. Whites eager for land to develop with slave labor felt entitled to displace the Indian owners, and they found allies in the federal government who, by the 1820s, were prepared to forcibly "remove" southeastern Indian nations from their homelands. The end of the War of 1812 also shepherded in America's full reimmersion in an Atlantic market economy. The market revolution promoted a capitalist political economy, intensified westward migration, transformed the work and home lives of many Americans, and threw into high relief the differences between the slaveholding South and the commercializing North. By the 1830s, the ideal of the commonwealth, of republican citizens seeking consensus, had given way to the aggressive competition of ideas in the marketplace of politics. And no issue plagued the antebellum political parties more than expansion into the West, in particular the contest between the North and South over slavery in the territories.

By the time the last of the sons of the founders had grown to manhood, then, their United States would in many ways have been unrecognizable to their fathers. Thomas Jefferson wrote John Adams about growing old in this new country: "When all our faculties have left, or are leaving us . . . and debility and malaise left in their places, when the friends of our youth are all gone, and a generation is risen around us whom we know not, is death an evil?"[2] Nothing had changed more between 1776 when Adams and Jefferson helped create an independent America and 1822 when Jefferson pondered this question than the spread of self-conscious sectionalism.

Which brings us back to John Palmer, who also exemplified the expansion of strident sectionalism in the antebellum decades. Palmer lauded John Calhoun as a courageous visionary during the nullification crisis, and he won a seat in the South Carolina General Assembly in 1832 running on a states' rights agenda. A relentless advocate of southern rights and unapologetic slaveholder from the 1830s through the Civil War, he praised his brother Samuel's participation in the 1850 Nashville Convention and proudly voted to abandon the Union at the South Carolina Secession Convention in 1860.

The decisions that southern leaders such as John Calhoun and James Hammond—and less renowned men like John Palmer—made between the Missouri crisis and the firing on Fort Sumter is a well-known and tragic tale. It is as familiar as the glorious triumphs of those other, earlier southern men, George Washington, Thomas Jefferson, and James Madison. How the leaders of the southern states went in a generation from designing the Republic to fomenting its destruction has been far less clear. Exploring the experiences of the southern sons coming of age between the 1790s and the 1820s helps answer that question.

Men of John Palmer's generation imagined themselves essential to the survival of their nation, their families' prominence, and the South's social order; they had been schooled from childhood in self-governance and the practiced domination of others; and they were obsessed with reputation. It was entirely predictable, then, given the events that unfolded under their watch in the antebellum era, that these sons of the Republic would become the chief architects of southern nationalism and the prime instigators of civil war. So too is it unsurprising, if heartrending, that they would raise their sons to understand that slavery, their manhood, and the South's survival were so inextricably bound as to be one and that no price, even death, was too high to pay in defense of that principle.

John Palmer was fifty-six when he voted for secession, too old, he reluctantly admitted, to fight the battle his actions seemed destined to spark. But he had many sons to courageously promote his southern cause. In November 1860, he wrote to one of those sons, James, a teenage student at the University of Virginia, about his excitement over participating in South Carolina's secession: "Oh, how I glory in our gallant little state." Disheartened that his age precluded military service, he declared that he would consider it "one of the highest honors to be ordered to fire the first gun if any one be fired." James, however, was just the right age, and so his father explained, "I intend on Wednesday to have Philip's, Tom's and Stephen's with your name put on the roll of the St. Stephens Volunteers." A telegraph would arrive in Charlottesville to let James know exactly when to report for duty.[5] As Palmer called his sons and nephews home from college to ready for the impending crisis, he and his wife set their daughters to preparing supplies and organizing farewell celebrations. With no conception of the fate that lay ahead for their family, the Palmers excitedly prepared for war. Five Palmer boys fought with the Confederate forces: brothers James, John Jr., Phillip, and Tommie, and their cousin, Stephen. In July 1862 John Palmer visited James in Richmond, where he was stationed. After touring the Confederate hospital, seeing the mangled bodies of anguished soldiers, and watching the trains roll away loaded with corpses, Dr. Palmer returned home devastated. And an almost unbearable personal cost was yet to come. James died just weeks after his father's visit, at Second Manassas. John Jr. and Stephen were killed in the summer of 1864. Three of five sons sacrificed, along with the family's estate and prominence, for the values that John Palmer and his contemporaries constructed and determined to defend at all costs. Despite all their parents' anxieties, this generation learned well the lessons of southern manhood. And, like John Palmer, they paid for it with the blood of their own southern sons.

Abbreviations

DUL	Duke University Special Collections Library
FHS	Filson Historical Society
GHS	Georgia Historical Society
NCC	North Carolina Collection at the University of North Carolina
SCHS	South Carolina Historical Society
SCL	South Caroliniana Library at the University of South Carolina
SHC	Southern Historical Collection at the University of North Carolina
TSL	Tennessee State Library and Archives
UKSCL	University of Kentucky Special Collections Library
UTSCL	University of Tennessee Special Collections Library
VHS	Virginia Historical Society

Introduction

1. Samuel DuBose to William DuBose, 25 June 1806, Samuel DuBose Papers, SHC. For a similar case, see John Ball Sr. to John Ball Jr., 12 August 1798, Ball Family Papers, SCHS.

2. William Barry to John Barry, 2 October 1810, William Taylor Barry Papers, FHS. See also Alice Izard to Henry Izard, 22 July 1807, Ralph Izard Papers, SCL; Thomas Todd to Charles Todd, 25 December 1812, Charles Stewart Todd Papers, FHS; Alexander Innes to Allen Quynn, 30 December 1784, in Dorothy Mackey Quynn and William Rogers Quynn, eds., "Letters of a Maryland Medical Student in Philadelphia and Edinburgh (1782–1784)," *Maryland Historical Magazine* 31 (September 1936): 212–14; John Palmer to Harriet Palmer, 3 June 1822, in Louis P. Towles, ed., *A World Turned Upside Down: The Palmers of South Santee, 1818–1881* (Columbia: University of South Carolina Press, 1996), 38; Henry DeSaussure to Jacob Read, 14 July 1798, Henry William DeSaussure Papers, SCL.

3. For honor, see especially Bertram Wyatt-Brown, *Southern Honor: Ethics and Behavior in the Old South* (New York: Oxford University Press, 1982). See also Edward L. Ayers, *Vengeance and Justice: Crime and Punishment in the Nineteenth-Century American South* (New York:

Oxford University Press, 1984), Kenneth S. Greenberg, *Masters and Statesmen: The Political Culture of American Slavery* (Baltimore: Johns Hopkins University Press, 1985); and Bertram Wyatt-Brown, *The Shaping of Southern Culture: Honor, Grace, and War, 1760s–1880s* (Chapel Hill: University of North Carolina Press, 2001). For honor in national values, see Joanne B. Freeman, *Affairs of Honor: National Politics in the New Republic* (New Haven: Yale University Press, 2001).

4. See, for example, Stephen M. Frank, *Life with Father: Parenthood and Masculinity in the Nineteenth-Century American North* (Baltimore: Johns Hopkins University Press, 1998); Shawn Johansen, *Family Men: Middle-Class Fatherhood in Early Industrializing America* (New York: Routledge, 2001); Anne S. Lombard, *Making Manhood: Growing Up Male in Colonial New England* (Cambridge: Harvard University Press, 2003); Lisa Wilson, *Ye Heart of a Man: The Domestic Life of Men in Colonial New England* (New Haven: Yale University Press, 1999); and especially E. Anthony Rotundo, *American Manhood: Transformations in Masculinity from the Revolution to the Modern Era* (New York: Basic Books, 1993). Two very recent exceptions to the southern honor model are Stephen W. Berry, *All That Makes a Man: Love and Ambition in the Civil War South* (New York: Oxford University Press, 2003); and Craig Thompson Friend and Lorri Glover, eds., *Southern Manhood: Perspectives on Masculinity in the Old South* (Athens: University of Georgia Press, 2004).

5. Wyatt-Brown indicated as much in his latest writings. Wyatt-Brown, *The Shaping of Southern Culture*, 301.

6. In addition to Bertram Wyatt-Brown's specific exploration of southern honor, cross-cultural and theoretical discussions of these general attributes of honor can be found in Lyman L. Johnson and Sonya Lipsett-Rivera, eds., *The Faces of Honor: Sex, Shame, and Violence in Colonial Latin America* (Albuquerque: University of New Mexico Press, 1998), introduction; William Ian Miller, *Humiliation and Other Essays on Honor, Social Discomfort, and Violence* (Ithaca: Cornell University Press, 1993); and J. G. Peristiany, ed., *Honour and Shame: The Values of Mediterranean Society* (London: Weidenfeld and Nicolson, 1965), esp. Julian Pitt-Rivers, "Honor and Social Status," 21–77. For an interrogation of the intersections of manhood and honor in French culture, see Robert A. Nye, *Masculinity and Male Codes of Honor in Modern France* (New York: Oxford University Press, 1993), esp. chap. 1.

7. David Gilmore found testing a ubiquitous (although not universal) component of manhood in his cross-cultural anthropological analysis. David G. Gilmore, *Manhood in the Making: Cultural Concepts of Masculinity* (New Haven: Yale University Press, 1990), esp. chap. 1. For the necessity of publicly earning manhood, see also Mark E. Kann, *The Gendering of American Politics: Founding Mothers, Founding Fathers, and Political Patriarchy* (Westport: Praeger, 1999), part 2; Kann, *A Republic of Men: The American Founders, Gendered Language, and Patriarchal Politics* (New York: New York University Press, 1998); and Michael Kimmel, *Manhood in America: A Cultural History* (New York: Free Press, 1996). For the imprecision of markers of maturation, see John Demos, "The Rise and Fall of Adolescence," in Demos, *Past, Present, and Personal: The Family and Life Course in American History* (New York: Oxford University Press, 1986), chap. 5; Harvey J. Graff, "Early Adolescence in Antebellum America: The Remaking of Growing Up," *Journal of Early Adolescence* 5: 411–27; and Joseph F. Kett, *Rites of Passage: Adolescence in America, 1790 to the Present* (New York: Basis Books, 1977), chap. 1.

8. Important studies of southern women in this era include Catherine Clinton, *The Plantation Mistress: Woman's World in the Old South* (New York: Pantheon Books, 1982); Elizabeth Fox-Genovese, *Within the Plantation Household: Black and White Women of the Old South* (Chapel Hill: University of North Carolina Press, 1988); and Cynthia A. Kierner, *Beyond the Household: Women's Place in the Early South, 1700–1835* (Ithaca: Cornell University Press, 1998). A pathbreaking work focusing on northern women in this era is Nancy F. Cott, *The Bonds of Womanhood: "Women's Sphere" in New England, 1780–1835* (New Haven: Yale University Press, 1977). See also Linda K. Kerber, "Separate Spheres, Female Worlds, Woman's Place: The Rhetoric of Women's History," *Journal of American History* 75 (June 1988): 9–39.

9. For the centrality of performance, see also Richard Bushman, *The Refinement of America: Persons, Houses, Cities* (New York: Knopf, 1992); and Jay Fliegelman, *Declaring Independence: Jefferson, Natural Language, and the Culture of Performance* (Stanford: Stanford University Press, 1993).

10. This story necessarily centers on the metaphorical, not the biological sons of the founders. Jefferson fathered only girls, at least in the white family he acknowledged. Washington and Madison helped to parent their wives' sons, but raised no children of their own. For analysis of this generation see also Joyce Appleby, *Inheriting the Revolution: The First Generation of Americans* (Cambridge: Harvard University Press, 2000); and Steven Watts, *The Republic Reborn: War and the Making of Liberal America, 1790–1820* (Baltimore: Johns Hopkins University Press, 1987). For the transforming effects of the American Revolution, see Gordon S. Wood, *The Radicalism of the American Revolution* (New York: Knopf, 1992). For the political anxieties Americans felt, see James Roger Sharp, *American Politics in the Early Republic: The New Nation in Crisis* (New Haven: Yale University Press, 1993).

One • The First Duties of a Southern Boy

1. Francis Ramsey to James G. M. Ramsey, 2 March 1813, James Gettys McGready Ramsey Papers, UTSCL.

2. John Randolph to Theodore Dudley, 15 February 1806, in Russell Kirk, *John Randolph of Roanoke* (Indianapolis: Liberty Press, 1978), 236.

3. In his analysis of young people's coming of age experiences, Harvey J. Graff found that elites were particularly hard on young people. Harvey J. Graff, *Conflicting Paths: Growing Up in America* (Cambridge: Harvard University Press, 1995), 184. For the elaborate expectations of elite southern parents, see also James Oakes, *The Ruling Race: A History of American Slaveholders* (New York: Knopf, 1982); Daniel Blake Smith, *Inside the Great House: Planter Family Life in Eighteenth-Century Chesapeake Society* (Ithaca: Cornell University Press, 1980), chap. 3; Brenda Stevenson, *Life in Black and White: Family and Community in the Slave South* (New York: Oxford University Press, 1996); Steven M. Stowe, *Intimacy and Power in the Old South: Ritual in the Lives of the Planters* (Baltimore: Johns Hopkins University Press, 1987); and Bertram Wyatt-Brown, *Southern Honor: Ethics and Behavior in the Old South* (New York: Oxford University Press, 1982). For the necessity of earning manhood, see also Craig Thompson Friend and Lorri Glover, eds., *Southern Manhood: Perspectives on Masculinity in the Old South* (Athens: University of Georgia Press, 2004); David G. Gilmore, *Manhood in the Making: Cultural Concepts of Masculinity* (New Haven: Yale University Press, 1990); Mark E.

Kann, *A Republic of Men: The American Founders, Gendered Language, and Patriarchal Politics* (New York: New York University Press, 1998); Michael Kimmel, *Manhood in America: A Cultural History* (New York: Free Press, 1996); and Anne S. Lombard, *Making Manhood: Growing Up Male in Colonial New England* (Cambridge: Harvard University Press, 2003).

4. Edward Rutledge to Henry Rutledge, 2 August 1796, in Marvin R. Zahniser, ed., "Edward Rutledge to His Son, August 2, 1796," *South Carolina Historical Magazine* 64 (1963): 69; Thomas Todd to Charles Todd, 25 September 1808, Charles Stewart Todd Papers, FHS.

5. Charles Anderson Memoir, Charles Anderson Papers, FHS. For the importance of this generation, see also Joyce Appleby, *Inheriting the Revolution: The First Generation of Americans* (Cambridge: Harvard University Press, 2000); Steven Watts, *The Republic Reborn: War and the Making of Liberal America, 1790–1820* (Baltimore: Johns Hopkins University Press, 1987), esp. 210–11, 152, 163; and David Waldstreicher, *In the Midst of Perpetual Fetes: The Making of American Nationalism, 1776–1820* (Chapel Hill: University of North Carolina Press, 1997), esp. 264.

6. For republican motherhood, see Linda K. Kerber, *Women of the Republic: Intellect and Ideology in Revolutionary America* (Chapel Hill: University of North Carolina, 1980); Mary Beth Norton, *Liberty's Daughters: The Revolutionary Experience of American Women, 1750–1800* (Boston: Little, Brown, 1980); and Rosemarie Zagarri, "Morals, Manners, and the Republican Mother," *American Quarterly* 44 (June 1992): 192–215.

7. Charles Anderson Memoir, Charles Anderson Papers, FHS; Noah Jones Composition Book, "On Ambition," 20 January 1805, SCL; Noah Jones Composition Book, "Epaminondas & Washington compared," undated [c. 1805–9], SCL.

8. Richard Bennehan to Thomas Bennehan, 5 March 1796, Cameron Family Papers, SHC; Arthur Alexander Morson to Ann Morson, 27 July 1819, Arthur Alexander Morson Papers, SHC; Phillip Hamilton, *The Making and Unmaking of a Revolutionary Family: The Tuckers of Virginia, 1752–1830* (Charlottesville: University of Virginia Press, 2003), 85.

9. Joanna Bowen Gillespie, *The Life and Times of Martha Laurens Ramsay, 1759–1811* (Columbia: University of South Carolina Press, 2001), 203.

10. John Wayles Eppes to Francis Eppes, 20 June 1818, John Wayles Eppes Letters, DUL.

11. Quoted in Clement Eaton, *Henry Clay and the Art of American Politics* (Boston: Little, Brown, 1957), 162.

12. Quoted in Watts, *Republic Reborn*, 163.

13. Robert Carter "Letter of Advice to My Children," 12–14 October 1803, Robert Carter Papers, VHS; Andrew Jackson to Rachel Jackson, 31 July 1814, in Harold D. Moser et al., eds., *The Papers of Andrew Jackson* (Knoxville: University of Tennessee Press, 1980-present), 3: 101. Born in 1808, Andrew Jackson Jr. was the biological son of Rachel's brother, Severn Donelson, and his wife, Elizabeth. For the rise of the affectionate family in the early South, see Smith, *Inside the Great House;* Jan Lewis, *The Pursuit of Happiness: Family and Values in Jefferson's Virginia* (Cambridge: Cambridge University Press, 1983); and Jane Turner Censer, *North Carolina Planters and Their Children, 1800–1860* (Baton Rouge: Louisiana State University Press, 1984).

14. Julia Mordecai to Solomon Mordecai, 26 July 1817, Mordecai Family Papers, SHC; Alfred Mordecai Memoir, reprinted in James A. Padgett, ed., "The Life of Alfred Mordecai, as

Related by Himself," *North Carolina Historical Review* 22 (1945): 64. For more on the Mordecais, see Emily Bingham, *Mordecai: An Early American Family* (New York: Hill and Wang, 2003). For sibling bonds among southern elites, see Lorri Glover, *All Our Relations: Blood Ties and Emotional Bonds among the Early South Carolina Gentry* (Baltimore: Johns Hopkins University Press, 2000).

15. Jane Ball to John Ball Jr., 12 October 1799 and 16 April 1800, both in Ball Family Papers, SCHS; Sterling Ruffin to Thomas Ruffin, 18 April 1802, Thomas Ruffin Papers, SHC; Henry Izard to Margaret Manigault, 28 March 1799, Ralph Izard Papers, SCL.

16. Reuben Grigsby to Hugh Blair Grigsby, 15 November 1824, in Fitzgerald Flournoy, "Hugh Blair Grigsby at Yale," *Virginia Magazine of History and Biography* 62 (1954): 167. For kinship bonds in the early South, see Joan Cashin, "The Structure of Antebellum Planter Families: 'The Ties that Bound us Was Strong,'" *Journal of Southern History* 56 (February 1990): 55–70; Glover, *All Our Relations;* Allan Kulikoff, *Tobacco and Slaves: The Development of Southern Cultures in the Chesapeake, 1680–1800* (Chapel Hill: University of North Carolina Press, 1986); and Smith, *Inside the Great House,* chaps. 1, 5.

17. Mary Adair to Mary McCalla, 16 March 1797, Adair-Hemphill Family Papers, FHS; Alicia Hopton Middleton to Nathaniel Russell Middleton, 28 July 1817, Middleton Family Papers, SCL.

18. Edward Rutledge open letter to family, 9 September 1799, John Rutledge Papers, SCL.

19. Andrew Jackson to Rachel Jackson, miscellaneous correspondence, 1814, *Papers of Andrew Jackson,* vol. 3.

20. George Henry Calvert, *Autobiographic Study* (Boston, 1885), quoted in Margaret Law Callcott, ed., *Mistress of Riversdale: The Plantation Letters of Rosalie Stier Calvert, 1795–1821* (Baltimore: Johns Hopkins University Press, 1991), 256; William Ruffin to Catherine Ruffin, 9 December 1824, Thomas Ruffin Papers, SHC; James McDowell to Suzanna Preston, 29 October 1813, McDowell Family Papers, VHS.

21. Andrew Jackson to Rachel Jackson, 8 January 1813, *Papers of Andrew Jackson,* 2: 353–54; Andrew Jackson to Rachel Jackson, 18 September 1816, *Papers of Andrew Jackson,* 4: 62.

22. Lemuel Kollock to George Jones Kollock, 2 November 1820, in Edith Duncan Johnston, ed., "The Kollock Letters, 1799–1850," *Georgia Historical Quarterly* 30 (1946): 228; John Ball Sr. to John Ball Jr., 15 September 1798, Ball Family Papers, SCHS. See also Lemuel Kollock to George Jones Kollock, 2 March 1820, in Johnston, ed., "Kollock Letters," 227; John Lloyd to Richard Champion, 4 June 1796, John Lloyd Letterbook, SCL; and William Read to Jacob Read, 18 December 1795, Read Family Papers, SCL.

23. Seaborn Jones to William Hart, 16 July 1806, in Seaborn Jones Family Papers, GHS; John Ball Sr. to John Ball Jr., 12 August 1798, Ball Family Papers, SCHS.

24. Robert Carter "Letter of Advice to My Children," 12–14 October 1803, Robert Carter Papers, VHS.

25. Ambler quoted in Lewis, *The Pursuit of Happiness,* 116; Henry Clay to Henry Clay Jr., 2 April 1827, in James F. Hopkins and Mary W. M. Hargreaves et al., eds., *The Papers of Henry Clay* (Lexington: University of Kentucky Press, 1959–1992), 6: 385.

26. James McDowell to Sarah McDowell, 12 October 1811, McDowell Family Papers, VHS; Francis Ramsey to James G. M. Ramsey, 25 March 1813, James Gettys McGready Ramsey

Papers, UTSCL; Edward Campbell to Phineas Kollock, 22 October 1823, in Johnston, ed., "Kollock Letters," 246; John Wayles Eppes to Francis Eppes, 28 June 1819, John Wayles Eppes Papers, DUL.

27. Mary Ann Harden to Edward Randolph Harden, undated [c. 1829], Harden Family Papers, DUL; Edward Harden to Edward Randolph Harden, 19 September 1829, Harden Family Papers, DUL. For another example, see the correspondence of John and Eliza Haywood to their son George, in Ernest Haywood Collection, SHC.

28. The best work on the tensions and later reconciliation between evangelicals and southern elites is Christine Leigh Heyrman, *Southern Cross: The Beginnings of the Bible Belt* (New York: Knopf, 1997). See also Stephen Aron, *How the West Was Lost: The Transformation of Kentucky from Daniel Boone to Henry Clay* (Baltimore: Johns Hopkins University Press, 1996); Appleby, *Inheriting the Revolution*, chaps. 7 and 8; John B. Boles, "Evangelical Protestantism in the Old South," in Charles Reagan Wilson, ed., *Religion in the South* (Jackson: University Press of Mississippi, 1985), 13–34; Boles, *The Great Revival, 1787–1804: The Origins of the Southern Evangelical Mind* (Lexington: University Press of Kentucky, 1972), esp. chap. 12; Janet Moore Lindman, "Acting the Manly Christian: White Evangelical Masculinity in Revolutionary Virginia," *William and Mary Quarterly* 57 (April 2000): 393–416; Cynthia Lynn Lyerly, *Methodism and the Southern Mind, 1770–1810* (New York: Oxford University Press, 1998); Donald G. Mathews, *Religion in the Old South* (Chicago: University of Chicago Press, 1977); Richard Rankin, *Ambivalent Churchmen and Evangelical Churchwomen: The Religion of the Episcopal Elite in North Carolina, 1800–1860* (Columbia: University of South Carolina Press, 1993); and Bertram Wyatt-Brown, *The Shaping of Southern Culture: Honor, Grace, and War, 1760s–1880s* (Chapel Hill: University of North Carolina Press, 2001), chap. 4.

29. Lyerly, *Methodism and the Southern Mind*, 73. See also Boles, "Evangelical Protestantism in the Old South," 26; Rhys Isaac, *The Transformation of Virginia, 1740–1790* (Chapel Hill: University of North Carolina Press, 1982); and Mathews, *Religion in the Old South*, 37–38. For the shift of evangelicals from antislavery to proslavery, see Heyrman, *Southern Cross*, chap. 5; Lyerly, *Methodism and the Southern Mind*, chap. 6; and Mathews, *Religion in the Old South*, chap. 4.

30. Mary McDonald to Charles McDonald, 16 and 17 November 1815, McDonald-Lawrence Family Papers, SHC.

31. Daniel A. Penick Papers, 1821–22 Diary, SHC; David Rice Sermons, UKSCL; Richard Watkins to Elizabeth Venable Watkins, 17 March 1831, in "The Watkins Letters," *Virginia Magazine of History and Biography* 41 (1933): 330–32. For additional examples of young men's spiritual awakenings, see Robert Morrison to James Morrison, 21 July 1823, Robert Hall Morrison Papers, SHC; Daniel Baker to George Palmes, 14 December 1811, George F. Palmes Papers, DUL.

32. See, for example, William Blanding Journal, 14 June 1807, SCL. For the mental perils of religious enthusiasm, see also Peter McCandless, *Moonlight, Magnolias, and Madness: Insanity in South Carolina from the Colonial Period to the Progressive Era* (Chapel Hill: University of North Carolina Press, 1996), 26.

33. Seaborn Jones to William Hart, 6 June 1807, Seaborn Jones Family Papers, GHS; Thomas Jefferson to Peter Carr, 10 August 1787, in Julian P. Boyd et al., eds., *Papers of Thomas*

Jefferson (Princeton: Princeton University Press, 1950-present), 12: 15–17. Southern gentlemen were not, of course, uniformly opposed to religious practices. Virginian Robert Carter, for example, expected his children to obey the Ten Commandments and read the New Testament. Robert Carter "Letter of Advice to My Children," 12–14 October 1803, Robert Carter Papers, VHS.

34. David Rice Sermons, UKSCL. For additional criticisms, see Edward Hooker to David Lilly, 8 May 1807, Edward Hooker Letters, SCL; Jeremiah Evarts to Henry Hill, 25 February 1826, in J. Orin Oliphant, ed., *Through the South and the West with Jeremiah Evarts in 1826* (Lewisburg, PA: Bucknell University Press, 1956), 104; Sarah Porter Hillhouse to Elisha Porter, 26 January 1787, in Marion Alexander Boggs, ed., *The Alexander Letters, 1787–1900* (Athens: University of Georgia Press, 1980), 16–17; James W. Patton, "Glimpses of North Carolina in the Writings of Northern and Foreign Travelers, 1783–1860," *North Carolina Historical Review* 45 (1968): 314; John Cook Wyllie, ed., "Observations Made during a Short Residence in Virginia: In a Letter from Thomas H. Palmer, May 30, 1814," *Virginia Magazine of History and Biography* 76 (October 1968): 409.

35. Charles Anderson Memoir, Charles Anderson Papers, FHS; Thomas Jefferson to Peter Carr, 19 August 1785, *Papers of Thomas Jefferson*, 8: 406. See also John Randolph to Theodore Dudley, 15 February 1806, in Kirk, *John Randolph of Roanoke*, 236.

36. Jane Ball to Isaac Ball, 30 May 1802 and 17 January 1803, Ball Family Papers, SCL; Elizabeth Brown Peyton to Robert Peyton, 20 March 1826, Peyton Family Papers, VHS; Anne Hart to William Hart, 7 November 1806, Oliver Hart Papers, SCL. For the centrality of women in nineteenth-century evangelical Protestantism, see Ann Douglas, *The Feminization of American Culture* (New York: Knopf, 1977), esp. 7–10; and Jean Friedman, *The Enclosed Garden: Women and Community in the Evangelical South, 1830–1900* (Chapel Hill: University of North Carolina Press, 1985). For the marginalization of women to legitimate evangelicalism in the eyes of elite men, see Heyrman, *Southern Cross,* chap. 4.

37. Micah Taul Memoir, p. 1, UKSCL.

38. Maria Campbell to George J. Kollock, 24 April 1826, in Johnston, ed., "Kollock Letters," 253; Mary McDonald to Charles McDonald, 16 and 17 November 1815, McDonald-Lawrence Family Papers, SHC; Frances Pinckney to Roger Pinckney, 14 July 1785, Roger Pinckney Correspondence, SCHS; Anne Hart to William Hart, 7 November 1806, Oliver Hart Papers, SCL.

39. Richard Watkins to William Watkins, 25 November and 12 December 1831, in "The Watkins Letters," *Virginia Magazine of History and Biography* 41 (1933): 332–34.

40. For the William and Mary incident, see Robert J. Brugger, *Beverley Tucker: Heart over Head in the Old South* (Baltimore: Johns Hopkins University Press, 1978), 16. For examples of derision, see Thomas Palmer Jr. to Joseph Palmer, 17 August 1821, Louis P. Towles, ed., *A World Turned Upside Down: The Palmers of South Santee, 1818–1881* (Columbia: University of South Carolina Press, 1996), 27; Lyerly, *Methodism and the Southern Mind*, 86; Paul C. Nagel, *The Lees of Virginia: Seven Generations of an American Family* (New York: Oxford University Press, 1990), 237.

41. John Wallace Jr. to Mary Wallace, 30 June 1808 and 27 February 1808, in Mary Savage Anderson, ed., "The Wallace Letters," *Georgia Historical Quarterly* 18 (1934): 177–78.

Two • Raising "Self Willed" Sons

1. William Ball to John Ball Jr., 17 April 1807, 15 June 1807, and 18 August 1807, all in William James Ball Family Correspondence, SCHS.

2. John Locke, *Some Thoughts concerning Education* (1693). See also Jay Fliegelman, *Prodigals and Pilgrims: The American Revolution against Patriarchal Authority, 1750–1800* (Cambridge: Cambridge University Press, 1982), 2, 12–15; C. Dallett Hemphill, *Bowing to Necessities: A History of Manners in America, 1620–1860* (New York: Oxford University Press, 1999), chap. 5, esp. 88; Gail S. Murray, "Rational Thought and Republican Virtues: Children's Literature, 1789–1820," *Journal of the Early Republic* 8 (Summer 1988): 159–77.

3. Seaborn Jones to William Hart, 9 June 1809, Seaborn Jones Family Papers, GHS; Harmer Gilmer to Peachy Gilmer, 12 October 1806, Peachy Ridgway Gilmer Papers, VHS; penmanship exercise, 28 April 1831, Thomas Lenoir Papers, DUL. See also Michael Zuckerman, "Penmanship Exercises for Saucy Sons: Some Thoughts on the Colonial Southern Family," *South Carolina Historical Magazine* 84 (July 1983): 152–66.

4. John Ball Sr. to John Ball Jr., 9 May 1802, Ball Family Papers, SCHS.

5. Charles Wilson Harris to Robert Wilson Harris, 5 December 1802, in J. G. DeRoulhac Hamilton and Henry McGilbert Wagstaff, eds., "The Harris Letters," *James Sprunt Historical Publications* 14 (1916). For the importance of reputation, see Richard Bushman, *The Refinement of America: Persons, Houses, Cities* (New York: Knopf, 1992); Craig Thompson Friend and Lorri Glover, eds., *Southern Manhood: Perspectives on Masculinity in the Old South* (Athens: University of Georgia Press, 2004); Hemphill, *Bowing to Necessities*; and Bertram Wyatt-Brown, *Southern Honor: Ethics and Behavior in the Old South* (New York: Oxford University Press, 1982).

6. For training girls, see Anne M. Boylan, "Growing Up Female in Young America, 1800–1860," in Joseph M. Hawes and N. Ray Hiner, eds., *American Childhood: A Research Guide and Historical Handbook* (Westport: Greenwood Press, 1985), 153–84; Catherine Clinton, "Equally Their Due: The Education of the Planter Daughter in the Early Republic," *Journal of the Early Republic* 2 (April 1982): 39–60; and Cynthia A. Kierner, *Beyond the Household: Women's Place in the Early South, 1700–1835* (Ithaca: Cornell University Press, 1998), 54–55; 147–61.

7. Francis Walker Gilmer to Peachy Gilmer, 30 May [1805?], Peachy Ridgway Gilmer Papers, VHS; Alfred Mordecai Memoir, reprinted in James A. Padgett, ed., "The Life of Alfred Mordecai, as Related by Himself," *North Carolina Historical Review* 22 (1945): 65; Louis P. Towles, ed., *A World Turned Upside Down: The Palmers of South Santee, 1818–1881* (Columbia: University of South Carolina Press, 1996), 19; G. Melvin Herndon, "Pinckney Horry, 1769–1828: Rebel without a Cause," *Georgia Historical Quarterly* 70 (Summer 1986): 232. Daniel Horry changed his name to Pinckney Horry.

8. Joel Lyle to William Lyle, 9 January 1827, Lyle Family Papers, UKSCL; Elias Horry to Thomas Horry, 16 November 1807, Letters to Thomas Horry, SCHS. See also Rosalie Stier Calvert to Isabelle van Havre, 12 December 1811, in Margaret Law Callcott, ed., *Mistress of Riversdale: The Plantation Letters of Rosalie Stier Calvert, 1795–1821* (Baltimore: Johns Hopkins University Press, 1991), 244.

9. Elijah Fletcher to Calvin Fletcher, 19 March 1830, in Martha von Briesen, ed., *The Letters of Elijah Fletcher* (Charlottesville: University Press of Virginia, 1965), 111. In his study

of early Mississippi, historian Christopher Morris found that when planters' sons played with poorer neighbors, they "brought extra food, ponies, guns, and fishing equipment for all to share." Christopher Morris, *Becoming Southern: The Evolution of a Way of Life, Warren County and Vicksburg, Mississippi, 1770–1860* (New York: Oxford University Press, 1995), 160.

10. See, for example, Charles Anderson Memoir, Charles Anderson Papers, FHS for play activities. See Cornelius Ayer to Lewis Malone Ayer, 8 March 1816, Lewis Malone Ayer Papers, SCL; and Hugh Swinton Ball to John Ball Jr., undated [c. 1823], John Ball Sr. and John Ball Jr. Papers, DUL for students using slaves.

11. David R. Roediger, "The Pursuit of Whiteness: Property, Terror, and Expansion, 1790–1860," *Journal of the Early Republic* 19 (Winter 1999): 582. See also Dana Nelson, *National Manhood: Capitalist Citizenship and the Imagined Fraternity of White Men* (Durham: Duke University Press, 1998); Lacy K. Ford Jr., "Making the 'White Man's Country' White: Race, Slavery, and State-Building in the Jacksonian South," *Journal of the Early Republic* 19 (Winter 1999): 713–37; and, for a critique of whiteness studies, Peter Kolchin, "Whiteness Studies: The New History of Race in America," *Journal of American History* 89 (June 2002): 154–73.

12. Quoted in Zuckerman, "Penmanship Exercises for Saucy Sons," 160.

13. Alice Izard to Margaret Izard Manigault, 2 March 1805, Manigault Family Papers, SCL; Alicia Hopton Middleton to Nathaniel Russell Middleton, 29 September 1817, Middleton Family Papers, SCL.

14. Quoted in Jan Lewis, *The Pursuit of Happiness: Family and Values in Jefferson's Virginia* (Cambridge: Cambridge University Press, 1983), 129. As Michael Zuckerman explained, parents in the South "might demand submissiveness, in letters and lectures, but they modeled autonomy, in life." Zuckerman, "Penmanship Exercises for Saucy Sons," 164.

15. Herndon, "Pinckney Horry," quotation from 235.

16. Ralph Wormeley to Warner Wormeley, 29 June 1801, Wormeley Family Papers, VHS; John Ball Sr. to John Ball Jr., 14 August 1800, Ball Family Papers, SCHS; Ralph Wormeley to Warner Wormeley, 29 June 1801, Wormeley Family Papers, VHS.

17. Edward Rutledge to Henry Rutledge, 2 August 1796, in Marvin R. Zahniser, ed., "Edward Rutledge to His Son, August 2, 1796," *South Carolina Historical Magazine* 64 (1963): 72.

18. Thomas Jefferson to Peter Carr, 11 December 1783, in Julian P. Boyd et al., eds., *Papers of Thomas Jefferson* (Princeton: Princeton University Press, 1950-present), 6: 379; Peter Carr to Thomas Jefferson, 20 April 1785, *Papers of Thomas Jefferson*, 8: 96.

19. Joanna Bowen Gillespie, *The Life and Times of Martha Laurens Ramsay, 1759–1811* (Columbia: University of South Carolina Press, 2001), 208; Elizabeth Brown Peyton to Robert Peyton, 30 December 1826, Peyton Family Papers, VHS; J. Wilson to Roger Pinckney, 16 May 1784, Roger Pinckney Correspondence, SCHS; Henry DeSaussure to John E. Colhoun Jr., 14 September 1810, Henry William DeSaussure Papers, SCL.

20. Alicia Hopton Middleton to Nathaniel Russell Middleton, 28 July 1817, Middleton Family Papers, SCL.

21. John Jones to Thomas Williamson Jones, 8 September 1813, Thomas Williamson Jones Papers, SHC.

22. William Cumming to Thomas Cumming, 8 April 1818, Alfred Cumming Papers, DUL; Sarah Gibbes to John Gibbes, 11 August 1783, Gibbes Family Papers, SCHS.

23. Anya Jabour, *Marriage in the Early Republic: Elizabeth and William Wirt and the*

Companionate Ideal (Baltimore: Johns Hopkins University Press, 1998), esp. 118; John Wayles Eppes to Francis Eppes, 11 December 1813 and 25 April 1815, John Wayles Eppes Papers, DUL. John Eppes married Martha Jones after Francis's mother, Maria Jefferson, died.

24. Robert Carter "Letter of Advice to My Children," 12–14 October 1803, Robert Carter Papers, VHS. For maternal authority over children, see also Jabour, *Marriage in the Early Republic*, 73–79; Joseph F. Kett, *Rites of Passage: Adolescence in America, 1790 to the Present* (New York: Basic Books, 1977), 14–16; E. Anthony Rotundo, *American Manhood: Transformations in Masculinity from the Revolution to the Modern Era* (New York: Basic Books, 1993), 28; Brenda Stevenson, *Life in Black and White: Family and Community in the Slave South* (New York: Oxford University Press, 1996), 97; and Wyatt-Brown, *Southern Honor*, 134.

25. John F. Grimké to Henry Grimké, 8 March 1818, Grimké Family Papers, SCHS; John Ball Sr. to John Ball Jr., 12 August 1798, Ball Family Papers, SCHS.

26. For father-son tensions, see Stevenson, *Life in Black and White*, 115; Shawn Johansen, *Family Men: Middle-Class Fatherhood in Early Industrializing America* (New York: Routledge, 2001), 153; Joyce Appleby, *Inheriting the Revolution: The First Generation of Americans* (Cambridge: Harvard University Press, 2000), 170; Jon L. Wakelyn, "Antebellum College Life and the Relations between Fathers and Sons," in Walter J. Fraser Jr., R. Frank Saunders Jr., and Jon L. Wakelyn, eds., *The Web of Southern Social Relations: Women, Family, and Education* (Athens: University of Georgia Press, 1985), 107–26; Wyatt-Brown, *Southern Honor*, 118; Daniel Blake Smith, *Inside the Great House: Planter Family Life in Eighteenth-Century Chesapeake Society* (Ithaca: Cornell University Press, 1980), chap. 3, esp. 100; and Zuckerman, "Penmanship Exercises for Saucy Sons," 161–63.

27. John Palmer to Harriett Palmer, 12 January 1822, in Towles, *A World Turned Upside Down*, 30. The evidence of what boys thought about their upbringing and the early demands of masculinity is far less voluminous than the advice offered by adults. Childhood writings are scarce; memoirs, although more common, are less reliable, since time can cloud memories and allow idealizations to replace reality. While teenage boys often corresponded with their relatives about college life, courtships, and careers, they were not a terribly self-reflective lot.

28. John McKnitt A. Ramsey to John McKnitt Alexander, 1 February 1803, James Gettys McGready Ramsey Papers, UTSCL; John Randolph to Frances Tucker, 27 September 1787, quoted in Smith, *Inside the Great House*, 112; Seaborn Jones to William Hart, 1 December 1804, Seaborn Jones Family Papers, GHS.

29. Thomas Cooper to Thomas Jefferson, 14 February 1822, Thomas Cooper Papers, SCL; Azel Backus to John Rutledge, 18 July 1805, John Rutledge Papers, SHC.

30. Clement Eaton, *Henry Clay and the Art of American Politics* (Boston: Little, Brown, 1957), 65–66. For northern tutors, see Elizabeth Brown Pryor, "An Anomalous Person: The Northern Tutor in Plantation Society, 1773–1860," *Journal of Southern History* 47 (August 1981): 363–92.

31. Gillespie, *The Life and Times of Martha Laurens Ramsay*, 121; Jane Ball to John Ball Jr., 12 October 1799 and 28 August 1799, both in Ball Family Papers, SCHS.

32. Joseph W. Barnwell, ed., "Diary of Timothy Ford," *South Carolina Historical and Genealogical Magazine* 13 (July 1912): 142–43; H. Roy Merrens, ed., "A View of Coastal Carolina in 1778: The Journal of Ebenezer Hazard," *South Carolina Historical Magazine* 73

(1972): 190; Jefferson quoted in William W. Freehling, *The Road to Disunion: Secessionists at Bay, 1776–1854* (New York: Oxford University Press, 1990), 125.

Three • *The Educational Aspirations of Southern Families*

1. Thomas Todd to Charles Todd, 9 March 1808, Charles Stewart Todd Papers, FHS.

2. For the importance of education to the future of the Republic, see Lawrence A. Cremin, *American Education: The National Experience, 1783–1876* (New York: Harper and Row, 1980), esp. chap. 4; Charles Crowe, "Bishop James Madison and the Republic of Virtue," *Journal of Southern History* 30 (February 1964): 58–70; Jay Fliegelman, *Prodigals and Pilgrims: The American Revolution against Patriarchal Authority, 1750–1800* (Cambridge: Cambridge University Press, 1982); Carl F. Kaestle, *Pillars of the Republic: Common Schools and American Society, 1780–1860* (New York: Hill and Wang, 1983); Gail S. Murray, "Rational Thought and Republican Virtues: Children's Literature, 1789–1820," *Journal of the Early Republic* (Summer 1988): 159–77; Gilman M. Ostrander, *Republic of Letters: The American Intellectual Community, 1775–1865* (Madison: Madison House, 1999); David W. Robson, *Educating Republicans: The College in the Era of the American Revolution, 1750–1800* (Westport: Greenwood Press, 1985); Bernard Wishy, *The Child and the Republic: The Dawn of Modern American Child Nurture* (Philadelphia: University of Pennsylvania Press, 1967), chaps. 1–2.

3. Henry DeSaussure to Ezekiel Pickens, 27 October 1805, Henry William DeSaussure Papers, SCL; Benjamin Rush, "Thoughts Upon the Mode of Education Proper in a Republic," in Frederick Rudolph, ed., *Essays on Education in the Early Republic* (Cambridge: Harvard University Press, 1965), 17; "Abraham Baldwin's Speech to the University of Georgia Trustees," *Georgia Historical Quarterly* 10 (1926): 328, 331. For the national significance of this generation, see Joyce Appleby, *Inheriting the Revolution: The First Generation of Americans* (Cambridge: Harvard University Press, 2000); Steven J. Novak, *The Rights of Youth: American Colleges and Student Revolt, 1798–1815* (Cambridge: Harvard University Press, 1977), esp. chap. 3; and Steven Watts, *The Republic Reborn: War and the Making of Liberal America, 1790–1820* (Baltimore: Johns Hopkins University Press, 1987). For colleges in the era, see Roger L. Geiger, ed., *The American College in the Nineteenth Century* (Nashville: Vanderbilt University Press, 2000); Jurgen Herbst, *From Crisis to Crisis: American College Government, 1636–1819* (Cambridge: Harvard University Press, 1982); J. David Hoeveler, *Creating the American Mind: Intellect and Politics in the Colonial Colleges* (New York: Rowman and Littlefield, 2003); Howard Miller, *The Revolutionary College: American Presbyterian Higher Education, 1707–1837* (New York: New York University Press, 1976); and Robson, *Educating Republicans.*

4. Gabriel Manigault to Mr. DuPont, 13 April 1807, Manigault Family Papers, SCL; Richard Beresford to unknown, 21 April 1785, Richard Beresford Papers, SCL.

5. For excellent syntheses, see Henry F. May, *The Enlightenment in America* (New York: Oxford University Press, 1976); Gordon S. Wood, *The Radicalism of the American Revolution* (New York: Knopf, 1992); and Charles Sellers, *The Market Revolution: Jacksonian America, 1815–1846* (New York: Oxford University Press, 1991).

6. St. George Tucker to Alexander Campbell, 7 July 1809, quoted in Phillip Hamilton, *The*

Making and Unmaking of a Revolutionary Family: The Tuckers of Virginia, 1752–1830 (Charlottesville: University of Virginia Press, 2003), 3.

7. Thomas Jefferson to Walker Maury, 19 August 1785, in Julian P. Boyd et al., eds., *Papers of Thomas Jefferson* (Princeton: Princeton University Press, 1950-present), 8: 409.

8. "Abraham Baldwin's Speech to the University of Georgia Trustees," 328, 332.

9. John Ball Sr. to John Ball Jr., 12 August 1798, Ball Family Papers, SCHS; Ralph Izard to Dr. Johnson, 20 December 1787, Ralph Izard Papers, SCL; Daniel Guerrant to Charles Guerrant, 4 May 1816, Guerrant Family Papers, VHS.

10. Kenneth Greenberg demonstrated that partisan activity was diminished throughout the South, largely because of the effects of slavery. Kenneth S. Greenberg, *Masters and Statesmen: The Political Culture of American Slavery* (Baltimore: Johns Hopkins University Press, 1985), 45. For a similar conclusion regarding religion, see Daniel Walker Howe, "Church, State, and Education in the Young American Republic," *Journal of the Early Republic* 22 (Spring 2002): 1–24, esp. 15; and David B. Potts, "American Colleges in the Nineteenth Century: From Localism to Denominationalism," *History of Education Quarterly* 11 (Winter 1971): 363–80.

11. John Ball Sr. to John Ball Jr., 9 May 1802, Ball Family Papers, SCHS; Rosalie Stier Calvert to H. J. Stier, 22 November 1819, in Margaret Law Callcott, ed., *Mistress of Riversdale: The Plantation Letters of Rosalie Stier Calvert, 1795–1821* (Baltimore: Johns Hopkins University Press, 1991), 354; John E. Colhoun Jr. to William Moultrie Reid, 25 March 1817, John Ewing Colhoun Papers, SHC.

12. See E. Anthony Rotundo, *American Manhood: Transformations in Masculinity from the Revolution to the Modern Era* (New York: Basic Books, 1993), for this shift in northern middle-class masculine values. For elite control of southern education, see Cremin, *American Education: The National Experience*, 177; Christie Anne Farnham, *The Education of the Southern Belle: Higher Education and Student Socialization in the Antebellum South* (New York: New York University Press, 1994), 3, 38–39; John Hope Franklin, *The Militant South, 1800–1860* (Cambridge: Harvard University Press, 1956), chap. 7; Kaestle, *Pillars of the Republic*, chap. 7; and Bertram Wyatt-Brown, *Southern Honor: Ethics and Behavior in the Old South* (New York: Oxford University Press, 1982), 94, 167.

13. Richard Bennehan to Thomas Bennehan, 11 December 1795, Cameron Family Papers, SHC; Edward Harden to Edward Randolph Harden, 19 September 1829, Harden Family Papers, DUL; Charlton DeSaussure Jr., ed., "Memoirs of General George Izard, 1825," *South Carolina Historical Magazine* 78 (1977): 44.

14. Ralph Izard to Mr. Bird, 25 June 1794, Ralph Izard Papers, SCL; John Wayles Eppes to Francis Eppes, 20 June 1818, John Wayles Eppes Letters, DUL; Charles Washington Goldsborough to Rosanna Harrington, 30 August 1811, in J. G. DeRoulhac Hamilton and Henry McGilbert Wagstaff, eds., "The Harrington Letters," *James Sprunt Historical Publications* 13 (1914): 28.

15. Sterling Ruffin to Thomas Ruffin, 5 May 1803, Thomas Ruffin Papers, SHC; unnamed cousin to Richard Hopkins, 27 May 1783, in "A Maryland Medical Student and His Friends," *Maryland Historical Magazine* 23 (1928); Theodorick Bland Jr. to Frances Randolph, 26 September 1777, quoted in Phillip Hamilton, "Education in the St. George Tucker Household: Change and Continuity in Jeffersonian Virginia," *Virginia Magazine of History and Biogra-*

phy 102 (April 1994): 182. See also Thomas Todd to Charles Todd, 9 March 1808, Charles Stewart Todd Papers, FHS; Sarah Gibbes to John Gibbes, 10 September 1783, Gibbes Family Papers, SCHS. For refinement, see Richard Bushman, *The Refinement of America: Persons, Houses, Cities* (New York: Knopf, 1992). For this pattern among medical students, see Daniel Kilbride, "Southern Medical Students in Philadelphia, 1800–1861: Science and Sociability in the 'Republic of Medicine,'" *Journal of Southern History* 65 (November 1999): 699–732.

16. B. Silliman to Alexander Morson, 6 May 1820, Arthur Alexander Morson Papers, SHC; Alice Izard to Margaret Izard Manigault, 24 June 1801, Manigault Family Papers, SCL.

17. John Ball Sr. to John Ball Jr., 22 February 1799, Ball Family Papers, SCHS; Richard Bennehan to Thomas Bennehan, 5 March 1796, Cameron Family Papers, SHC; John Ball Sr. to John Ball Jr., 21 October 1801, Ball Family Papers, SCHS.

18. For masculine values on the southern frontier, see Stephen Aron, *How the West Was Lost: The Transformation of Kentucky from Daniel Boone to Henry Clay* (Baltimore: Johns Hopkins University Press, 1996); Joan Cashin, *A Family Venture: Men and Women on the Southern Frontier* (New York: Oxford University Press, 1991); Elliott J. Gorn, "'Gouge and Bite, Pull Hair and Scratch': The Social Significance of Fighting in the Southern Backcountry," *American Historical Review* 90 (February 1985): 18–43; Elizabeth Perkins, *Border Life: Experience and Memory in the Revolutionary Ohio Valley* (Chapel Hill: University of North Carolina Press, 1998); and Nathaniel Shiedley, "Unruly Men: Indians, Settlers, and the Ethos of Frontier Patriarchy in the Upper Tennessee Watershed, 1763–1815" (Ph.D. dissertation, Princeton University, 1999).

19. George William Respess Corlis to John Corlis, 4 December 1814, Corlis-Respess Family Papers, FHS; Charles M. Thruston to Buckner Thruston, 5 November 1812 and 15 June 1813, both in Thruston Family Papers, FHS.

20. Thomas Armstrong to Martin Armstrong, 6 December 1815, Martin W. B. Armstrong Papers, SHC; Ralph Wormeley to Warner Wormeley, 16 December 1801 and 16 May 1802, Wormeley Family Papers, VHS; John F. Grimké to Henry Grimké, 8 March 1818, Grimké Family Papers, SCHS.

21. John Haywood to George W. Haywood, 24 August 1819 and 5 March 1816, Ernest Haywood Collection, SHC; Richard V. Watkins to William M. Watkins, 25 November 1831, in "Watkins Letters," *Virginia Magazine of History and Biography* 41 (1933): 333.

22. Sarah Gibbes to John Gibbes, 11 August 1783, Gibbes Family Papers, SCHS; John Stacy to John W. Stacy, 13 September 1817, John Stacy Papers, GHS; George Jones to Noble Wimberly Jones, 23 October 1805, Jones Family Papers, GHS. For examples of housing autonomy, see John Pettigrew to Charles Pettigrew, 23 February 1795, Pettigrew Family Papers, SHC; and Thomas Bennehan to Rebecca Bennehan, 22 July 1799, Cameron Family Papers, SHC.

23. Thomas Todd to Charles Todd, 25 September 1808, Charles Stewart Todd Papers, FHS.

24. John F. Grimké to Henry Grimké, 8 March 1818, Grimké Family Papers, SCHS; John Stacy to John W. Stacy, 13 September 1817, John Stacy Papers, GHS; George Jones to Noble Wimberly Jones, 17 September 1805, Jones Family Papers, GHS.

25. George Swain to David Swain, 7 June 1822, David Lowry Swain Papers, NCC; Joanna Bowen Gillespie, *The Life and Times of Martha Laurens Ramsay, 1759–1811* (Columbia: University of South Carolina Press, 2001), 207. See also Rosalie Stier Calvert to Charles J. Stier,

24 February 1813, in Callcott, *Mistress of Riversdale*, 254; John Minor to William Lorman, undated [c. 1811], John Minor Letterbook, VHS.

26. George Jones to Noble Wimberly Jones, 25 June 1807, Jones Family Papers, GHS; Alice Izard to Ralph Izard, 4 November 1794, Ralph Izard Papers, SCL.

27. Charles Pettigrew to John and Ebenezer Pettigrew, 19 September 1795, Pettigrew Family Papers, SHC; John Randolph to Theodore Dudley, 15 February 1806, in Russell Kirk, *John Randolph of Roanoke* (Indianapolis: Liberty Press, 1978), 237. For John Randolph's upbringing, see Robert Dawidoff, *The Education of John Randolph* (New York: W. W. Norton, 1979).

28. Seaborn Jones to William Hart, 1 December 1804, Seaborn Jones Family Papers, GHS.

29. John Ball Jr. to Hugh Swinton Ball, 15 January 1824, John Ball Sr. and John Ball Jr. Papers, DUL.

30. John McDowell to James McDowell, 25 September 1804, McDowell Family Papers, VHS.

31. Charles Wilkins Short Papers, FHS; John Rutledge Papers, SHC; Matthew Cary Whitaker Papers, SHC. For kin networks in the colonial South, see Lorri Glover, *All Our Relations: Blood Ties and Emotional Bonds among the Early South Carolina Gentry* (Baltimore: Johns Hopkins University Press, 2000); Michael Zuckerman, "William Byrd's Family," *Perspectives in American History* 12 (1979); Darrett and Anita Rutman, *A Place in Time: Middlesex County, Virginia, 1650–1750* (New York: W. W. Norton, 1984); and Daniel Blake Smith, *Inside the Great House: Planter Family Life in Eighteenth-Century Chesapeake Society* (Ithaca: Cornell University Press, 1980), chap. 5.

32. See Emily Bingham, *Mordecai: An Early American Family* (New York: Hill and Wang, 2003); William Barlow and David O. Powell, "A Dedicated Medical Student: Solomon Mordecai, 1819–1822," *Journal of the Early Republic* 7 (Winter 1987): 377–97; and for the family's female boarding academy, Jean E. Friedman, *Ways of Wisdom: Moral Education in the Early National Period* (Athens: University of Georgia Press, 2001).

33. Alexander Morson to unknown, 2 July 1819, Arthur Alexander Morson Papers, SHC; Ralph Izard to Edward Rutledge, 16 March 1789, Ralph Izard Papers, SCL. See also unknown to Thomas Ruffin, 15 May 1825, Thomas Ruffin Papers, SHC; Henry DeSaussure to John E. Colhoun Jr., 20 January 1808, Henry William DeSaussure Papers, SCL.

34. Ralph Izard to [Charles?] Pinckney, 22 February 1793 and 3 December 1794, Ralph Izard Papers, SCL; Thomas Todd to Charles Todd, 9 March 1808, Charles Stewart Todd Papers, FHS.

35. Rudolphus Bogert to William Page, 14 January 1812 and William Page to Benjamin Cater, 12 May 1813, both in William Page Papers, SHC.

Four • *Creating Southern Schools for Southern Sons*

1. Thomas Jefferson to Charles Yancey, 6 January 1816, quoted in Robert E. Shalhope, *John Taylor of Caroline: Pastoral Republican* (Columbia: University of South Carolina Press, 1980), 195. Abraham Baldwin, a founder of the University of Georgia, similarly insisted that "to send them [southern students] abroad to foreign countries for their education will always be the cause of so great foreign attachment that could our national pride brook such a dependence, upon principles of good policy it would be insufferable. To send them to other States . . . is too

humiliating an acknowledgment of the ignorance and inferiority of our own." "Abraham Baldwin's Speech to the University of Georgia Trustees," *Georgia Historical Quarterly* 10 (1926): 329.

2. Thomas Jefferson to James Breckenridge, 15 February 1821, quoted in John S. Ezell, "A Southern Education for Southrons," *Journal of Southern History* 17 (August 1951): 303.

3. M. F. Bryan to William Ruffin, 19 June 1828, Thomas Ruffin Papers, SHC.

4. For the history of Harvard, see Gilman M. Ostrander, *Republic of Letters: The American Intellectual Community, 1775–1865* (Madison: Madison House, 1999), 168–78; and Ronald Story, *The Forging of an Aristocracy: Harvard and the Boston Upper Class, 1800–1870* (Middletown: Wesleyan University Press, 1980). For Yale, see Lawrence A. Cremin, *American Education: The National Experience, 1783–1876* (New York: Harper and Row, 1980), 404–6. For Princeton, see Howard Miller, *The Revolutionary College: American Presbyterian Higher Education, 1707–1837* (New York: New York University Press, 1976); and Mark A. Noll, *Princeton and the Republic, 1768–1822: The Search for a Christian Enlightenment in the Era of Samuel Stanhope Smith* (Princeton: Princeton University Press, 1989). For medical education in the early United States, see Thomas Neville Bonner, *Becoming a Physician: Medical Education in Britain, France, Germany, and the United States, 1750–1945* (New York: Oxford University Press, 1995), 175–81.

5. George Swain to David Swain, 7 June 1822, David Lowry Swain Papers, NCC. See also William Barry to John Barry, 23 September 1803, William Taylor Barry Papers, FHS; and Daniel C. Edwards to William Moultrie Reid, 4 September 1815, William Moultrie Reid Papers, SCL.

6. Samuel DuBose to William DuBose, undated [c. 1805], Samuel DuBose Papers, SHC. Similar apprehension emerged over girls' education in this era. Upon touring northern female academies, one southern planter reported that "girls here are imbibing habits and manners not so perfectly congenial with those of the people of the South, where they are destined to live." Catherine Clinton, "Equally Their Due: The Education of the Planter Daughter in the Early Republic," *Journal of the Early Republic* 2 (April 1982): 59.

7. Edmund Ruffin Jr., 8 October 1828, in Mrs. Kirkland Ruffin, ed., "School-Boy Letters of Edmund Ruffin, Jr., 1828–29," *North Carolina Historical Review* 10 (1933): 293–96. See also Bertram Wyatt-Brown, *Lewis Tappan and the Evangelical War against Slavery* (Cleveland: Press of Case Western Reserve University, 1969).

8. The 1796 report quoted in John Maclean, *History of the College of New Jersey, from its Origin in 1746 to the Commencement of 1854* (Philadelphia: J. B. Lippincott, 1877), 15.

9. While several states granted charters and made plans for schools earlier, these represent the dates of the first classes of the respective colleges. For general information on the founding of these and other southern state colleges in the early national era, see Donald G. Tewksbury, *The Founding of American Colleges and Universities before the Civil War, With Particular Reference to the Religious Influences Bearing upon the College Movement* (New York: Archon Books, 1965), 175–91.

10. Two of the other three early national state schools were founded in Ohio, while Vermont created the third. Tewksbury, *The Founding of American Colleges and Universities before the Civil War*, 32–38, 167–70.

11. John E. Colhoun Jr. to William Moultrie Reid, 10 December 1818, John Ewing Colhoun

Papers, SHC; Richard Hopkins to Elizabeth Thomas Hopkins, 7 January 1784, in "A Maryland Medical Student and His Friends," *Maryland Historical Magazine* 23 (1928): 286.

12. John Ball Sr. to John Ball Jr., 29 September 1799, Ball Family Papers, SCHS. See also Lorri Glover, "An Education in Southern Masculinity: The Ball Family of South Carolina in the New Republic," *Journal of Southern History* 69 (February 2003): 39–70.

13. Edmund Wilcox Hubard to B. Walker, 26 July 1825, Hubard Family Papers, SHC; Moses Waddel to Joseph Brevan, 14 March 1825, Moses Waddel Papers, SHC; Charles Wilson Harris to Joseph Caldwell, 24 July 1796, in J. G. DeRoulhac Hamilton and Henry McGilbert Wagstaff, eds., "The Harris Letters," *James Sprunt Historical Publications* 14 (1916): 30.

14. George Swain to David Swain, c. June 1822, David Lowry Swain Papers, NCC; John Pettigrew to Charles Pettigrew, 27 June 1797, Pettigrew Family Papers, SHC.

15. Henry Clay to [probably Horace Holley], 24 December 1819, in James F. Hopkins and Mary W. M. Hargreaves et al., eds., *The Papers of Henry Clay* (Lexington: University of Kentucky Press, 1959–1992), 2: 735; Charles Henry Warfield to William Bullitt, 14 December 1808, Bullitt Family Papers, FHS; Pryor Lee to Charles Coffin, 30 October 1826, Pryor Lee Letter, TSL.

16. See, for example, Lacy K. Ford Jr., *Origins of Southern Radicalism: The South Carolina Upcountry, 1800–1860* (New York: Oxford University Press, 1988); Kenneth S. Greenberg, *Masters and Statesmen: The Political Culture of American Slavery* (Baltimore: Johns Hopkins University Press, 1985); Manisha Sinha, *The Counterrevolution of Slavery: Politics and Ideology in Antebellum South Carolina* (Chapel Hill: University of North Carolina Press, 2000); and Jeffrey Robert Young, *Domesticating Slavery: The Master Class in Georgia and South Carolina, 1670–1837* (Chapel Hill: University of North Carolina Press, 1999).

17. Wayne K. Durrill, "The Power of Ancient Words: Classical Teaching and Social Change at South Carolina College, 1804–1860," *Journal of Southern History* 65 (August 1999): 469–98, quotation from p. 471. See also Michael Sugrue, " 'We desired our future rulers to be educated men': South Carolina College, the Defense of Slavery, and the Development of Secessionist Politics," *History of Higher Education Annual* 14 (1994): 43–44; and Joyce Appleby, *Inheriting the Revolution: The First Generation of Americans* (Cambridge: Harvard University Press, 2000), 49.

18. John Drayton to General Assembly, 23 November 1801, quoted in Sugrue, "We desired our future rulers," 39. For additional contemporary assessments of South Carolina College, see Lowell Harrison, "South Carolina's Educational System in 1822," *South Carolina Historical and Genealogical Magazine* 51 (January 1950): 1–9. See also Daniel Walker Howe, "Church, State, and Education in the Young American Republic," *Journal of the Early Republic* 22 (Spring 2002): 11–12; Louis P. Towles, "A Matter of Honor at South Carolina College, 1822," *South Carolina Historical Magazine* 94 (January 1993): 9; Greenberg, *Masters and Statesmen,* 77; and Drew Gilpin Faust, *James Henry Hammond and the Old South: A Design for Mastery* (Baton Rouge: Louisiana State University Press, 1982), 13.

19. Quoted in Richard Beale Davis, *Intellectual Life in Jefferson's Virginia* (Knoxville: University of Tennessee Press, 1972), 66–67. For more about William and Mary, see Steven J. Novak, *The Rights of Youth: American Colleges and Student Revolt, 1798–1815* (Cambridge: Harvard University Press, 1977), 96–106; and J. David Hoeveler, *Creating the American Mind: Intellect and Politics in the Colonial Colleges* (New York: Rowman and Littlefield, 2003),

chaps. 4 and 11. For more on the University of Virginia, see Davis, *Intellectual Life in Jefferson's Virginia*, 61–69; and Mark R. Wenger, "Thomas Jefferson, the College of William and Mary, and the University of Virginia," *Virginia Magazine of History and Biography* 103 (July 1995): 339–74.

20. Roger L. Geiger, ed., *The American College in the Nineteenth Century* (Nashville: Vanderbilt University Press, 2000), 20.

21. For military schools, including the masculine cultures that emerged there, see John Hope Franklin, *The Militant South, 1800–1860* (Cambridge: Harvard University Press, 1956), chap. 8; Jennifer R. Green, "'Stout Chaps Who Can Bear the Distress': Young Men in Antebellum Military Academies," in Craig Thompson Friend and Lorri Glover, eds., *Southern Manhood: Perspectives on Masculinity in the Old South* (Athens: University of Georgia Press, 2004), 174–95; Anya Jabour, "Masculinity and Adolescence in Antebellum America: Robert Wirt at West Point, 1820–1821," *Journal of Family History* 23 (October 1998): 393–416; Harry S. Laver, "Rethinking the Social Role of the Militia: Community Building in Antebellum Kentucky," *Journal of Southern History* 58 (November 2002): 777–816; and Stephen A. Ross, "To 'Prepare our Sons for All that May Lie before Them': The Hillsborough Military Academy and Military Education in Antebellum North Carolina," *North Carolina Historical Review* 79 (January 2002): 1–27. For a later era, see Rod Andrew Jr., *Long Gray Lines: The Southern Military School Tradition, 1839–1915* (Chapel Hill: University of North Carolina Press, 2001). For denominational schools, see Novak, *The Rights of Youth*, chap. 4, and Tewksbury, *The Founding of American Colleges and Universities before the Civil War*, chap. 2.

22. For the significance of oratory in the South, see also Greenberg, *Masters and Statesmen*, 12; and in the young nation, see Jay Fliegelman, *Declaring Independence: Jefferson, Natural Language, and the Culture of Performance* (Stanford: Stanford University Press, 1993).

23. Robert Curtis, "The Bingham School and Classical Education in North Carolina, 1793–1873," *North Carolina Historical Review* 73 (July 1996): 328–77. See also Miller, *The Revolutionary College*, 169–73, 280–83; Robert F. Pace, *Halls of Honor: College Men in the Old South* (Baton Rouge: Louisiana State University Press, 2004); and Bertram Wyatt-Brown, *Southern Honor: Ethics and Behavior in the Old South* (New York: Oxford University Press, 1982), 92–95. For classical education at female schools, see Christie Anne Farnham, *The Education of the Southern Belle: Higher Education and Student Socialization in the Antebellum South* (New York: New York University Press, 1994), 21–23, 30–31.

24. John Pettigrew Copybook, 1795–1797, Pettigrew Family Papers, SHC; Circular of the South Carolina College, June 1821, SCL.

25. Durrill, "Classical Teaching at South Carolina College," 478.

26. Novak, *The Rights of Youth*, 127.

27. George Wilson McPhail to Mary Grigsby, 18 August 1834, Carrington Family Papers, VHS. For the observations of Henry Adams regarding his southern classmates at Harvard in the 1850s, see Henry Adams, *The Education of Henry Adams: An Autobiography* (Boston: Houghton, Mifflin, 1918), 57.

28. Address, Southern Rights Association, University of Virginia, 1851, typescript, SCL.

29. Sugrue, "We desired our future leaders," 62–63. See also Stephen W. Berry II, *All That Makes a Man: Love and Ambition in the Civil War South* (New York: Oxford University

Press, 2003), 152–56; and Leroy Youmans, "The Historical Significance of South Carolina College," *Proceedings of the Centennial Celebration of South Carolina College* (Columbia: The State Company, 1905), 161–62.

30. John Pettigrew Copybook, 1795–1797, Pettigrew Family Papers, SHC; William Ruffin to Thomas Ruffin, miscellaneous correspondence, 1824–25, Thomas Ruffin Papers, SHC.

31. Cassius Clay to Brutus Clay, 10 February 1828, Clay Family Papers, UKSCL.

32. E. Merton Coulter, *College Life in the Old South* (Athens: University of Georgia Press, 1928), 60.

33. Circular Letter of Board of Trustees, University of North Carolina, 15 December 1802, Ernest Haywood Collection, SHC.

34. Coulter, *College Life in the Old South,* 101.

35. Circular Letter of Board of Trustees, University of North Carolina, 15 December 1802, Ernest Haywood Collection, SHC; University of Virginia printed letter to parents and guardians, 1 September 1827, Ambler Family Papers, VHS.

36. Martin Armstrong to Thomas Armstrong, 19 March 1819; Thomas Armstrong to Martin Armstrong, 5 April 1819, Martin W. B. Armstrong Papers, SHC.

37. William J. Grayson, "The Character of a Gentleman," *Southern Quarterly Review* (January 1853): 69, quoted in Sugrue, "We desired our future rulers," 45; Isaac Coles to David Watson, 21 March 1798, in "Letters from William and Mary College, 1795–1799," *Virginia Magazine of History and Biography* 30 (July 1922): 241; Abner Stith to Thomas Williamson Jones, 31 March 1814, Thomas Williamson Jones Papers, SHC. For the difficulty of disciplining students, see also Joseph F. Kett, *Rites of Passage: Adolescence in America, 1790 to the Present* (New York: Basic Books, 1977), 48, 51–59.

38. University of North Carolina to John Hughes, 4 December 1823, Leander Hughes Papers, SHC.

39. William Hooper to Thomas Ruffin, 23 May 1828, Thomas Ruffin Papers, SHC.

40. Thomas Jefferson to Hugh Lawson White, et al., 6 May 1810, Hugh Lawson White Papers, UTSCL.

41. For the University of Georgia, see Coulter, *College Life in the Old South.* For Virginia, see Novak, *The Rights of Youth,* 127. For presidents' networks, see Miller, *The Revolutionary College,* 268.

42. Thomas Cooper, 25 February 1831, Thomas Cooper Papers, SHC; Thomas Jefferson, 7 February 1826, quoted in Davis, *Intellectual Life in Jefferson's Virginia,* 69.

Five • *The (Mis)Behaviors of Southern Collegians*

1. William Davie quoted in Steven J. Novak, *The Rights of Youth: American Colleges and Student Revolt, 1798–1815* (Cambridge: Harvard University Press, 1977), 84. For youth culture generally, see also John Demos, *Past, Present, and Personal: The Family and Life Course in American History* (New York: Oxford University Press, 1986), chap. 5; Harvey J. Graff, *Conflicting Paths: Growing Up in America* (Cambridge: Harvard University Press, 1995); Joseph F. Kett, *Rites of Passage: Adolescence in America, 1790 to the Present* (New York: Basic Books, 1977); and E. Anthony Rotundo, *American Manhood: Transformations in Masculinity from the Revolution to the Modern Era* (New York: Basic Books, 1993).

2. John Pettigrew to Charles Pettigrew, 23 February 1795, Pettigrew Family Papers, SHC; miscellaneous correspondence, 1783–1788, in Julian P. Boyd et al., eds., *Papers of Thomas Jefferson* (Princeton: Princeton University Press, 1950-present), vols. 6–13.

3. Arthur Alexander Morson to Alexander Morson, 17 September 1818, Arthur Alexander Morson Papers, SHC; Thomas Johnson to Elizabeth Johnson, 19 August 1810, David Johnson Papers, SCL; John Grimball to William Moultrie Reid, 13 October 1816, John Berkley Grimball Papers, SCL; Solomon Mordecai to Ellen Mordecai, 6 November 1819, Mordecai Family Papers, SHC. For additional examples, see Robert Blow to Fanny Blow, 18 September 1826, Blow Family Papers, VHS; Alfred Beckley to James Love, 2 October 1819, James Young Love and Thomas Love Papers, FHS; Daniel Baker to George Palmes, 30 August 1811, George F. Palmes Papers, DUL; Edmund Mason to John Mason, 27 April 1823, Mason Family Papers, VHS; and John E. Colhoun Jr. to William Moultrie Reid, 13 August 1816, John Ewing Colhoun Papers, SHC.

4. Richard Hopkins to Elizabeth Thomas Hopkins, 7 January 1784, in "A Maryland Medical Student and His Friends," *Maryland Historical Magazine* 23 (1928). For examples of family health concerns, see James Legaré to Jedediah Morse, 11 November 1811, Thomas Legaré Papers, DUL; Anne Hart to William Hart, 7 November 1806, Oliver Hart Papers, SCL; John Ball Sr. to John Ball Jr., miscellaneous correspondence, Ball Family Papers, SCHS; and George Jones to Noble Wimberly Jones, 28 January 1804, Jones Family Papers, GHS.

5. William Ball to John Ball Sr., 11 October 1808, William James Ball Family Correspondence, SCHS.

6. Charles Carter Lee to "dear mamma," 26 April 1818, Lee and Marshall Family Papers, SHC.

7. Francis Walker Gilmer to Peachy Gilmer, 30 April 1809, Peachy Ridgway Gilmer Papers, VHS; Thomas Bennehan to mother, 14 December 1799, Cameron Family Papers, SHC.

8. William Ball to John Ball Sr., 12 December 1805, William James Ball Family Correspondence, SCHS.

9. Miscellaneous correspondence, quotation from John Palmer to Harriet Palmer, 31 December 1818, in Louis P. Towles, ed., *A World Turned Upside Down: The Palmers of South Santee, 1818–1881* (Columbia: University of South Carolina Press, 1996), 23.

10. William Quynn to Allen Quynn, 23 October 1782, in Dorothy Mackay Quynn and William Rogers Quynn, eds., "Letters of a Maryland Medical Student in Philadelphia and Edinburgh (1782–1784)," *Maryland Historical Magazine* 31 (September 1936): 185; Edmund Mason to John Mason, 27 April 1823, Mason Family Papers, VHS; Richard Randolph to Frances Tucker, 12 April 1787 and 8 March 1787, Tucker Coleman Papers, College of William and Mary, quoted in Daniel Blake Smith, *Inside the Great House: Planter Family Life in Eighteenth-Century Chesapeake Society* (Ithaca: Cornell University Press, 1980), 103. Randolph later attended Princeton.

11. Edward Marshall to Robert Peyton, 8 March 1826, Peyton Family Papers, VHS; Walter Raleigh Lenoir to General William Lenoir, 31 October 1801, Lenoir Family Papers, SHC.

12. James Henry Hammond, 1852 unpublished memoir, Hammond Family Papers, SCL; Thomas Jefferson Withers to James Henry Hammond, 14 April 1826, Hammond Family Papers, SCL. See also John Haywood to George W. Haywood, 3 February 1816, Ernest Haywood Collection, SHC; and Henry DeSaussure to John E. Colhoun Jr., 14 September 1810, Henry William DeSaussure Papers, SCL.

13. Drew Gilpin Faust, *James Henry Hammond and the Old South: A Design for Mastery* (Baton Rouge: Louisiana State University Press, 1982), 16.

14. Alfred Mordecai to Solomon Mordecai, 24 February 1819, Mordecai Family Papers, SHC; Ellen Mordecai to Solomon Mordecai, 12 July 1821, Mordecai Family Papers, SHC; Alfred Mordecai to L. Mordecai, 4 March 1819, Jacob Mordecai Papers, DUL.

15. For father-son tensions, see also Joyce Appleby, *Inheriting the Revolution: The First Generation of Americans* (Cambridge: Harvard University Press, 2000), 170; Shawn Johansen, *Family Men: Middle-Class Fatherhood in Early Industrializing America* (New York: Routledge, 2001), 153; Brenda Stevenson, *Life in Black and White: Family and Community in the Slave South* (New York: Oxford University Press, 1996), 115; Jon L. Wakelyn, "Antebellum College Life and the Relations between Fathers and Sons," in Walter J. Fraser Jr., R. Frank Saunders Jr., and Jon L. Wakelyn, eds., *The Web of Southern Social Relations: Women, Family, and Education* (Athens: University of Georgia Press, 1985), 107–26; and Bertram Wyatt-Brown, *Southern Honor: Ethics and Behavior in the Old South* (New York: Oxford University Press, 1982), 118.

16. A number of scholars have pointed out that youth generally marked the stage of life between dependence and independence. See Demos, *Past, Present, and Personal,* 105; Harvey J. Graff, "Early Adolescence in Antebellum America: The Remaking of Growing Up," *Journal of Early Adolescence* 5: 413, 422; and Kett, *Rites of Passage,* 14–31.

17. Anya Jabour, *Marriage in the Early Republic: Elizabeth and William Wirt and the Companionate Ideal* (Baltimore: Johns Hopkins University Press, 1998), 117.

18. Hugh Blair Grigsby to parents, 16 February 1825, in Fitzgerald Flournoy, "Hugh Blair Grigsby at Yale," *Virginia Magazine of History and Biography* 62 (1954): 166; Joseph Watson to David Watson, 9 February 1799, in "Letters from William and Mary College, 1798–1801," *Virginia Magazine of History and Biography* 29 (April 1921): 140; William Ball to John Ball Jr., 24 November 1806, William James Ball Family Correspondence, SCHS.

19. William S. Powell, *The First State University: A Pictorial History of the University of North Carolina,* 3rd ed. (Chapel Hill: University of North Carolina Press, 1992), 49.

20. John Randolph to Frances Tucker, 20 June 1786, in Mrs. George P. Coleman, ed., "Randolph and Tucker Letters," *Virginia Magazine of History and Biography* 42 (1934): 48.

21. Jonathan Maxcy to president of South Carolina College Board of Trustees, 26 November 1813, Jonathan Maxcy Papers, SCL. See also John Jaquelin Ambler to John Ambler, 9 March 1818, Ambler Family Papers, VHS, for a similar incident at the College of William and Mary.

22. Quoted in E. Merton Coulter, *College Life in the Old South* (Athens: University of Georgia Press, 1928), 77.

23. John Grimball to William Moultrie Reid, 7 September 1817, John Berkley Grimball Papers, SCL. For a case study of friendships among southern boys carried into adulthood, see Anya Jabour, "Male Friendship and Masculinity in the Early National South: William Wirt and His Friends," *Journal of the Early Republic* 20 (Spring 2000): 83–111. For comparison to middle-class northerners, see Karen Hansen, " 'Our Eyes Beheld Each Other': Masculinity and Intimate Friendship in Antebellum New England," in Peter Nardi, ed., *Men's Friendships* (London: Sage, 1992); E. Anthony Rotundo, "Boy Culture: Middle-Class Boyhood in Nineteenth-Century America," in Mark C. Carnes and Clyde Griffen, eds., *Meanings for Manhood: Constructions of*

Masculinity in Victorian America (Chicago: University of Chicago Press, 1990), 15–36; and Donald Yacovone, " 'Surpassing the Love of Women': Victorian Manhood and the Language of Fraternal Love," in Laura McCall and Donald Yacovone, eds., *A Shared Experience: Men, Women, and the History of Gender* (New York: New York University Press, 1998), 195–221. For southern girls, see Christie Anne Farnham, *The Education of the Southern Belle: Higher Education and Student Socialization in the Antebellum South* (New York: New York University Press, 1994), chap. 7; and Anya Jabour, " 'College Girls': The Female Academy and Female Identity in the Old South," in Bruce L. Clayton and John A. Salmond, eds., *"Lives Full of Struggle and Triumph": Southern Women, Their Institutions, and Their Communities* (Gainesville: University Press of Florida, 2003), 74–92.

24. Daniel Baker to George Palmes, 30 August 1811 and 5 October 1811, both in George F. Palmes Papers, DUL. For analysis see Carroll Smith-Rosenberg, "The Female World of Love and Ritual: Relations between Women in Nineteenth-Century America," *Signs: Journal of Women in Culture and Society* 1 (1975): 1–29; Hansen, "Our Eyes Beheld Each Other"; and Yacovone, "Surpassing the Love of Women."

25. See, for example, Thomas Todd to Charles Todd, 9 March 1808, Charles Stewart Todd Papers, FHS; Robert Blow to Fanny Blow, 18 September 1826, Blow Family Papers, VHS; William Cumming to Thomas Cumming, 17 August 1806, Alfred Cumming Papers, DUL; and Edmund Mason to John Mason, 27 April 1823, Mason Family Papers, VHS.

26. Frances Pinckney to Roger Pinckney, 18 March 1786, Roger Pinckney Correspondence, SCHS.

27. Joel Lyle to William Lyle, 11 July 1826, Lyle Family Papers, UKSCL; John Ball Sr. to John Ball Jr., 7 November 1798, 19 June 1799, and 19 August 1801, Ball Family Papers, SCHS.

28. For the best overview of student disorder in the early national universities, see Novak, *The Rights of Youth.* See also Leon Jackson, "The Rights of Man and the Rites of Youth: Fraternity and Riot at Eighteenth-Century Harvard," in Roger L. Geiger, ed., *The American College in the Nineteenth Century* (Nashville: Vanderbilt University Press, 2000), esp. 47; Kett, *Rites of Passage,* 47–61; Howard Miller, *The Revolutionary College: American Presbyterian Higher Education, 1707–1837* (New York: New York University Press, 1976), 260; and Gilman M. Ostrander, *Republic of Letters: The American Intellectual Community, 1775–1865* (Madison: Madison House, 1999), 29. For examples from the antebellum era, see Robert F. Pace, *Halls of Honor: College Men in the Old South* (Baton Rouge: Louisiana State University Press, 2004), 86–89.

29. Coulter, *College Life in the Old South,* 67, 70–74; annual evaluations 1824–1827, Thomas Cooper Papers, SCL. For more on Cooper, see Thomas Cooper Papers, SCL; and Dumas Malone, *Public Life of Thomas Cooper, 1783–1839* (New Haven: Yale University Press, 1926).

30. Edmund Wilcox Hubard to Robert Thruston Hubard, 8 November 1825, Hubard Family Papers, SHC; Thomas Amis to Ebenezer Pettigrew, 6 August 1798, Pettigrew Family Papers, SHC; William Grayson quoted in Louis P. Towles, "A Matter of Honor at South Carolina College, 1822," *South Carolina Historical Magazine* 94 (January 1993): 12; William Barry to John Barry, 6 February 1804, William Taylor Barry Papers, FHS. For additional examples, see Joseph Watson to David Watson, 9 February 1799, in "Letters from William and Mary College, 1798–1801," *Virginia Magazine of History and Biography* 29 (April 1821): 139;

Robert J. Brugger, *Beverley Tucker: Heart over Head in the Old South* (Baltimore: Johns Hopkins University Press, 1978), 20; and Faust, *James Henry Hammond and the Old South*, 17.

31. Thomas Cooper to Thomas Jefferson, 14 February 1822, Thomas Cooper Papers, SCL; Abner Stith to Thomas Williamson Jones, 31 March 1814, Thomas Williamson Jones Papers, SHC; Edmund Wilcox Hubard to Robert Thruston Hubard, 15 December 1824, Hubard Family Papers, SHC.

32. George Swain to David Swain, 26 April 1822, David Lowry Swain Papers, NCC; Brugger, *Beverley Tucker*, 20.

33. Kenneth Silverman, *Edgar A. Poe: Mournful and Never-Ending Remembrance* (New York: Harper Collins, 1991), 32–34; Ralph Ketcham, *James Madison: A Biography* (New York: Macmillan, 1971), 616.

34. Severn Eyre Diary, 22 August 1785, VHS.

35. John Brown Cutting to John Rutledge, 4 February 1787, John Rutledge Papers, SHC; and Arney R. Childs, ed., "William Hasell Gibbes' Story of His Life," *South Carolina Historical and Genealogical Magazine* 50 (1949): 61, both quoted in Maurie D. McInnis, ed., *In Pursuit of Refinement: Charlestonians Abroad, 1740–1860* (Columbia: University of South Carolina Press, 1999), 12.

36. Hugh Swinton Ball to John Ball Jr., 24 December 1823, John Ball Sr. and John Ball Jr. Papers, DUL; Edward Ball, *Slaves in the Family* (New York: Farrar, Straus, and Giroux, 1998), 298–300.

37. Leander Hughes to John Hughes, 2 October 1824 and 23 August 1823, Leander Hughes Papers, SHC.

38. Joseph Caldwell to Martin W. B. Armstrong, 3 May 1819, Martin W. B. Armstrong Papers, SHC (first and third quotations); C. D. Donoho to Martin W. B. Armstrong, 8 May 1819, Martin W. B. Armstrong Papers, SHC (second quotation).

39. For analyses of dueling in the early South, see Appleby, *Inheriting the Revolution*, 40–45; Dickson D. Bruce Jr., *Violence and Culture in the Antebellum South* (Austin: University of Texas Press, 1979), chap. 1; Kenneth S. Greenberg, *Masters and Statesmen: The Political Culture of American Slavery* (Baltimore: Johns Hopkins University Press, 1985), chap. 2; Kett, *Rites of Passage*, 54; Steven M. Stowe, *Intimacy and Power in the Old South: Ritual in the Lives of the Planters* (Baltimore: Johns Hopkins University Press, 1987), chap. 1; and Wyatt-Brown, *Southern Honor*, 166–67, 350–61. Novak argues that dueling was common in the early national South, but he cites four instances at William and Mary between 1802 and 1809 as evidence of the level of frequency. Novak, *The Rights of Youth*, 100.

40. John Pettigrew to Charles Pettigrew, 3 October 1795, Pettigrew Family Papers, SHC.

41. Chapman Johnson to David Watson, 18 May 1800, in "Letters to David Watson," *Virginia Magazine of History and Biography* 29 (July 1921): 268–69; Novak, *The Rights of Youth*, 20–21, 77–79 (regarding Transylvania); Thomas Cooper to Board of Trustees of South Carolina College, 12 March 1827, Thomas Cooper Papers, SCL. For similar (but unsuccessful) activism at the University of North Carolina, see Iveson Brookes to Jonathan Brookes, September 1816, Iveson Lewis Brookes Papers, SHC.

42. Paul Carrington to John Mason, 18 April [n.y.], Mason Family Papers, VHS; Towles, "A Matter of Honor at South Carolina College," 15.

43. Abner Stith to Thomas Williamson Jones, 31 March 1814, Thomas Williamson Jones

Papers, SHC; Thomas Cooper, public notice to Trustees, 12 March 1827, Thomas Cooper Papers, SCL.

44. Thomas Cooper to Thomas Jefferson, 14 February 1822, Thomas Cooper Papers, SCL.

45. Samuel Lewis to Isaac L. Baker, 30 May 1807, Isaac L. Baker Papers, SHC (regarding Princeton); Novak, *The Rights of Youth*, 7 (regarding Harvard). For disorder at Princeton, see also Thomas J. Wertenbaker, *Princeton, 1746–1896* (Princeton: Princeton University Press, 1946), 135–42; 155–58; 167–68; 176–77.

46. Charles M. Thruston to Buckner Thruston, 19 October 1813, Thruston Family Papers, FHS.

47. First quotation from Thomas Neville Bonner, *Becoming a Physician: Medical Education in Britain, France, Germany, and the United States, 1750–1945* (New York: Oxford University Press, 1995), 75; second quotation from Kett, *Rites of Passage*, 51.

48. Edward Hooker to Addin Lewis, 4 June 1807, Edward Hooker Letters, SCL; Thomas Cooper to Thomas Jefferson, 14 February 1822, Thomas Cooper Papers, SCL.

49. Wertenbaker, *Princeton, 1746–1896*, 135. For the involvement of this group of Virginians, see Richard Beale Davis, *Intellectual Life in Jefferson's Virginia* (Knoxville: University of Tennessee Press, 1972), 49.

50. Hugh Blair Grigsby to family, 1 May 1825, in Fitzgerald Flournoy, "Hugh Blair Grigsby at Yale," *Virginia Magazine of History and Biography* 62 (1954): 167; Joanna Bowen Gillespie, *The Life and Times of Martha Laurens Ramsay, 1759–1811* (Columbia: University of South Carolina Press, 2001), 212.

51. David M. Lees, essay c. 1826, David McMichen Lees Papers, SHC; Joseph C. Cabell to David Baillie Warden, 1 April 1823, in William D. Hoyt Jr., ed., "Mr. Cabell, Mr. Warden, and the University, 1823," *Virginia Magazine of History and Biography* 49 (1941): 351–53.

52. Thomas Cooper to Thomas Jefferson, 14 February 1822, Thomas Cooper Papers, SCL.

53. Davis Thacher Diary, November 1817, SCL.

54. Thomas Cooper to Board of Trustees of South Carolina College, 22 April 1821, Thomas Cooper Papers, SCL; Georgian quoted in Coulter, *College Life in the Old South*, 36.

55. Charles Pettigrew to Mr. Caldwell, 10 November 1797, Pettigrew Family Papers, SHC; Robert E. Shalhope, *John Taylor of Caroline: Pastoral Republican* (Columbia: University of South Carolina Press, 1980), 113; Edward Hooker to Samuel Whitman, 5 May 1807, Edward Hooker Letters, SCL. See also Richard Furman Sermon, 1799, Richard Furman Papers, SCL.

56. David Swain to George Swain, 2 May 1822, David Lowry Swain Papers, NCC.

57. Robert Carter III to James Manning, 9 February 1786, in Louis Morton, *Robert Carter of Nomini Hall: A Virginia Tobacco Planter of the Eighteenth Century* (Colonial Williamsburg, 1941), 257.

58. George Swain to David Swain, undated [c. June 1822], David Lowry Swain Papers, NCC.

59. Severn Eyre Diary, 15 August 1785 and 8 January 1785, VHS; William Barry to John Barry, 23 February 1804, William Taylor Barry Papers, FHS.

60. Edmund Ruffin Jr., 17 November 1828, in Mrs. Kirkland Ruffin, ed., "School-Boy Letters of Edmund Ruffin, Jr., 1828–29," *North Carolina Historical Review* 10 (1933): 303–4; John C. Calhoun to unknown, c. November 1802, in Robert L. Meriwether et al., eds., *Papers of John C. Calhoun* (Columbia: University of South Carolina Press, 1959–2003), 1: 5; Alfred

Beckley to George Washington Love, 2 April 1820, James Young Love and Thomas Love Papers, FHS.

61. William Dickinson Martin Diary, 1809, SCL. See also Edmund Ruffin Jr., 28 March 1829 and 6 November 1828, in "School-Boy Letters of Edmund Ruffin, Jr."; and Elijah Fletcher to Jesse Fletcher Jr., 29 August 1810, in Martha von Briesen, ed., *The Letters of Elijah Fletcher* (Charlottesville: University Press of Virginia, 1965), 10–15.

62. For examples, see Hugh Ball to John Ball Jr., 20 November 1823, John Ball Sr. and John Ball Jr. Papers, DUL; and Edmund Ruffin Jr., 6 November 1828, in "School-Boy Letters of Edmund Ruffin, Jr."

63. E. Mitchell to Duncan Cameron, 18 May 1824, Cameron Family Papers, SHC; J. Alebb[?] to Duncan Cameron, 20 May 1824, Cameron Family Papers, SHC; Brugger, *Beverley Tucker,* 11.

64. E. F. Campbell to Phineas Kollock, 22 October 1823, in Edith Duncan Johnston, ed., "The Kollock Letters, 1799–1850," *Georgia Historical Quarterly* 30 (1946): 245.

65. Thomas Jefferson Withers to James Henry Hammond, undated, partial letter c. 1827 and 11 July 1827, both in Hammond Family Papers, SCL.

Six • *The Southern Code of Gentlemanly Conduct*

1. For the importance of social performance in the early South, see also Steven M. Stowe, *Intimacy and Power in the Old South: Ritual in the Lives of the Planters* (Baltimore: Johns Hopkins University Press, 1987); Bertram Wyatt-Brown, *Southern Honor: Ethics and Behavior in the Old South* (New York: Oxford University Press, 1982), chap. 4; Charlene M. Boyer Lewis, *Ladies and Gentlemen on Display: Planter Society at the Virginia Springs, 1790–1860* (Charlottesville: University Press of Virginia, 2001); and John Mayfield, " 'The Soul of a Man!': William Gilmore Simms and the Myths of Southern Manhood," *Journal of the Early Republic* 15 (Fall 1995): 477–500. For the North, see Richard Bushman, *The Refinement of America: Persons, Houses, Cities* (New York: Knopf, 1992); and Jay Fliegelman, *Declaring Independence: Jefferson, Natural Language, and the Culture of Performance* (Stanford: Stanford University Press, 1993).

2. Thomas Jefferson to Peter Carr, 19 August 1785, in Julian P. Boyd et al., eds., *The Papers of Thomas Jefferson* (Princeton: Princeton University Press, 1950-present), 8: 405; John Haywood to George W. Haywood, 24 August 1819, Ernest Haywood Collection, SHC; Edward Harden to Edward Randolph Harden, 19 September 1829, Harden Family Papers, DUL. See also William Ballard Lenoir to Albert Lenoir, 4 June 1819, Lenoir Family Papers, SHC; and John Wayles Eppes to Francis Eppes, 20 June 1818, John Wayles Eppes Letters, DUL.

3. Harmer Gilmer to Peachy Gilmer, 12 October 1806, Peachy Ridgway Gilmer Papers, VHS; Thomas T. Armstrong to Martin W. B. Armstrong, 6 December 1815, Martin W. B. Armstrong Papers, SHC. See also Anne Hart to William Hart, 7 November 1806, Oliver Hart Papers, SCL; and Seaborn Jones to William Hart, 17 February 1808, Seaborn Jones Family Papers, GHS.

4. Arthur M. Schlesinger, *Learning How to Behave: A Historical Study of American Etiquette Books* (New York: Cooper Square, 1968), 6.

5. For middle-class conduct and values, see Bushman, *The Refinement of America;* C. Dallett Hemphill, *Bowing to Necessities: A History of Manners in America, 1620–1860* (New

York: Oxford University Press, 1999); John Kasson, *Rudeness and Civility: Manners in Nineteenth-Century Urban America* (New York: Hill and Wang, 1990); Sarah E. Newton, *Learning to Behave: A Guide to American Conduct Books before 1900* (Westport: Greenwood Press, 1994); and Schlesinger, *Learning How to Behave*. For northern masculinity, see E. Anthony Rotundo, *American Manhood: Transformations in Masculinity from the Revolution to the Modern Era* (New York: Basic Books, 1993); and Michael Kimmel, *Manhood in America: A Cultural History* (New York: Free Press, 1996), 13–78. See also Richard D. Brown, *Knowledge Is Power: The Diffusion of Information in Early America, 1700–1865* (New York: Oxford University Press, 1989), chap. 9; and Joyce Appleby, *Inheriting the Revolution: The First Generation of Americans* (Cambridge: Harvard University Press, 2000), esp. 133–34, 157.

6. Quoted in William R. Taylor, *Cavalier and Yankee: The Old South and American National Character* (New York: George Braziller, 1961), 97.

7. Raymond A. Mohl, ed., "'The Grand Fabric of Republicanism': A Scotsman Describes South Carolina, 1810–1811," *South Carolina Historical Magazine* 71 (June 1970): 184; Elijah Fletcher to Jesse Fletcher, 1 October 1810, in Martha Von Briesen, ed., *The Letters of Elijah Fletcher* (Charlottesville: University Press of Virginia, 1965), 17; "Henry Bernard Travel Account," 25 March 1833, *Maryland Historical Magazine* 13 (1918): 326; Joseph W. Barnwell, ed., "The Diary of Timothy Ford, 1785–1786," *South Carolina Historical and Genealogical Magazine* 13 (July 1912): 143.

8. See also Wyatt-Brown, *Southern Honor*, 152–53; Edward L. Ayers, *Vengeance and Justice: Crime and Punishment in the Nineteenth-Century American South* (New York: Oxford University Press, 1984), 10; and Brenda Stevenson, *Life in Black and White: Family and Community in the Slave South* (New York: Oxford University Press, 1996), 112.

9. For the importance of England in the elite culture of the plantation South, see Michal J. Rozbicki, *The Complete Colonial Gentleman: Cultural Legitimacy in Plantation America* (Charlottesville: University Press of Virginia, 1998). For the artifacts of refinement and the immersion of British Americans in the material culture of the empire, see J. Thomas Savage and Robert A. Leath, "Buying British: Merchants, Taste, and Charleston Consumerism," in Maurice D. McInnis, ed., *In Pursuit of Refinement: Charlestonians Abroad, 1740–1860* (Columbia: University of South Carolina Press, 1999), 55–64; Timothy H. Breen, "An Empire of Goods: The Anglicanization of Colonial America, 1690–1776," *Journal of British Studies* 25 (October 1986): 467–99; and Breen, *The Marketplace of Revolution: How Consumer Politics Shaped American Independence* (New York: Oxford University Press, 2004).

10. The often-printed letters of Philip Dormer Stanhope, fourth Earl of Chesterfield, to his son and namesake were widely read by Americans and Britons. Numerous reprints include R. K. Root, ed., *Lord Chesterfield's Letters to His Son* (London: J. M. Dent, 1929).

11. Philip Stanhope to Philip Stanhope, 9 December 1749, in *Lord Chesterfield's Letters to His Son*, 138–39.

12. For self-mastery and male autonomy in the South, see also Ayers, *Vengeance and Justice*; Wyatt-Brown, *Southern Honor*; and Michael Zuckerman, "Penmanship Exercises for Saucy Sons: Some Thoughts on the Colonial Southern Family," *South Carolina Historical Magazine* 84 (July 1983): 152–66. For northern perceptions of self-mastery, see Hemphill, *Bowing to Necessity*, 101–2.

13. John Ball Sr. to John Ball Jr., 14 April 1799, Ball Family Papers, SCHS; John Ramsey to

Thomas Jones, 26 May 1810, Thomas Williamson Jones Papers, SHC; Noah Jones Composition Book, "On Ambition," 20 January 1805, SCL; Winifred Green to Jack Green, 5 July 1823, Green Family Papers, FHS. Chesterfield was not without critics. His advice regarding dalliances with French women, for example, sparked controversy. See, for example, John Ball Sr. to John Ball Jr., 14 April 1799, Ball Family Papers, SCHS; and Edmund Hayes, "Mercy Otis Warren versus Lord Chesterfield, 1779," *William and Mary Quarterly* 40 (July 1983): 616–21.

14. Sidney Walter Martin, ed., "A New Englander's Impressions of Georgia in 1817–1818: Extracts from the Diary of Ebenezer Kellogg," *Journal of Southern History* 12 (May 1946): 253; Julein Dwight Martin, ed., "The Letters of Charles Caleb Cotton, 1798–1802," *South Carolina Historical and Genealogical Magazine* 51 (July 1950): 133, 140; John Cook Wyllie, ed., "Observations Made during a Short Residence in Virginia: In a Letter from Thomas H. Palmer, May 30, 1814," *Virginia Magazine of History and Biography* 76 (October 1968): 389. This hospitality was also highly exclusive. Generally, only visitors with ties to elite families received such gracious receptions. See Joseph W. Barnwell, ed., "The Diary of Timothy Ford, 1785–1786," *South Carolina Historical and Genealogical Magazine* 13 (July 1912): 146; Elijah Fletcher to Jesse Fletcher, 31 October 1810, in *The Letters of Elijah Fletcher*, 21; and unknown to Thomas Ruffin, 21 January 1805, Thomas Ruffin Papers, SHC.

15. Thomas Todd to Charles Todd, 5 February 1812, Charles Stewart Todd Papers, FHS.

16. Sterling Ruffin to Thomas Ruffin, 5 May 1803, Thomas Ruffin Papers, SHC; William Barry to John Barry, 23 September 1801, William Taylor Barry Papers, FHS; Washington quoted in Hunter Dickinson Farish, ed., *Journal and Letters of Philip Vickers Fithian, 1773–1774: A Plantation Tutor of the Old Dominion* (Williamsburg: Colonial Williamsburg, 1957), xvii.

17. C. H. Manigault to Gabriel Manigault, 27 April 1800, Manigault Family Papers, SCL; Charlton DeSaussure Jr., ed., "Memoirs of General George Izard, 1825," *South Carolina Historical Magazine* 78 (1977): 45; James Strobhart to John Kirk, 22 June [n.y.], Kirk Family Papers, SCHS.

18. John Ball Sr. to John Ball Jr., 9 May 1802, Ball Family Papers, SCHS; John C. Calhoun to [unknown], c. November 1802, in Robert L. Meriwether et al., eds., *The Papers of John C. Calhoun* (Columbia: University of South Carolina Press, 1959–2003), 1: 5.

19. P. J. Staudenraus, ed., "Letters from South Carolina, 1821–1822" [Samuel Sitgraves Travel Account], *South Carolina Historical Magazine* 58 (1957): 215; Elijah Fletcher to Jesse Fletcher, 31 October 1810, in *The Letters of Elijah Fletcher*, 20–21.

20. Thomas T. Armstrong to Martin W. B. Armstrong, 6 December 1815, Martin W. B. Armstrong Papers, SHC; Andrew Jackson to Andrew Jackson Donelson, 24 February 1817, Harold D. Moser et al., eds., *The Papers of Andrew Jackson* (Knoxville: University of Tennessee Press, 1980-present), 4: 91. See also Daniel Guerrant to Charles Guerrant, 4 May 1816, Guerrant Family Papers, VHS; George Swain to David Swain, undated [June 1822], David Lowry Swain Papers, NCC; and Thomas Todd to Charles Todd, 4 June 1808, Charles Stewart Todd Papers, FHS.

21. William Ballard Lenoir to Albert Lenoir, 4 June 1819, Lenoir Family Papers, SHC; Harriott Pinckney Horry Letterbook, 28 February 1786, Harriott Horry Ravenel Papers, SCHS. See also A. Abbot to Phineas Kollock, 6 May 1823, Kollock Family Papers, GHS; Azel

Backus to John Rutledge, 18 July 1805, John Rutledge Papers, SHC; and Edward Harden to Edward Randolph Harden, 19 September 1829, Harden Family Papers, DUL.

22. Sterling Ruffin to Thomas Ruffin, 18 April 1802, Thomas Ruffin Papers, SHC; St. George Tucker to John and Richard Randolph, 12 June 1787, Tucker-Coleman Papers, Swem Library, College of William and Mary, quoted in Daniel Blake Smith, *Inside the Great House: Planter Family Life in Eighteenth-Century Chesapeake Society* (Ithaca: Cornell University Press, 1980), 96–97. See also Francis Corbin to David English, 13 June [c. 1820], Beverley Family Papers, VHS; William Short to Charles Wilkins Short, 8 July 1813, Charles Wilkins Short Papers, FHS.

23. Quotation from Martin, ed., "The Letters of Charles Caleb Cotton," 219. For additional assessments, see James Gallaway to Melchizedek Spragins, 16 February 1815, Melchizedek Spragins Papers, DUL; Chapman Johnson to David Watson, 19 December 1799, in "Letters to David Watkins," *Virginia Magazine of History and Biography* 29 (July 1921): 266; Robert J. Parker, "A Chapter in the Early Life of Thomas Oliver Larkin," *California Historical Society Quarterly* 16 (March 1937): 19.

24. Joan Cashin, *A Family Venture: Men and Women on the Southern Frontier* (New York: Oxford University Press, 1991). See also Stephen Aron, *How the West Was Lost: The Transformation of Kentucky from Daniel Boone to Henry Clay* (Baltimore: Johns Hopkins University Press, 1996); and Elizabeth Perkins, *Border Life: Experience and Memory in the Revolutionary Ohio Valley* (Chapel Hill: University of North Carolina Press, 1998).

25. Quoted in Perkins, *Border Life,* 135.

26. Aron, *How the West Was Lost,* 56.

27. William Cumming to [mother], September 1815, Alfred Cumming Papers, DUL.

28. Thomas Todd to Charles Todd, 25 September 1808, Charles Stewart Todd Papers, FHS.

29. An excellent analysis of letter writing among antebellum elite southern families can be found in Steven M. Stowe, "The Rhetoric of Authority: The Making of Social Values in Planter Family Correspondence," *Journal of American History* 73 (March 1987): 916–33. Tamara Plakins Thornton offers a fascinating investigation of handwriting in *Handwriting in America: A Cultural History* (New Haven: Yale University Press, 1996). See also Bushman, *The Refinement of America,* 90–95; William Merrill Decker, *Epistolary Practices: Letter Writing in America before Telecommunications* (Chapel Hill: University of North Carolina Press, 1998); and Konstantin Dierks, "Letter Writing, Masculinity, and American Men of Science, 1750–1800," *Pennsylvania History* 65 (1998): 167–98.

30. David M. Lees to Hugh Lees, 17 March 1829, David McMichen Lees Papers, SHC.

31. Francis Ramsey to James G. M. Ramsey and William B. A. Ramsey, 24 June 1815, James Gettys McGready Ramsey Papers, UTSCL.

32. David M. Lees to Hugh Lees, 17 March 1829, David McMichen Lees Papers, SHC; Green Clay to Sidney Clay, 2 September 1818, Green Clay Papers, FHS; Edmund Ruffin Jr. to mother, 11 February 1829, in Mrs. Kirkland Ruffin, ed., "School-Boy Letters of Edmund Ruffin, Jr.," *North Carolina Historical Review* 10 (1933): 313.

33. Sterling Ruffin to Thomas Ruffin, 18 April 1802, Thomas Ruffin Papers, SHC.

34. Robert Thruston Hubard to Edmund Wilcox Hubard, 19 November 1824 and 13

December 1824, both in Hubard Family Papers, SHC; Peter Guerrant to Charles Guerrant, 8 September 1818, Guerrant Family Papers, VHS.

35. Ralph Wormeley to Warner Wormeley, 16 December 1801, Wormeley Family Papers, VHS; Margaret Izard Manigault to Charles Izard Manigault, 2 February 1812, Manigault Family Papers, SCL; John Randolph to Theodore Dudley, 31 January 1806, in Russell Kirk, *John Randolph of Roanoke* (Indianapolis: Liberty Press, 1978), 233.

36. Robert Thruston Hubard to Edmund Wilcox Hubard, 13 January 1825, Hubard Family Papers, SHC; Francis Ramsey to James G. M. Ramsey and William B. A. Ramsey, 24 June 1815, James Gettys McGready Ramsey Papers, UTSCL.

37. Willie Jones to Willie William Jones, 7 May 1798, in William Dana Hoyt Jr., ed., "Letters from Willie Jones to His Son at the University of North Carolina, 1796–1801," *North Carolina Historical Review* 19 (1942): 376–80; J. Wilson to Roger Pinckney, 16 May 1784, Roger Pinckney Correspondence, SCHS; Sterling Ruffin to Thomas Ruffin, 18 April 1802, Thomas Ruffin Papers, SHC.

38. John Ball Sr. to John Ball Jr., 14 April 1799, Ball Family Papers, SCHS; Cassius Clay to Brutus Clay, 18 December 1827, Clay Family Papers, UKSCL.

39. Mary Cochran to Charles Cochran, 16 August 1779, Cochran Family Papers, SCHS; Sterling Ruffin to Thomas Ruffin, 7 June 1805, Thomas Ruffin Papers, SHC. See also Lemuel Kollock to George Kollock, [c. December 1820], in Edith Duncan Johnston, ed., "The Kollock Letters, 1799–1850," *Georgia Historical Quarterly* 30 (1946): 228; and Margaretta Brown to Orlando Brown, 21 June 1820, Brown Family Papers, FHS.

40. John Guerrant to Charles Guerrant, 10 January 1817, Guerrant Family Papers, VHS; Annie C. Bullitt to William Bullitt, 14 December 1808, Bullitt Family Papers, FHS.

41. John Ball Sr. to John Ball Jr., 15 September 1798, Ball Family Papers, SCHS; George Swain to David Swain, miscellaneous correspondence, David Lowry Swain Papers, NCC.

Seven • *Acting the Part of a Gentleman*

1. John Palmer to President and Faculty of South Carolina College, 7 May 1822, in Louis P. Towles, ed., *A World Turned Upside Down: The Palmers of South Santee, 1818–1881* (Columbia: University of South Carolina Press, 1996), 33; William Quynn to Allen Quynn, 12 November 1783, in Dorothy Mackay Quynn and William Rogers Quynn, eds., "Letters of a Maryland Medical Student in Philadelphia and Edinburgh (1782–1784)," *Maryland Historical Magazine* 31 (September 1936): 195.

2. Joseph Shelton Watson to David Watson, 9 February 1799, in "Letters from William and Mary College, 1798–1801," *Virginia Magazine of History and Biography* 29 (April 1921): 139.

3. Cornelius Ayer to F. C. Ayer, 10 May 1819, Lewis Malone Ayer Papers, SCL; J. Wilson to Roger Pinckney, 23 March 1784, Roger Pinckney Correspondence, SCHS.

4. Richard Bushman, *The Refinement of America: Persons, Houses, Cities* (New York: Knopf, 1992), 69–71.

5. William Quynn to Allen Quynn, 11 November 1782, in "Letters of a Maryland Medical Student," 186; Edmund Ruffin Jr. to Edmund Ruffin, 26 May 1829, in Mrs. Kirkland Ruffin, ed., "School-Boy Letters of Edmund Ruffin, Jr.," *North Carolina Historical Review* 10 (1933): 327.

6. Joyce Appleby, *Inheriting the Revolution: The First Generation of Americans* (Cambridge: Harvard University Press, 2000), 141.

7. Joanne B. Freeman, *Affairs of Honor: National Politics in the New Republic* (New Haven: Yale University Press, 2001), 6.

8. Mary Ann Harden to Edward Randolph Harden, 15 July 1829, Harden Family Papers, DUL; John Ball Sr. to John Ball Jr., 17 June 1799, Ball Family Papers, SCHS; Richard T. Brown to George Frederick Brown and Richard Henry Brown, 16 May 1825, Richard T. Brown Papers, VHS.

9. Charles Cochran to Mary Cochran, 22 December 1779, Cochran Family Papers, SCHS. See also Joseph L. C. Hardy to "Aunt Reid," 13 July 1815, William Moultrie Reid Papers, SCL; Martin W. B. Armstrong to Thomas T. Armstrong, undated [c. March 1819], Martin W. B. Armstrong Papers, SHC.

10. Severn Eyre Diary, 15 August 1785, VHS; William Ruffin to Thomas Ruffin, 29 December 1824, Thomas Ruffin Papers, SHC.

11. Leonidas Polk to [mother], 10 March 1822, Leonidas Polk Papers, SHC.

12. Joanna Bowen Gillespie, *The Life and Times of Martha Laurens Ramsay, 1759–1811* (Columbia: University of South Carolina Press, 2001), 219.

13. John Ball Sr. to John Ball Jr., 10 November 1799 and 22 May 1801, both in Ball Family Paper, SCHS; Ralph Wormeley to Warner Wormeley, 8 September 1803, Wormeley Family Papers, VHS.

14. Thomas Bennehan to Rebecca Bennehan, August 1799, Cameron Family Papers, SHC; Thomas Pinckney Jr. to Harriott Pinckney, 2 February 1802, in Anna Wells Rutledge, ed., "Letters from Thomas Pinckney Jr. to Harriott Pinckney," *South Carolina Historical and Genealogical Magazine* 41 (July 1940): 113; Charles Wilson Harris to Robert Wilson Harris, 6 April 1800 (quotation); and Charles Wilson Harris to Robert Wilson Harris, 5 October 1800, both in J. G. DeRoulhac Hamilton and Henry McGilbert Wagstaff, eds., "The Harris Letters," *James Sprunt Historical Publications* 14 (1916).

15. John Wallace Jr. to Sarah Wallace, undated [c. 1810], in Mary Savage Anderson, ed., "The Wallace Letters," *Georgia Historical Quarterly* 18 (1934): 181; Jane Pinckney to Roger Pinckney, 18 March 1786, Roger Pinckney Correspondence, SCHS; Ralph Wormeley to Warner Wormeley, 8 September 1803, Wormeley Family Papers, VHS.

16. Thomas Amis to Thomas Bennehan, 3 October 1795, Cameron Family Papers, SHC; Thomas Jefferson to Peter Carr, 19 August 1785, in Julian P. Boyd et al., ed., *The Papers of Thomas Jefferson* (Princeton: Princeton University Press, 1950-present), 8: 407–8; George Jones to Noble Cunningham Jones, 17 September 1805, Jones Family Papers, GHS. See also Robert Thruston Hubard to Edmund Wilcox Hubard, 1 December 1824, Hubard Family Papers, SHC; and Rebecca Bennehan to Thomas Bennehan, 20 June 1797, Cameron Family Papers, SHC.

17. See, for example, Hugh Grigsby Diary, miscellaneous entries, 1830–31, Hugh Blair Grigsby Papers, VHS; Edmund Ruffin Jr. to "My Dear Sister," n.d. October 1828, in "School-Boy Letters of Edmund Ruffin, Jr.," 299.

18. Kenneth S. Greenberg, *Masters and Statesmen: The Political Culture of American Slavery* (Baltimore: Johns Hopkins University Press, 1985), 12. See also Appleby, *Inheriting the Revolution*, 246; Richard Beale Davis, *Intellectual Life in Jefferson's Virginia, 1790–1830*

(Knoxville: University of Tennessee Press, 1972), 41–42; Jay Fliegelman, *Declaring Independence: Jefferson, Natural Language, and the Culture of Performance* (Stanford: Stanford University Press, 1993), 30; and Bertram Wyatt-Brown, *Southern Honor: Ethics and Behavior in the Old South* (New York: Oxford University Press, 1982).

19. Quoted in Michael Sugrue, " 'We desired our future rulers to be educated men': South Carolina College, the Defense of Slavery, and the Development of Secessionist Politics," *History of Higher Education Annual* 14 (1994): 43.

20. Joel Lyle to William Lyle, 12 February 1828, Lyle Family Papers, UKSCL; John Ball Sr. to John Ball Jr., 21 October 1798, Ball Family Papers, SCHS; John Randolph to Theodore Dudley, 15 February 1806, in Russell Kirk, *John Randolph of Roanoke* (Indianapolis: Liberty Press, 1978), 237. See also Alicia Hopton Middleton to Nathaniel Russell Middleton, 29 September 1817, Middleton Family Papers, SCL; Francis Gilmer to Peachy Gilmer, 30 May [180?], Peachy Ridgway Gilmer Papers, VHS; George Clarke, 1802 student notebook, Beverley Family Papers, VHS.

21. Hugh Grigsby Diary, 14 May 1830, Hugh Blair Grigsby Papers, VHS; Francis Gilmer to Peachy Gilmer, 7 November 1810, Peachy Ridgway Gilmer Papers, VHS.

22. For studies of travel, see also Charlene M. Boyer Lewis, *Ladies and Gentlemen on Display: Planter Society at the Virginia Springs, 1790–1860* (Charlottesville: University Press of Virginia, 2001); and Maurie D. McInnis, ed., *In Pursuit of Refinement: Charlestonians Abroad, 1740–1860* (Columbia: University of South Carolina Press, 1999).

23. William Barry to Susan Barry, 25 May 1826 and 14 June 1820, both in William Taylor Barry Papers, FHS; Charles M. Thruston to Buckner Thruston, 19 June 1813, Thruston Family Papers, FHS. See also George Jones to Noble Jones, 1 September 1804, Jones Family Papers, GHS; Green Clay to Sidney Clay, 2 September 1818, Green Clay Papers, FHS; Sarah Gibbes to John Gibbes, 10 September 1783, Gibbes Family Papers, SCHS. Thomas Jefferson, conversely, recommended against travel at a young age. Thomas Jefferson to Peter Carr, 10 August 1787, *Papers of Thomas Jefferson*, 12: 17.

24. For the leisured lifestyles of southern elites, see Lewis, *Ladies and Gentlemen on Display*; Steven M. Stowe, *Intimacy and Power in the Old South: Ritual in the Lives of the Planters* (Baltimore: Johns Hopkins University Press, 1987); and Wyatt-Brown, *Southern Honor*.

25. John Cook Wyllie, ed., "Observations Made during a Short Residence in Virginia: In a Letter from Thomas H. Palmer, May 30, 1814," *Virginia Magazine of History and Biography* 76 (October 1968): 389. See also J. Fred Rippy, ed., "A View of the Carolinas in 1783," *North Carolina Historical Review* 6 (1929): 368, 363; Elijah Fletcher to Jesse Fletcher, 4 August 1810, in *Letters of Elijah Fletcher*, 8; and Raymond A. Mohl, ed., " 'The Grand Fabric of Republicanism': A Scotsman Describes South Carolina, 1810–1811," *South Carolina Historical Magazine* 71 (June 1970): 182–83.

26. James W. Patton, "Glimpses of North Carolina in the Writings of Northern and Foreign Travelers, 1783–1860," *North Carolina Historical Review* 45 (1968): 322.

27. Thomas Jefferson to Peter Carr, 19 August 1785, *Papers of Thomas Jefferson*, 8: 407. For analysis of hunting, see Dickson D. Bruce Jr., *Violence and Culture in the Antebellum South* (Austin: University of Texas Press, 1979), chap. 9; and Nicholas Proctor, *Bathed in Blood: Hunting and Mastery in the Old South* (Charlottesville: University Press of Virginia, 2002).

28. Mohl, "The Grand Fabric of Republicanism," 183.

29. Ralph Ketcham, *James Madison: A Biography* (New York: Macmillan, 1971), 616; Kenneth Silverman, *Edgar Allan Poe: Mournful and Never-ending Remembrance* (New York: HarperCollins, 1991), 32–34. For gambling, see also Wyatt-Brown, *Southern Honor*, 339–45.

30. Joel Lyle to William Lyle, 24 December 1828, Lyle Family Papers, UKSCL; J. Wilson to Roger Pinckney, 16 May 1784, Roger Pinckney Correspondence, SCHS; Ralph Wormeley to Warner Wormeley, 8 September 1803, Wormeley Family Papers, VHS.

31. John Wayles Eppes to Francis Eppes, 17 May [1817?], John Wayles Eppes Letters, DUL.

32. Ralph Wormeley to Warner Wormeley, 17 February 1804 and 29 June 1801, Wormeley Family Papers, VHS.

33. Miscellaneous correspondence, 1814–1815, William Page Papers, SHC. Quotation from Rudolphus Bogert to William Page, 29 May 1815, William Page Papers, SHC.

34. William Quynn to Allen Quynn, 9 December 1782, in "Letters of a Maryland Medical Student," 189–90. See also John Palmer to Harriet Palmer, 15 January 1820, in Towles, ed., *A World Turned Upside Down*, 26; William Ball to John Ball Jr., 12 January 1808, William James Ball Family Correspondence, SCHS.

35. Bertram Wyatt-Brown, *The Shaping of Southern Culture: Honor, Grace, and War, 1760s–1880s* (Chapel Hill: University of North Carolina Press, 2001), 62. For general discussions of duels in this era, see Appleby, *Inheriting the Revolution*, 40–45; Edward L. Ayers, *Vengeance and Justice: Crime and Punishment in the Nineteenth-Century American South* (New York: Oxford University Press, 1984); Bruce, *Violence and Culture in the Antebellum South*, chap. 1; Freeman, *Affairs of Honor*, chap. 4; Greenberg, *Masters and Statesmen*, chap. 2; Stowe, *Intimacy and Power*, chap. 1; Wyatt-Brown, *The Shaping of Southern Culture*, chap. 3; and Wyatt-Brown, *Southern Honor*, 350–61.

36. William E. Walker, "The South Carolina College Duel of 1833," *South Carolina Historical and Genealogical Magazine* 52 (1951): 140–42.

37. John Palmer to Harriett Palmer, 7 May 1822, in Towles, ed., *A World Turned Upside Down*, 34–36. The conflict continued until James Gregg, a school trustee and "mutual friend" of Cooper and Palmer, interceded and issued an apology ostensibly from Cooper. James R. Gregg to John Palmer, 24 June 1822, in Towles, ed., *A World Turned Upside Down*, 40–41. See also Louis P. Towles, "A Matter of Honor at South Carolina College, 1822," *South Carolina Historical Magazine* 94 (January 1993).

38. Henry Clay Jr. to Henry Clay, 7 May 1827, in James F. Hopkins and Mary W. M. Hargreaves, et al., eds., *The Papers of Henry Clay* (Lexington: University of Kentucky Press, 1959–1992), 6: 524–25; miscellaneous correspondence, *Papers of Andrew Jackson*, 4: 253–63; Ralph Izard Jr. to Alice Izard, July 1801, Izard Family Papers, SCHS.

39. Sterling Ruffin to Thomas Ruffin, 29 December 1803, Thomas Ruffin Papers, SHC; Andrew Jackson to Joseph Gardner Swift, 12 January 1817, *Papers of Andrew Jackson*, 4: 84.

40. James Thruston Hubard to William Hubard, 30 October 1797 and undated, both in Hubard Family Papers, SHC. See also William Ball to John Ball Sr., 9 April 1806, William James Ball Family Correspondence, SCHS; William Quynn to Allen Quynn, 9 September 1783 and 9 December 1782, both in "Letters of a Maryland Medical Student," 189–91; Arthur Morson to Alexander Morson, 9 October 1819, Arthur Alexander Morson Papers, SHC.

41. Robert W. Hill, ed., "A Virginian at Harvard, 1819–1823: Edward T. Tayloe's College Expenses," *Virginia Magazine of History and Biography* 52 (1944): 262–66.

42. George Izard to Gabriel Manigault, 29 May 1804, Ralph Izard Papers, SCL.

43. Robert Thruston Hubard to Edmund Wilcox Hubard, 22 March 1825, Hubard Family Papers, SHC; George Swain to David Swain, 7 June 1822, David Lowry Swain Papers, NCC.

44. John Randolph to Theodore Dudley, 15 February 1806, in Kirk, *John Randolph of Roanoke*, 235.

45. Charles Pettigrew to John Pettigrew, 8 October 1797, Pettigrew Family Papers, SHC; Frances Pinckney to Roger Pinckney, 14 July 1785, Roger Pinckney Correspondence, SCHS; Ralph Wormeley to Warner Wormeley, 29 June 1801, Wormeley Family Papers, VHS.

46. Henry Clay to Henry Clay Jr., 25 December 1827, *Papers of Henry Clay,* 6: 1,380; Charlton DeSaussure Jr., ed., "Memoirs of General George Izard, 1825," *South Carolina Historical Magazine* 78 (1977): 45; Spier Whitaker to Matthew Cary Whitaker, 13 December 1823, Matthew Cary Whitaker Papers, SHC.

47. William Quynn to Allen Quynn, 16 March 1784, in "Letters of a Maryland Medical Student," 203; Cornelius Ayer to Lewis Malone Ayer, 8 March 1819, Lewis Malone Ayer Papers, SCL.

48. Joseph Cabell Breckinridge to John Breckinridge, 16 April 1806, quoted in Lowell W. Harrison, "A Young Kentuckian at Princeton, 1806–1810: Joseph Cabell Breckinridge," *Filson Club History Quarterly* 38 (October 1964): 294; Martin W. B. Armstrong to Thomas T. Armstrong, undated [c. March 1819], Martin W. B. Armstrong Papers, SHC; Charles Carter Lee to [mother], 20 June 1819, Lee and Marshall Family Papers, SHC.

Eight • Supervising Suitors

1. William Barry to John Barry, 20 September 1805, William Taylor Barry Papers, FHS. For explorations of courtship and marriage in the early-nineteenth-century South, see Jane Turner Censer, *North Carolina Planters and Their Children, 1800–1860* (Baton Rouge: Louisiana State University Press, 1984), chap. 4; Brenda Stevenson, *Life in Black and White: Family and Community in the Slave South* (New York: Oxford University Press, 1996), 47–58; Steven M. Stowe, *Intimacy and Power in the Old South: Ritual in the Lives of the Planters* (Baltimore: Johns Hopkins University Press, 1987), chap. 2; and Bertram Wyatt-Brown, *Southern Honor: Ethics and Behavior in the Old South* (New York: Oxford University Press, 1982), chap. 8. For the North, see Karen Lystra, *Searching the Heart: Women, Men, and Romantic Love in Nineteenth-Century America* (New York: Oxford University Press, 1989); and Ellen K. Rothman, *Hands and Hearts: A History of Courtship in America* (New York: Basic Books, 1984).

2. For strategic marriages in the colonial South, see Lorri Glover, *All Our Relations: Blood Ties and Emotional Bonds among the Early South Carolina Gentry* (Baltimore: Johns Hopkins University Press, 2000). While some scholars have emphasized the rise of romantic individualism in southern marriages, their subjects overwhelmingly married within a limited pool of elites. See Daniel Blake Smith, *Inside the Great House: Planter Family Life in Eighteenth-Century Chesapeake Society* (Ithaca: Cornell University Press, 1980), chap. 4; and Jan Lewis, *The Pursuit of Happiness: Family and Values in Jefferson's Virginia* (Cambridge: Cambridge University Press, 1983), chap. 5. For a revealing case study of marriage in the early national South, see Anya Jabour's *Marriage in the Early Republic: Elizabeth and William Wirt and the Companionate Ideal* (Baltimore: Johns Hopkins University Press, 1998).

3. William Barry to John Barry, 20 September 1805, William Taylor Barry Papers, FHS. See also John Wallace Jr. to "dear Mag," 1 September 1814, in Mary Savage Anderson, ed., "The Wallace Letters," *Georgia Historical Quarterly* 18 (1934): 189; Agnes Lind to Jane Bruce, 29 July 1786, Jane Bruce Jones Papers, SCL.

4. Arthur Lee Campbell to Matthew Monroe Campbell, 31 July 1831, Arthur Lee Campbell Papers, FHS; Joel Reid Lyle to William C. Lyle, 29 November 1826, Lyle Family Papers, UKSCL.

5. Charles Wilson Harris to Robert Wilson Harris, 6 April 1800, in J. G. DeRoulhac Hamilton and Henry McGilbert Wagstaff, eds., "The Harris Letters," *James Sprunt Historical Publications* 14, no. 1 (1916): 68.

6. Edward Rutledge to Ralph Izard, 28 September 1792, Ralph Izard Papers, SCL. See also Robert Carter "Letter of Advice to My Children," 12–14 October 1803, Robert Carter Papers, VHS; Thomas Todd to Charles Todd, 23 August 1808, Charles Stewart Todd Papers, FHS.

7. John E. Colhoun Jr. to William Moultrie Reid, 12 April 1818, John Ewing Colhoun Papers, SHC.

8. Unknown to Edward Randolph Harden, 15 May 1830, Harden Family Papers, DUL; Robert Anderson to Maria Latham, 2 January 1827, Anderson Family Papers, FHS; Chapman Johnson to David Watson, 19 December 1799, in "Letters to David Watson," *Virginia Magazine of History and Biography* 29 (July 1921): 266.

9. John Lloyd to Richard Champion, 22 April 1794, John Lloyd Letterbook, SCL.

10. Thomas Jefferson Withers to James Henry Hammond, 8 June 1826, Hammond Family Papers, SCL.

11. Sarah Gilbert to Adam Alexander, 8 April 1822, in Marion Alexander Boggs, ed., *The Alexander Letters, 1787–1900* (Athens: University of Georgia Press, 1980), 54; Sarah Gibbes to John Gibbes, 10 September 1783, Gibbes Family Papers, SCHS.

12. Anne Randolph to St. George Tucker, 23 September 1788, in Mrs. George P. Coleman, ed., "Randolph and Tucker Letters," *Virginia Magazine of History and Biography* 42 (1934): 49.

13. For the history of divorce, see Norma Basch, *Framing American Divorce: From the Revolutionary Generation to the Victorians* (Berkeley: University of California Press, 1999); Thomas E. Buckley, *The Great Catastrophe of My Life: Divorce in the Old Dominion* (Chapel Hill: University of North Carolina Press, 2002); Nancy F. Cott, *Public Vows: A History of Marriage and the Nation* (Cambridge: Harvard University Press, 2000); Hendrik Hartog, *Man and Wife in America: A History* (Cambridge: Harvard University Press, 2000); and Glenda Riley, *Divorce: An American Tradition* (New York: Oxford University Press, 1991).

14. Anne Randolph to St. George Tucker, 23 September 1788, in "Randolph and Tucker Letters," 49. Judith would have been wise to heed her mother's advice. Instead, she married Richard Randolph, who, rumor held, got her sister Nancy pregnant in 1792 and embroiled the family in a scandal they did not escape for decades. See Christopher L. Doyle, "The Randolph Scandal in Early National Virginia, 1792–1815: New Voices in the 'Court of Honor,'" *Journal of Southern History* 69 (May 2003): 283–318; and Cynthia A. Kierner, *Scandal at Bizarre: Rumor and Reputation in Jefferson's Virginia* (New York: Palgrave Macmillan, 2004).

15. Miscellaneous correspondence, Ball Family Papers, SCHS, quotation from John Ball Sr. to John Ball Jr., 22 February 1799; Sarah Gibbes to John Gibbes, 10 September 1783, Gibbes Family Papers, SCHS.

16. Elizabeth Shippen Izard to William Shippen, 11 August 1816, quoted in Wylma Wates, "Precursor to the Victorian Age: The Concept of Marriage and Family as Revealed in the Correspondence of the Izard Family of South Carolina," in Carol Bleser, ed., *In Joy and in Sorrow: Women, Family, and Marriage in the Victorian South, 1830–1900* (New York: Oxford University Press, 1991), 14; Robert J. Parker, "A Chapter in the Early Life of Thomas Oliver Larkin," *California Historical Society Quarterly* 16 (March 1937): 19.

17. Lambert Gough Lance to Hext McCall, [n.d.] 1801, Lambert Lance Papers, SCHS; Fabius Haywood to Eliza Haywood, 10 April 1825, Ernest Haywood Collection, SHC; John Grimball to William Moultrie Reid, 13 October 1816, John Berkley Grimball Papers, SCL. See also Daniel C. Edwards to William Moultrie Reid, 4 September 1815, William Moultrie Reid Papers, SCL; Paul Carrington to John Mason, 18 April [n.y.], Mason Family Papers, VHS.

18. John E. Colhoun Jr. to William Moultrie Reid, 10 December 1818, John Ewing Colhoun Papers, SHC.

19. Robert Anderson to Maria Latham, 8 October 1825, Anderson Family Papers, FHS; Charles Carter Lee to "dear mamma," 31 January 1819, Lee and Marshall Family Papers, SHC.

20. Edward Marshall to Robert Peyton, 29 November 1825, Peyton Family Papers, VHS; Rachel Mordecai to Moses Mordecai, 4 October 1817, Mordecai Family Papers, SHC.

21. Margaret Law Callcott, ed., *Mistress of Riversdale: The Plantation Letters of Rosalie Stier Calvert, 1795–1821* (Baltimore: Johns Hopkins University Press, 1991), 19–20; Jabour, *Marriage in the Early Republic*, 16.

22. See, for example, Lystra, *Searching the Heart;* and Rothman, *Hands and Hearts.*

23. For white wives, see Catherine Clinton, *The Plantation Mistress: Woman's World in the Old South* (New York: Pantheon Books, 1982); and Cynthia A. Kierner, *Beyond the Household: Women's Place in the Early South, 1700–1835* (Ithaca: Cornell University Press, 1998). For widows negotiating this order, see Kirsten E. Wood, *Masterful Women: Slaveholding Widows from the American Revolution to the Civil War* (Chapel Hill: University of North Carolina Press, 2004).

24. William Short to Charles Wilkins Short, 22 August 1815 and 28 June 1815, both in Charles Wilkins Short Papers, FHS.

25. Callcott, *Mistress of Riversdale,* 375, 377.

26. Robert J. Brugger, *Beverley Tucker: Heart over Head in the Old South* (Baltimore: Johns Hopkins University Press, 1978), 34. When the couple did marry in early 1809, St. George Tucker did not attend. See also Phillip Hamilton, *The Making and Unmaking of a Revolutionary Family: The Tuckers of Virginia, 1752–1830* (Charlottesville: University of Virginia Press, 2003), 120–22.

27. John Lloyd to Richard Champion, 3 July 1794, 28 June 1794, 22 April 1794, and 16 August 1794, in John Lloyd Letterbook, SCL.

28. Joseph W. Barnwell, ed., "Diary of Timothy Ford, 1785–1786," *South Carolina Historical and Genealogical Magazine* 13 (July 1912): 137–38.

29. William Short to Charles Wilkins Short, miscellaneous correspondence. Quotations from William Short to Charles Wilkins Short, 20 June 1815 and 28 April 1813, both in Charles Wilkins Short Papers, FHS.

30. Barnwell, ed., "Diary of Timothy Ford," 192.

31. Philip Hopkins to Richard Hopkins, 7 November 1784, in "A Maryland Medical Student and His Friends," *Maryland Historical Magazine* 23 (1928): 26; Thomas Jefferson Withers to James Henry Hammond, 11 July 1827, Hammond Family Papers, SCL.

32. Rebecca Tayloe Beverley to Robert Beverley, 8 March 1819, Beverley Family Papers, VHS.

33. Miscellaneous correspondence, Jane Bruce Jones Papers, SCL.

34. Joseph Manigault to Gabriel Manigault, 18 March 1784, Manigault Family Papers, SCL; John Ball Sr. to John Ball Jr., 14 April 1799, Ball Family Papers, SCHS.

35. For sexual restraint, see G. J. Barker-Benfield, *The Horrors of the Half-Known Life: Male Attitudes toward Women and Sexuality in Nineteenth-Century America* (New York: Harper and Row, 1976), 56–57; John D'Emilio and Estelle B. Freedman, *Intimate Matters: A History of Sexuality in America* (New York: Harper and Row, 1988), 67–69; Mark E. Kann, *A Republic of Men: The American Founders, Gendered Language, and Patriarchal Politics* (New York: New York University Press, 1998), 60–61; and Michael Kimmel, *Manhood in America: A Cultural History* (New York: Free Press, 1996), 44–47. For sexual incapacity and imperiled manhood, see Thomas A. Foster, "Deficient Husbands: Manhood, Sexual Incapacity, and Male Marital Sexuality in Seventeenth-Century New England," *William and Mary Quarterly* 56 (October 1999): 723–44. For imaginative new approaches to recovering early American sexual values and practices, see "Sexuality in Early America," *William and Mary Quarterly* 60 (January 2003).

36. As Nancy Cott has demonstrated, throughout early America the "informal public" of kin and neighbors policed aberrant sexual behaviors. Criminal prosecutions operated as extensions of rather than independent from local values systems. Cott, *Public Vows*, 40. For the most comprehensive discussion of female sexual deviance in the early South, see Victoria E. Bynum, *Unruly Women: The Politics of Social and Sexual Control in the Old South* (Chapel Hill: University of North Carolina Press, 1992). See also Martha Hodes, *White Women, Black Men: Illicit Sex in the Nineteenth-Century South* (New Haven: Yale University Press, 1997); and Joshua D. Rothman, *Notorious in the Neighborhood: Sex and Families across the Color Line in Virginia, 1787–1861* (Chapel Hill: University of North Carolina Press, 2003). For incest in the nineteenth-century South, see Peter Bardaglio, " 'An Outrage upon Nature': Incest and the Law in the Nineteenth-Century South," in Bleser, ed., *In Joy and in Sorrow*, esp. 32–43.

37. For slave women and sexual exploitation, see Thelma Jennings, " 'Us Colored Women Had to Go through a Plenty': Sexual Exploitation of African-American Slave Women," *Journal of Women's History* 1 (1990): 45–74; Jacqueline Jones, *Labor of Love, Labor of Sorrow: Black Women, Work, and the Family from Slavery to the Present* (New York: Basic Books, 1985); Melton A. McLaurin, *Celia: A Slave* (Athens: University of Georgia Press, 1991); Marie Jenkins Schwartz, *Born in Bondage: Growing Up Enslaved in the Antebellum South* (Cambridge: Harvard University Press, 2000); Stevenson, *Life in Black and White*, esp. 137–38, 236–38; and Deborah Gray White, *"Ar'n't I a Woman?": Female Slaves in the Plantation South* (New York: W. W. Norton, 1985). For the Jefferson-Hemings controversy, see Jan Ellen Lewis and Peter S. Onuf, eds., *Sally Hemings and Thomas Jefferson: History, Memory, and Civic Culture* (Charlottesville: University Press of Virginia, 1999).

38. D'Emilio and Freedman, *Intimate Matters*, 95; Lee W. Ryan, *French Travelers in the Southeastern United States, 1775–1800* (Bloomington: Principia Press, 1939), 93.

39. See Bynum, *Unruly Women;* Hodes, *White Women, Black Men;* and Rothman, *Notorious in the Neighborhood.*

40. William James Ball to Isaac Ball, 28 January 1805, Ball Family Papers, SCL; Samuel DuBose to William DuBose, 14 October 1806, Samuel DuBose Papers, SHC.

41. Severn Eyre Diary, 22 August 1785, 25 September 1785, and 5 September 1785, VHS. For analyses of prostitution, see D'Emilio and Freedman, *Intimate Matters,* 140–45; Karen Halttunen, *Confidence Men and Painted Women: A Study of Middle-Class Culture in America, 1830–1870* (New Haven: Yale University Press, 1982); and Christine Stansell, *City of Women: Sex and Class in New York, 1789–1860* (New York: Knopf, 1986).

42. Miscellaneous correspondence, 1814–15, William Page Papers, SHC. Quotation from Benjamin Cater to William Page, 24 September 1814.

43. Paul Nagel, *The Lees of Virginia: Seven Generations of an American Family* (New York: Oxford University Press, 1990), 207–9. For a surprisingly similar case in another prominent Virginia family, see Kierner, *Scandal at Bizarre.*

44. Callcott, *Mistress of Riversdale,* 377. Eugenia Calvert did marry Charles Henry Carter in November 1830.

45. In my review of over two hundred collections of family papers in archival repositories throughout the southeast as well as published volumes, I discovered only two substantial discussions of homosexual or homoerotic behavior (discussed below).

46. John C. Calhoun to Floride Colhoun, 24 August 1810 and 7 September 1810, both in Robert L. Meriwether et al., eds., *Papers of John C. Calhoun* (Columbia: University of South Carolina Press, 1959–2003), 1: 53, 55.

47. Thomas Jefferson Withers to James Henry Hammond, 14 April, 4 May, 15 May, and 24 September 1826, Hammond Family Papers, SCL. Carol Bleser and Drew Faust have both written extensively about James Henry Hammond, and they both dismiss the Withers letters as so much youthful exaggeration. Drew Gilpin Faust, *James Henry Hammond and the Old South: A Design for Mastery* (Baton Rouge: Louisiana State University, 1982), 18–19; Carol K. Bleser, ed., *Secret and Sacred: The Diaries of James Henry Hammond, a Southern Slaveholder* (New York: Oxford University Press, 1988), 5. Martin Baulm Duberman presents a contradictory argument in "'Writhing Bedfellows': 1826—Two Young Men from Antebellum South Carolina's Ruling Elite Share 'Extravagant Delight,'" *Journal of Homosexuality* 6 (Fall/Winter 1980–81): 85–101. See also Karen Hansen, "'Our Eyes Beheld Each Other': Masculinity and Intimate Friendship in Antebellum New England," in Peter Nardi, ed., *Men's Friendships* (London: Sage, 1992), 35–58; Clare A. Lyons, "Mapping an Atlantic Sexual Culture: Homoeroticism in Eighteenth-Century Philadelphia," *William and Mary Quarterly* 60 (January 2003): 119–54; and Donald Yacovone, "'Surpassing the Love of Women': Victorian Manhood and the Language of Fraternal Love," in Laura McCall and Donald Yacovone, eds., *A Shared Experience: Men, Women, and the History of Gender* (New York: New York University Press, 1998), 195–221. For women, see Carroll Smith-Rosenberg, "The Female World of Love and Ritual: Relations between Women in Nineteenth-Century America," *Signs: Journal of Women in Culture and Society* 1 (1975): 1–29.

48. Samuel DuBose to William DuBose, 14 October 1806, Samuel DuBose Papers, SHC.

Nine • Winning a Wife

1. Nancy F. Cott, *Public Vows: A History of Marriage and the Nation* (Cambridge: Harvard University Press, 2000), 10, 18–19. See also Michael Grossberg, *Governing the Hearth: Law and Family in Nineteenth-Century America* (Chapel Hill: University of North Carolina Press, 1985); Hendrik Hartog, *Man and Wife in America: A History* (Cambridge: Harvard University Press, 2000); Mark E. Kann, *A Republic of Men: The American Founders, Gendered Language, and Patriarchal Politics* (New York: New York University Press, 1998), 79–104. Kann, *The Gendering of American Politics: Founding Mothers, Founding Fathers, and Political Patriarchy* (Westport: Praeger, 1999), 74, 82–85. For the colonial era, see Anne S. Lombard, *Making Manhood: Growing Up Male in Colonial New England* (Cambridge: Harvard University Press, 2003), chap. 4; and Lisa Wilson, *Ye Heart of a Man: The Domestic Lives of Men in Colonial New England* (New Haven: Yale University Press, 1999). John Randolph of Roanoke, who in his teens was stricken by an illness that left him beardless and probably impotent, is an important exception. See Robert Dawidoff, *The Education of John Randolph* (New York: W.W. Norton, 1979); and Russell Kirk, *John Randolph of Roanoke* (Indianapolis: Liberty Press, 1978).

2. For links between race and gender in southern social hierarchy, see Kathleen M. Brown, *Good Wives, Nasty Wenches, and Anxious Patriarchs: Gender, Race, and Power in Colonial Virginia* (Chapel Hill: University of North Carolina Press, 1996); Catherine Clinton, *The Plantation Mistress: Woman's World in the Old South* (New York: Pantheon Books, 1982); and Stephanie McCurry, "The Two Faces of Republicanism: Gender and Proslavery Politics in Antebellum South Carolina," *Journal of American History* 78 (March 1992): 1,245–64.

3. James Henry Hammond, 1852 unpublished memoir, Hammond Family Papers, SCL; miscellaneous correspondence, 1805–06, Izard Family Papers, SCHS.

4. John C. Calhoun to Floride Colhoun, 28 September 1810, in Robert L. Meriwether et al., eds., *Papers of John C. Calhoun* (Columbia: University of South Carolina Press, 1959–2003), 1: 57–58; Joseph Daviess Hamilton to Sally Hamilton, 15 May 1821, Mary Hamilton Thompson Orr Papers, TSL. See also Anya Jabour, *Marriage in the Early Republic: Elizabeth and William Wirt and the Companionate Ideal* (Baltimore: Johns Hopkins University Press, 1998), 73; and Cynthia A. Kierner, *Beyond the Household: Women's Place in the Early South, 1700–1835* (Ithaca: Cornell University Press, 1998), 169–70.

5. Quotation from Kierner, *Beyond the Household*, 114. See also John McCurdy, " 'The Rank of Men Called Bachelors': The Political Identity of Single Men in Early America" (Ph.D. dissertation, Washington University, 2004).

6. Thomas Jefferson Withers to James Henry Hammond, 4 May 1826, Hammond Family Papers, SCL; Solomon Mordecai to Ellen Mordecai, 17 August 1817, Mordecai Family Papers, SHC; Carter Henry Harrison to David Watson, 11 June 1797, in "Letters from William and Mary, 1795–1799," *Virginia Magazine of History and Biography* 30 (July 1922): 227; William Ball to Isaac Ball, 24 November 1806, Ball Family Papers, SCL. See also John Guerrant to Charles Guerrant, 13 September 1819, Guerrant Family Papers, VHS; Thomas Pinckney Jr. to Harriott Pinckney, 2 January 1802, in Anna Wells Rutledge, ed., "Letters from Thomas Pinckney Jr. to Harriott Pinckney," *South Carolina Historical and Genealogical Magazine* 41

(July 1940): 106; Joseph L. C. Hardy to William Moultrie Reid, 29 October 1820, William Moultrie Reid Papers, SCL.

7. Edward Marshall to Robert Peyton, 8 March 1826, Peyton Family Papers, VHS. For rituals in the antebellum South, see Jane Turner Censer, *North Carolina Planters and Their Children, 1800–1860* (Baton Rouge: Louisiana State University Press, 1984), chap. 4; Brenda Stevenson, *Life in Black and White: Family and Community in the Slave South* (New York: Oxford University Press, 1996), 47–58; Steven M. Stowe, *Intimacy and Power in the Old South: Ritual in the Lives of the Planters* (Baltimore: Johns Hopkins University Press, 1987), chap. 2; and Bertram Wyatt-Brown, *Southern Honor: Ethics and Behavior in the Old South* (New York: Oxford University Press, 1982), chap. 8. For the North, see Karen Lystra, *Searching the Heart: Women, Men, and Romantic Love in Nineteenth-Century America* (New York: Oxford University Press, 1989); and Ellen K. Rothman, *Hands and Hearts: A History of Courtship in America* (New York: Basic Books, 1984).

8. Margaret Law Callcott, ed., *Mistress of Riversdale: The Plantation Letters of Rosalie Stier Calvert, 1795–1821* (Baltimore: Johns Hopkins University Press, 1991), 18–19.

9. Edward Marshall to Robert Peyton, 8 March 1826, Peyton Family Papers, VHS; Thomas Jefferson Withers to James Henry Hammond, 8 June 1826, Hammond Family Papers, SCL; Margaret Izard quoted in Wylma Wates, "Precursor to the Victorian Age: The Concept of Marriage and Family as Revealed in the Correspondence of the Izard Family of South Carolina," in Carol Bleser, ed., *In Joy and in Sorrow: Women, Family, and Marriage in the Victorian South, 1830–1900* (New York: Oxford University Press, 1991), 7.

10. Joseph Manigault to Gabriel Manigault, 18 December 1786, Manigault Family Papers, SCL.

11. Thomas Pinckney Jr. to Harriott Pinckney, 23 January 1802, in Rutledge, ed., "Letters from Thomas Pinckney Jr. to Harriott Pinckney," 110–12. He eventually overcame his failures and married Elizabeth Izard in 1803.

12. Charlton DeSaussure Jr., ed., "Memoirs of General George Izard, 1825," *South Carolina Historical Magazine* 78 (1977): 48–49.

13. Louis Goldsborough to Elizabeth Wirt, miscellaneous letters, quotation from 24 September 1830, Louis Malesherbes Goldsborough Papers, DUL; Felix Gilbert to Sarah Hillhouse, 12 May, 20 June, and 28 July 1802, in Marion Alexander Boggs, ed., *The Alexander Letters, 1787–1900* (Athens: University of Georgia Press, 1980).

14. James Lyons to Henrietta Watkins, miscellaneous correspondence, quotation from 19 September 1821, James Lyons Papers, SHC.

15. See also Clinton, *The Plantation Mistress*, 63–64; Jabour, *Marriage in the Early Republic*, 16; and Wyatt-Brown, *Southern Honor*, 211. An expansive discussion of marital relations among southern gentry couples is beyond the scope of this project and already clearly in evidence in other works, particularly Clinton, *The Plantation Mistress*; Kierner, *Beyond the Household*, esp. chap. 5; and Stevenson, *Life in Black and White*, esp. chap. 3.

16. Alfred Beckley to George Washington Love, 2 April 1820, James Young Love and Thomas Love Papers, FHS. Stephen Berry discovered a similar pattern among his Civil War subjects. Stephen W. Berry Jr., *All That Makes a Man: Love and Ambition in the Civil War South* (New York: Oxford University Press, 2003), 86.

17. William Ball to Isaac Ball, 22 June 1806 and 8 January 1807, Ball Family Papers, SCL;

John C. Calhoun to Floride Colhoun, 28 September 1810, *Papers of John C. Calhoun*, 1: 58; Isaac Coles to David Watson, in "Letters from William and Mary, 1795–1799," 241. For additional examples, see Louis Goldsborough to Elizabeth Wirt, 24 September 1830, Louis Malesherbes Goldsborough Papers, DUL; Thomas Jefferson Withers to James Henry Hammond, 23 April 1826, Hammond Family Papers, SCL; Joel Reid Lyle to William C. Lyle, 10 December 1829, Lyle Family Papers, UKSCL; and Thomas Pinckney Jr. to Harriott Pinckney, 23 January 1802, in Rutledge, ed., "Letters from Thomas Pinckney Jr. to Harriott Pinckney," 112.

18. John C. Calhoun to Floride Colhoun, 7 September 1810, *Papers of John C. Calhoun*, 1: 54.

19. Martin W. B. Armstrong to Thomas Armstrong, 19 March 1819, Martin W. B. Armstrong Papers, SHC; Daniel C. Edwards to William Moultrie Reid, 10 May 1815, William Moultrie Reid Papers, SCL; Felix Gilbert to Sarah Hillhouse, 11 July 1804, in Boggs, ed., *The Alexander Letters*, 27.

20. Thomas Jefferson to Peter Carr, 11 December 1783, in Julian P. Boyd et al., eds., *Papers of Thomas Jefferson* (Princeton: Princeton University Press, 1950-present), 6: 379; Sterling Ruffin to Thomas Ruffin, 11 May 1805, Thomas Ruffin Papers, SHC.

21. Andrew Jackson to Andrew Jackson Donelson, 24 February 1817, in Harold D. Moser et al., eds., *The Papers of Andrew Jackson* (Knoxville: University of Tennessee Press, 1980-present), 4: 92; John Haywood to Richard Dobbs Spaight [?], 20 January 1796, Ernest Haywood Collection, SHC. See also Ralph Wormeley to Warner Wormeley, 16 December 1801, Wormeley Family Papers, VHS; Eliza Grimball to John Grimball, 29 August 1821, John Berkley Grimball Papers, SCL; W. W. Burrows to Alice Izard, 12 November 1802, Izard Family Papers, SCHS; Sterling Ruffin to Thomas Ruffin, 7 June 1805, Thomas Ruffin Papers, SHC; William Barry to John Barry, 6 February 1804, William Taylor Barry Papers, FHS.

22. James A. Strobhart to John W. Kirk, 22 June [n.y.], Kirk Family Letters, SCHS.

23. William Ball to John Ball Jr., 2 October 1805, 18 August 1807, and 16 December 1807, in William James Ball Family Correspondence, SCHS; William Ball to Isaac Ball, 27 September 1807, Ball Family Papers, SCL.

24. Miscellaneous correspondence, "Letters from William and Mary, 1795–1799," 223–49. David Watson eventually married Sarah Minor.

25. John Grimball to William Moultrie Reid, 10 June 1818, William Moultrie Reid Papers, SCL. See also Henry Ravenel Diary, miscellaneous entries, 1812, Henry Ravenel Papers, SCHS; and Alfred Beckley to George Washington Love, 2 April 1820, James Young Love and Thomas Love Papers, FHS.

26. Thomas Pinckney Jr. to Harriott Pinckney, miscellaneous letters, in Rutledge, ed., "Letters from Thomas Pinckney Jr. to Harriott Pinckney," 99–116.

27. William Ball to Isaac Ball, 9 April 1806, Ball Family Papers, SCL; Thomas Jefferson Withers to James Henry Hammond, 11 July 1827, Hammond Family Papers, SCL. See also Daniel C. Edwards to William Moultrie Reid, 10 May 1815, William Moultrie Reid Papers, SCL.

28. Alfred Beckley to George Washington Love, 11 December 1819, James Young Love and Thomas Love Papers, FHS; Richard Stockett to John Leigh, 10 December 1795 and 10 January 1796, both in Lucy Leigh Bowie, ed., "Young Men in Love, 1795 and 1823," *Maryland*

Historical Magazine 41 (1946): 222–23; John Wallace Jr. to Sarah Wallace, 5 September 1810, in Mary Savage Anderson, ed., "The Wallace Letters," *Georgia Historical Quarterly* 18 (1934): 180.

29. William Barry to John Barry, 20 September 1805, William Taylor Barry Papers, FHS; John Palmer to Esther Simons, 28 November 1829, in Louis P. Towles, ed., *A World Turned Upside Down: The Palmers of South Santee, 1818–1881* (Columbia: University of South Carolina Press, 1996), 51; John C. Calhoun to Floride Colhoun, 20 January 1810, *Papers of John C. Calhoun*, 1: 47; DeSaussure, ed., "Memoirs of General George Izard," 50.

30. James Lyons to Henrietta Watkins, 3 February 1821, James Lyons Papers, SHC.

31. David Swain to Eleanor White, 2 January 1826, David Lowry Swain Papers, NCC; William Barry to John Barry, 20 September 1805, William Taylor Barry Papers, FHS.

32. Samuel Hinton to John Haywood, 13 June 1796, Ernest Haywood Collection, SHC. See also F. W. Armstrong to William C. Mynatt, 30 April 1819, Mynatt Family Papers, UTSCL.

33. Thomas Todd to Charles Todd, 18 February 1812, Charles Stewart Todd Papers, FHS; Alfred Beckley to George Washington Love, 11 December 1819, James Young Love and Thomas Love Papers, FHS.

34. J. W. Johnstone to Mary Ann Bullitt, c. 1823, Bullitt Family Papers, FHS; Joseph Richardson to John Leigh, undated letter 1795, in Bowie, ed., "Young Men in Love," 224.

35. Joseph Richardson to John Leigh, 27 June 1795, in Bowie, ed., "Young Men in Love," 225.

36. Louis Goldsborough to Elizabeth Wirt, 11 March 1831, Louis Malesherbes Goldsborough Papers, DUL.

Ten • *Professions and the "Circle about Every Man"*

1. St. George Tucker to John and Richard Randolph, 12 June 1787, quoted in Daniel Blake Smith, *Inside the Great House: Planter Family Life in Eighteenth-Century Chesapeake Society* (Ithaca: Cornell University Press, 1980), 96–97. For the women's sphere concept, see Nancy F. Cott, *The Bonds of Womanhood: "Women's Sphere" in New England, 1780–1835* (New Haven: Yale University Press, 1977); and Linda K. Kerber, "Separate Spheres, Female Worlds, Woman's Place: The Rhetoric of Women's History," *Journal of American History* 75 (June 1988): 9–39.

2. John C. Calhoun to John Ewing Colhoun, 26 November 1820, in Robert L. Meriwether et al., eds., *Papers of John C. Calhoun* (Columbia: University of South Carolina Press, 1959–2003), 5: 454; Marvin R. Zahniser, ed., "Edward Rutledge to His Son, August 2, 1796," *South Carolina Historical Magazine* 64 (1963): 71; Charles Wilson Harris to Robert Wilson Harris, 22 September 1797 and 29 October 1797, both in J. G. DeRoulhac Hamilton and Henry McGilbert Wagstaff, eds., "The Harris Letters," *James Sprunt Historical Publications* 14 (1916); Thomas S. Grimké to Henry Grimké, February 1818, Grimké Family Papers, SCHS.

3. Thomas S. Grimké to Henry Grimké, February 1818, Grimké Family Papers, SCHS. See also John F. Grimké to Henry Grimké, 8 March 1818, Grimké Family Papers, SCHS.

4. Andrew Jackson to Andrew Jackson Donelson, 17 September 1819, in Harold D. Moser et al., eds., *The Papers of Andrew Jackson* (Knoxville: University of Tennessee Press, 1980–present), 4: 323. For the centrality of entering professional life to independence and manhood,

see also Joseph F. Kett, *Rites of Passage: Adolescence in America, 1790 to the Present* (New York: Basic Books, 1977), 31–35; and Lisa Wilson, *Ye Heart of a Man: The Domestic Lives of Men in Colonial New England* (New Haven: Yale University Press, 1999), chap. 1. For the importance of fathers launching sons into successful careers, see also Shawn Johansen, *Family Men: Middle-Class Fatherhood in Early Industrializing America* (New York: Routledge, 2001), 144–45; Mark E. Kann, *A Republic of Men: The American Founders, Gendered Language, and Patriarchal Politics* (New York: New York University Press, 1998), 88; Anne S. Lombard, *Making Manhood: Growing Up Male in Colonial New England* (Cambridge: Harvard University Press, 2003), 39; and Bertram Wyatt-Brown, *Southern Honor: Ethics and Behavior in the Old South* (New York: Oxford University Press, 1982), 175.

5. Ralph Izard Jr. to Alice Izard, 9 December 1802, Izard Family Papers, SCHS; Memoir of Micah Taul, pp. 12, 18, UKSCL; Hamilton and Wagstaff, eds., "The Harris Letters," 7; James Henry Hammond, 1852 unpublished memoir, Hammond Family Papers, SCL; Steven Watts, *The Republic Reborn: War and the Making of Liberal America, 1790–1820* (Baltimore: Johns Hopkins University Press, 1987), 88. This pattern marked a continuation from the revolutionary era. Edward Rutledge, for example, represented South Carolina at the first Continental Congress at age twenty-five.

6. George Swain to David Swain, 10 May 1822, David Lowry Swain Papers, NCC; Anne Deas to Ralph Izard Jr., 9 May 1802, Ralph Izard Papers, SCL; Alice Izard to William Burrows, 20 May 1801, Izard Family Papers, SCHS; J. Wilson to Roger Pinckney, 16 May 1784, Roger Pinckney Correspondence, SCHS.

7. Thomas Grimké to Henry Grimké, February 1818, Grimké Family Papers, SCHS. For non-elite men see, for example, L. Diane Barnes, "Fraternity and Masculine Identity: The Search for Respectability among White and Black Artisans in Petersburg, Virginia," in Craig Thompson Friend and Lorri Glover, eds., *Southern Manhood: Perspectives on Masculinity in the Old South* (Athens: University of Georgia Press, 2004), 71–91.

8. William Hartwell Allen to William Huntington, 26 April 1817, William Huntington Papers, VHS; Green Clay to Sidney Clay, 2 September 1818, Green Clay Papers, FHS; Martin W. B. Armstrong to Thomas Armstrong, 8 December 1817, Martin W. B. Armstrong Papers, SHC.

9. Southerners, of course, had long enthusiastically participated in markets. From the early eighteenth century, Virginia planters and South Carolina merchants embraced the "empire of goods" and consumer culture that bound the colonies to the imperial center. See T. H. Breen, *Tobacco Culture: The Mentality of the Great Tidewater Planters on the Eve of the American Revolution* (Princeton: Princeton University Press, 1985); T. H. Breen, *The Marketplace of Revolution: How Consumer Politics Shaped American Independence* (New York: Oxford University Press, 2004), esp. part 1; and Joyce E. Chaplin, *An Anxious Pursuit: Agricultural Innovation and Modernity in the Lower South, 1730–1815* (Chapel Hill: University of North Carolina Press, 1993). For the persistence of this disjuncture between rhetoric and reality into the Civil War era, see Stephen W. Berry II, *All That Makes a Man: Love and Ambition in the Civil War South* (New York: Oxford University Press, 2003), 18.

10. John Randolph to Theodore Dudley, 30 December 1821, in Russell Kirk, *John Randolph of Roanoke* (Indianapolis: Liberty Press, 1978), 280; Sterling Ruffin to Thomas Ruffin, 7 June 1805, Thomas Ruffin Papers, SHC.

11. Joseph W. Barnwell, ed., "Diary of Timothy Ford, 1785–1786," *South Carolina Historical and Genealogical Magazine* 13 (July 1912): 143; (October 1912), 203. See also Susan-Mary Grant, *North over South: Northern Nationalism and American Identity in the Antebellum Era* (Lawrence: University Press of Kansas, 2000); and Linda K. Kerber, *Federalists in Dissent: Imagery and Ideology in Jeffersonian America* (Ithaca: Cornell University Press, 1970), chap. 2.

12. Elizabeth Brown Pryor, "An Anomalous Person: The Northern Tutor in Plantation Society, 1773–1860," *Journal of Southern History* 47 (August 1981): 363–92.

13. Thomas S. Grimké to Henry Grimké, February 1818, Grimké Family Papers, SCHS.

14. Charles Wilson Harris to John Conrad Otto, 1 June 1796, in Hamilton and Wagstaff, eds., "The Harris Letters"; John W. Brown Diary, 9 March 1822, SHC; James Strobart to John Kirk, 22 June [n.y.], Kirk Family Papers, SCHS.

15. For analyses of planters in southern society, see Eugene D. Genovese, *The Political Economy of Slavery: Studies in the Economy and Society of the Slave South* (New York: Vintage, 1967), and Genovese, *The World the Slaveholders Made: Two Essays in Interpretation* (New York: Pantheon, 1969); Kenneth S. Greenberg, *Masters and Statesmen: The Political Culture of American Slavery* (Baltimore: Johns Hopkins University Press, 1985); James Oakes, *The Ruling Race: A History of American Slaveholders* (New York: Knopf, 1982); William Kauffman Scarborough, *Masters of the Big House: Elite Slaveholders in the Mid-Nineteenth-Century South* (Baton Rouge: Louisiana State University Press, 2003); Steven M. Stowe, *Intimacy and Power: Ritual in the Lives of the Planters* (Baltimore: Johns Hopkins University Press, 1987); Wyatt-Brown, *Southern Honor;* and Jeffrey Robert Young, *Domesticating Slavery: The Master Class in Georgia and South Carolina, 1670–1837* (Chapel Hill: University of North Carolina Press, 1999).

16. Henry Izard to Margaret Manigault, 28 March 1799, Ralph Izard Papers, SCL; John C. Calhoun to Andrew Pickens Jr., 21 January 1803, *Papers of John C. Calhoun,* 1: 8; Kirk, *John Randolph of Roanoke,* 31.

17. John Ball Sr. to John Ball Jr., miscellaneous correspondence, Ball Family Papers, SCHS.

18. John W. Brown Diary, 26 October 1821, SHC. For general discussions of professional training, see Thomas Neville Bonner, *Becoming a Physician: Medical Education in Britain, France, Germany, and the United States, 1750–1945* (New York: Oxford University Press, 1995), esp. chaps. 4 and 5; Michael Grossberg, "Institutionalizing Masculinity: The Law as Masculine Profession," in Mark C. Carnes and Clyde Griffen, eds., *Meanings for Manhood: Constructions of Masculinity in Victorian America* (Chicago: University of Chicago Press, 1990), 133–51; and Lawrence A. Cremin, *American Education: The National Experience, 1783–1876* (New York: Harper and Row, 1980), 353–60. See also Toby L. Ditz, "Shipwrecked; or, Masculinity Imperiled: Mercantile Representations of Failure and the Gendered Self in Eighteenth-Century Philadelphia," *Journal of American History* 81 (June 1994): 51–80.

19. Cary Whitaker to Matthew Cary Whitaker, 31 January 1824, Matthew Cary Whitaker Papers, SHC; Benjamin Cater to William Page, 25 June 1814, William Page Papers, SHC; John Randolph to Theodore Dudley, 31 January 1806, in Kirk, *John Randolph of Roanoke,* 231.

20. William Barlow and David O. Powell, "A Dedicated Medical Student: Solomon Mordecai, 1819–1822," *Journal of the Early Republic* 7 (Winter 1987): 378. For medical students' experiences, see also "A Maryland Medical Student and His Friends," *Maryland Historical Magazine* 23 (1928): 279–92 and 23–30; Severn Eyre Diary, VHS; and Mordecai Family

Papers, SHC (regarding Solomon Mordecai). For analysis, see Daniel Kilbride, "Southern Medical Students in Philadelphia, 1800–1860: Science and Sociability in the 'Republic of Medicine,'" *Journal of Southern History* 65 (November 1999): 697–732.

21. Zahniser, ed., "Edward Rutledge to His Son, August 2, 1796," 71; Frances Pinckney to Roger Pinckney, 18 March 1786, Roger Pinckney Correspondence, SCHS.

22. John C. Calhoun to Andrew Pickens Jr., 23 May 1803, *Papers of John C. Calhoun*, 1: 9–10; John C. Calhoun to Floride Colhoun, 6 April 1809, *Papers of John C. Calhoun*, 1: 41; Louis P. Towles, ed., *A World Turned Upside Down: The Palmers of South Santee, 1818–1881* (Columbia: University of South Carolina Press, 1996), 49.

23. John Floyd to Mary Floyd, 7 October 1813 and 19 September 1813, both in "Letters of John Floyd, 1813–1838," *Georgia Historical Quarterly* 33 (1949): 231, 230.

24. Robert J. Brugger, *Beverley Tucker: Heart over Head in the Old South* (Baltimore: Johns Hopkins University Press, 1978), 45; William Cumming to Thomas Cumming, 11 November 1814, Alfred Cumming Papers, DUL.

25. Watts, *The Republic Reborn*. For military culture in the early Republic, see Lawrence Delbert Cress, *Citizens in Arms: The Army and the Militia in American Society to the War of 1812* (Chapel Hill: University of North Carolina Press, 1982). See also Donald J. Morzek, "The Habit of Victory: The American Military and the Cult of Manliness," in J. A. Mangan and James Walvin, eds., *Manliness and Morality: Middle-Class Masculinity in Britain and the United States, 1800–1940* (Manchester: Manchester University Press, 1987), 220–39; and Todd D. Smith, "The Problematics of Absence: Looking for the Male Body in the War of 1812," in Janet Moore Lindman and Michele Lise Tarter, eds., *A Centre of Wonders: The Body in Early America* (Ithaca: Cornell University Press, 2001).

26. Henry Clay quoted in Watts, *The Republic Reborn*, 91; John Floyd to Mary Floyd, 13 December 1814, in "Letters of John Floyd," 243. For service in the War of 1812, see also Edmund Bryan Journal, Bryan and Leventhorpe Papers, SHC; and "Journal of William K. Beall, July-August, 1812," *American Historical Review* 17 (July 1912): 783–808.

27. Henry Clay Jr. to Henry Clay, 27 March 1827, in James F. Hopkins and Mary W. M. Hargreaves et al., eds., *The Papers of Henry Clay* (Lexington: University of Kentucky Press, 1959–1992), 6: 366.

28. Izard Family Papers, SCHS. For more on the military and southern culture, see Dickson D. Bruce Jr., *Violence and Culture in the Antebellum South* (Austin: University of Texas Press, 1979).

29. George Jones to Noble Jones, 23 February 1806, Jones Family Papers, GHS.

30. Anonymous essayist quoted in Watts, *The Republic Reborn*, 210; Zahniser, ed., "Edward Rutledge to His Son, August 2, 1796," 68–69.

31. For additional discussions of the struggle between duty and autonomy in the lives of early American men, see Kann, *A Republic of Men;* Dana Nelson, *National Manhood: Capitalist Citizenship and the Imagined Fraternity of White Men* (Durham: Duke University Press, 1998); E. Anthony Rotundo, *American Manhood: Transformations in Masculinity from the Revolution to the Modern Era* (New York: Basic Books, 1993); Smith, *Inside the Great House*, chap. 3; and Stowe, *Intimacy and Power*, chap. 3.

32. George Swain to David Swain, 10 May 1822 and 12 July 1822, both in David Lowry Swain Papers, NCC; William Short to Charles Wilkins Short, 8 July 1813, Charles Wilkins

Short Papers, FHS; Charles Wilson Harris to Robert Wilson Harris, 22 September 1797, in Hamilton and Wagstaff, eds., "The Harris Letters."

33. Henry Clay to Henry Clay Jr., 6 February 1828, *Papers of Henry Clay,* 7: 80; Thomas Jefferson to Peter Carr, 19 August 1785, in Julian P. Boyd et al., eds., *Papers of Thomas Jefferson* (Princeton: Princeton University Press, 1950-present), 8: 405. See also Thomas S. Grimké to Henry Grimké, February 1818, Grimké Family Papers, SCHS; and John Palmer to Harriet Palmer, 12 January 1822, in Towles, ed., *A World Turned Upside Down,* 30.

34. William Ball to John Ball Sr., 16 March 1808, William James Ball Family Correspondence, SCHS; Frances Pinckney to Roger Pinckney, 18 March 1786, Roger Pinckney Correspondence, SCHS; Charles Wilson Harris to Robert Wilson Harris, 27 November 1797, in Hamilton and Wagstaff, eds., "The Harris Letters."

35. Ralph Wormeley to Warner Wormeley, 3 June 1804, Wormeley Family Papers, VHS; James McDowell to James McDowell, 30 January 1821, McDowell Family Papers, VHS; Thomas Jefferson to Peter Carr, 22 June 1792, *Papers of Thomas Jefferson,* 24: 108.

36. William James Ball to Isaac Ball, 12 January 1808 and 8 January 1807, both in Ball Family Papers, SCL; Margaretta Brown to Orlando Brown, 13 April 1820, Brown Family Papers, FHS.

37. Margaretta Brown to Ebenezer Mason, 14 March 1821, Brown Family Papers, FHS; Ralph Wormeley to Warner Wormeley, 8 November 1803, Wormeley Family Papers, VHS.

38. Martin W. B. Armstrong to Thomas Armstrong, 8 December 1817, Martin W. B. Armstrong Papers, SHC; Peter Carr to Thomas Jefferson, 1 May 1791, *Papers of Thomas Jefferson,* 20: 331; Peter Carr to Thomas Jefferson, 28 May 1792, *Papers of Thomas Jefferson,* 23: 548.

39. Thomas Jefferson Withers to James Henry Hammond, 8 June 1826, 10 January 1828, and 5 May 1827, all in Hammond Family Papers, SCL.

40. John Howard Jr. to Henry A. DeSaussure, 26 March 1807, Henry William DeSaussure Papers, SCL. See also Benjamin Howard to David Watson, 14 July 1797, in "Letters from William and Mary College, 1795–1799," *Virginia Magazine of History and Biography* 30 (July 1922): 229; and Charlton DeSaussure Jr., ed., "Memoirs of General George Izard, 1825," *South Carolina Historical Magazine* 78 (1977): 46.

41. Miscellaneous correspondence, Hamilton and Wagstaff, eds., "The Harris Letters"; Thomas Jefferson to Peter Carr, miscellaneous correspondence, *Papers of Thomas Jefferson;* miscellaneous correspondence, Charles Wilkins Short Papers, FHS; Ralph Izard Jr. to Alice Izard, 10 January 1803, Izard Family Papers, SCHS. For young men's complaints about inattentive relatives, see John Wallace to Sarah Wallace, 20 February 1811, in Mary Savage Anderson, ed., "The Wallace Letters," *Georgia Historical Quarterly* 18 (1934): 182; and James Gallaway to Melchizedek Spragins, 17 June 1815, Melchizedek Spragins Papers, DUL.

42. Richard Beale Davis, *Intellectual Life in Jefferson's Virginia, 1790–1830* (Knoxville: University of Tennessee Press, 1972), 356; Barnwell, ed., "Diary of Timothy Ford," 199.

43. Thomas Jefferson to Peter Carr, 10 November 1793, *Papers of Thomas Jefferson,* 27: 338; Thomas Todd to Charles Todd, 18 February 1812, Charles Stewart Todd Papers, FHS; William Burrows to Alice Izard, 12 November 1802, Izard Family Papers, SCHS.

44. Charles Wilkins Short to William Short, 18 August 1813, Charles Wilkins Short Papers, FHS; Samuel DuBose to William DuBose, March 1805, Samuel DuBose Papers, SHC.

45. William Quynn to Allen Quynn, 4 March 1784, in "Letters of a Maryland Medical Student."

46. Thomas S. Grimké to Henry Grimké, February 1818, and John F. Grimké to Henry Grimké, 8 March 1818, both in Grimké Family Papers, SCHS.

47. John Boyle to Henry Clay, 10 January 1825, *Papers of Henry Clay*, 4: 13; John Boyle to Henry Clay, 1 October 1825, *Papers of Henry Clay*, 4: 705; Henry Clay to Henry Clay Jr., 2 April 1827, *Papers of Henry Clay*, 6: 385.

48. Eliza Pinckney to Daniel Horry Jr., 16 April 1782, quoted in G. Melvin Herndon, "Pinckney Horry, 1769–1828: Rebel without a Cause," *Georgia Historical Quarterly* 70 (Summer 1986): 237–38.

49. Rudolphus Bogert to William Page, 29 May 1815, William Page Papers, SHC.

50. Ball Family Papers, SCHS; *Papers of Thomas Jefferson*. See also the correspondences of James McDowell and James McDowell, McDowell Family Papers, VHS; and William Short and Charles Wilkins Short, Charles Wilkins Short Papers, FHS.

51. John W. Brown Diary, 9 March 1822, SHC.

Eleven • Slaveholding and the Destiny of the Republic's Southern Sons

1. Madison was specifically referring to debates over the international slave trade. Calhoun's comments came during a congressional address, quoted in Russell Kirk, *John Randolph of Roanoke* (Indianapolis: Liberty Press, 1978), 156.

2. A full discussion of political culture is beyond the scope of this book. For the effects of slavery on southern politics, see William W. Freehling, *The Road to Disunion: Secessionists at Bay, 1776–1854* (New York: Oxford University Press, 1990); Kenneth S. Greenberg, *Masters and Statesmen: The Political Culture of American Slavery* (Baltimore: Johns Hopkins University Press, 1985); and Manisha Sinha, *The Counterrevolution in Slavery: Politics and Ideology in Antebellum South Carolina* (Chapel Hill: University of North Carolina Press, 2000). For proslavery positions, see Paul Finkelman, ed., *Defending Slavery: Proslavery Thought in the Old South. A Brief History with Documents.* The Bedford Series in History and Culture (New York: Bedford, St. Martin's, 2003), intro.; and Larry E. Tise, *Proslavery: A History of the Defense of Slavery in America, 1701–1840* (Athens: University of Georgia Press, 1987).

3. Works stressing the significance of these decades include Lacy K. Ford Jr., "Making the 'White Man's Country' White: Race, Slavery, and State-Building in the Jacksonian South," *Journal of the Early Republic* 19 (Winter 1999): 713–37; Susan-Mary Grant, *North over South: Northern Nationalism and American Identity in the Antebellum Era* (Lawrence: University Press of Kansas, 2000); Louis P. Masur, *1831: Year of Eclipse* (New York: Hill and Wang, 2001); Richard S. Newman, *The Transformation of American Abolitionism: Fighting Slavery in the Early Republic* (Chapel Hill: University of North Carolina Press, 2002); Christopher J. Olsen, *Political Culture and Secession in Mississippi: Masculinity, Honor, and the Antiparty Tradition, 1830–1860* (New York: Oxford University Press, 2000); Sinha, *The Counterrevolution in Slavery*; Tise, *Proslavery*; and Jeffrey Robert Young, *Domesticating Slavery: The Master Class in Georgia and South Carolina, 1670–1837* (Chapel Hill: University of North Carolina Press, 1999).

4. John Adams to Jeremy Belknap, 22 October 1795, quoted in Newman, *Transformation of*

American Abolitionism, 33. See also Ira Berlin, *Many Thousands Gone: The First Two Centuries of Slavery in North America* (Cambridge: Harvard University Press, 1998); and Joanne Pope Melish, *Disowning Slavery: Gradual Emancipation and "Race" in New England, 1780–1860* (Ithaca: Cornell University Press, 1998).

5. See Melish, *Disowning Slavery;* and Grant, *North over South.*

6. First quotation from Robert E. Shalhope, *John Taylor of Caroline: Pastoral Republican* (Columbia: University of South Carolina Press, 1980), 50; second and third quotations from Newman, *Transformation of American Abolitionism,* 55, 81. For regional tensions at the Constitutional Convention, see Jack P. Greene, "The Constitution of 1787 and the Question of Southern Distinctiveness," in Greene, *Imperatives, Behaviors, and Identities: Essays in Early American Cultural History* (Charlottesville: University Press of Virginia, 1992), 327–47. For sectional tensions in the early national era, see Joyce Appleby, *Inheriting the Revolution: The First Generation of Americans* (Cambridge: Harvard University Press, 2000), esp. chap. 8; Joanne B. Freeman, *Affairs of Honor: National Politics in the New Republic* (New Haven: Yale University Press, 2001), esp. 230, 217; Linda K. Kerber, *Federalists in Dissent: Imagery and Ideology in Jeffersonian America* (Ithaca: Cornell University Press, 1970), chap. 2; and David Waldstreicher, *In the Midst of Perpetual Fetes: The Making of American Nationalism, 1776–1820* (Chapel Hill: University of North Carolina Press, 1997), chap. 5.

7. Ezekiel Haynie to Martin Haynie, 18 June 1788, in Doris Maslin Cohn, ed., "The Haynie Letters," *Maryland Historical Magazine* 36 (1941): 212.

8. Kerber, *Federalists in Dissent,* 29–30, 25, 35.

9. Phillip Hamilton, *The Making and Unmaking of a Revolutionary Family: The Tuckers of Virginia, 1752–1830* (Charlottesville: University of Virginia Press, 2003).

10. Robert J. Brugger, *Beverley Tucker: Heart over Head in the Old South* (Baltimore: Johns Hopkins University Press, 1978), 12, 18; Hamilton, *The Making and Unmaking of a Revolutionary Family,* 155, 203.

11. The pathbreaking work of James Oakes is particularly revealing on this front. James Oakes, *The Ruling Race: A History of American Slaveholders* (New York: Knopf, 1982). For yeomen, see Stephanie McCurry, *Masters of Small Worlds: Yeoman Households, Gender Relations, and the Political Culture of the Antebellum South Carolina Low Country* (New York: Oxford University Press, 1995).

12. For further discussion of the internal divisions within the South and the preeminence of Virginians in early national antislavery, see Freehling, *Road to Disunion,* chap. 7; Ford, "Making the 'White Man's Country' White"; and Shalhope, *John Taylor,* 42–43. For South Carolina's strident, unrelenting defense of slaveholding, see Freehling, *Road to Disunion,* chaps. 12 and 13; Greenberg, *Masters and Statesmen;* and Sinha, *The Counterrevolution in Slavery.*

13. Robert Carter "Letter of Advice to My Children," 12–14 October 1803, Robert Carter Papers, VHS. See also Sterling Ruffin to Thomas Ruffin, 17 June 1804, Thomas Ruffin Papers, SHC.

14. Both men quoted in Joyce Appleby, ed., *Recollections of the Early Republic: Selected Autobiographies* (Boston: Northeastern University Press, 1997), 200, 62. See also Margaretta Mason Brown to unknown, 27 February 1811, Brown Family Papers, FHS; and David Barrow Diary, 1795, FHS.

15. For the most persuasive analysis of slaveholding and white family life on the southern frontier, see Joan Cashin, *A Family Venture: Men and Women on the Southern Frontier* (New York: Oxford University Press, 1991). See also Edward E. Baptist, *Creating an Old South: Middle Florida's Plantation Frontier before the Civil War* (Chapel Hill: University of North Carolina Press, 2002).

16. 1793 essay, Anthony Walke Papers, FHS.

17. Quoted in Appleby, *Recollections of the Early Republic*, 208–9.

18. Thomas Jefferson quoted in Freehling, *Road to Disunion*, 125.

19. Quoted in Melish, *Disowning Slavery*, xiv.

20. Ralph Wormeley to Warner Wormeley, 16 May 1802, Wormeley Family Papers, VHS; Jefferson quoted in Freehling, *Road to Disunion*, 125; Jefferson and Mason quoted in Philip D. Morgan, *Slave Counterpoint: Black Culture in the Eighteenth-Century Chesapeake and Lowcountry* (Chapel Hill: University of North Carolina Press, 1998), 380.

21. Freehling, *Road to Disunion*, 226–27; Joanna Bowen Gillespie, *The Life and Times of Martha Laurens Ramsay, 1759–1811* (Columbia: University of South Carolina Press, 2001), 220, 213; M. A. DeWolfe Howe, ed., "Journal of Josiah Quincy Jr., 1773," *Proceedings of the Massachusetts Historical Society* 49 (June 1916): 456.

22. For examples of these other critiques, see William Eaton to Alexander Sessions, 24 June 1804, in Louis B. Wright, ed., "William Eaton Takes a Dismal View of Virginia," *William and Mary Quarterly* 5 (1958): 106; H. Roy Merrens, ed., "A View of Coastal South Carolina in 1778: The Journal of Ebenezer Hazard," *South Carolina Historical Magazine* 73 (1972): 190.

23. Merrens, ed., "A View of Coastal South Carolina in 1778," 190; Fred Shelley, ed., "The Journal of Ebenezer Hazard in Georgia, 1778," *Georgia Historical Quarterly* 41 (1957): 319.

24. Joseph W. Barnwell, ed., "Diary of Timothy Ford, 1785–1786," *South Carolina Historical and Genealogical Magazine* 13 (July 1912): 143; Raymond A. Mohl, ed., " 'The Grand Fabric of Republicanism': A Scotsman Describes South Carolina, 1810–1811," *South Carolina Historical Magazine* 71 (July 1970): 182.

25. "Henry Bernard Travel Account," 25 March 1833, in *Maryland Historical Magazine* 13 (1918): 326; James W. Patton, "Glimpses of North Carolina in the Writings of Northern and Foreign Travelers, 1783–1860," *North Carolina Historical Review* 45 (1968): 322; Ralph D. Gray, ed., "A Tour of Virginia in 1827: Letters of Henry D. Gilpin to His Father," *Virginia Magazine of History and Biography* 76 (1968): 450; Robert J. Parker, "A Chapter in the Early Life of Thomas Oliver Larkin," *California Historical Society Quarterly* 16 (March 1937): 145; Eliza Cope Harrison, ed., *Best Companions: Letters of Eliza Middleton Fisher and Her Mother, Mary Hering Middleton, from Charleston, Philadelphia, and Newport, 1839–1846* (Columbia: University of South Carolina Press, 2001), 20.

26. Sidney Walter Martin, ed., "Ebenezer Kellogg's Visit to Charleston, 1817," *South Carolina Historical and Genealogical Magazine* 49 (January 1948): 6, 9.

27. Martin, "Ebenezer Kellogg's Visit to Charleston, 1817," 10; John Hammond Moore, ed., "The Abiel Abbot Journals: A Yankee Preacher in Charleston Society, 1818–1827," *South Carolina Historical Magazine* 68 (1967): 68.

28. Barnwell, "Diary of Timothy Ford," 142–43.

29. Thomas Jefferson to John Taylor, 14 February 1821, quoted in Shalhope, *John Taylor*, 200.

30. Catherine Read to "my dear Betsy," 8 December [n.y.], Read Family Papers, SCL.

31. John Ball Sr. to John Ball Jr., 29 September 1799 and 6 October 1801, both in Ball Family Papers, SCHS; Sterling Ruffin to Thomas Ruffin, 17 June 1804, Thomas Ruffin Papers, SHC; Charles Warren Harris to Robert Wilson Harris, 18 September 1800, in J. G. DeRoulhac Hamilton and Henry McGilbert Wagstaff, eds., "The Harris Letters," *James Sprunt Historical Publications* 14 (1916).

32. Sterling Ruffin to Thomas Ruffin, 17 June 1804, Thomas Ruffin Papers, SHC.

33. John Ball Sr. to John Ball Jr., 22 May 1800, Ball Family Papers, SCHS; Charles Pettigrew to Ebenezer Pettigrew, 19 May 1802, Pettigrew Family Papers, SHC.

34. John Ball Sr. to John Ball Jr., 6 October 1801 and 11 August 1799, both in Ball Family Papers, SCHS; Sarah Gibbes to John Gibbes, 11 August 1783 and 10 September 1783, both in Gibbes Family Papers, SCHS.

35. William Ball to John Ball Jr., 24 November 1806, William James Ball Family Correspondence, SCHS.

36. John Wallace Jr. to Mary Wallace, 27 February 1808, in Mary Savage Anderson, ed., "The Wallace Letters," *Georgia Historical Quarterly* 18 (1934): 178; Clement Eaton, *Henry Clay and the Art of American Politics* (Boston: Little, Brown, 1957), 66. Kendall became a prominent newspaperman in Kentucky and a political ally of Andrew Jackson.

37. Parker, "A Chapter in the Early Life of Thomas Oliver Larkin," 28; Jefferson quoted in Pauline Maier, *American Scripture: Making the Declaration of Independence* (New York: Knopf, 1997), 185.

38. Quoted in Kirk, *John Randolph of Roanoke*, 156.

39. James Henry Hammond, quoted in Young, *Domesticating Slavery*, 232; Thomas Dew, "Abolition of Negro Slavery," *American Quarterly Review* 12 (1832): 189–265, quoted in Ford, "Making the 'White Man's Country' White," 723.

Epilogue

1. Louis P. Towles, ed., *A World Turned Upside Down: The Palmers of South Santee, 1818–1881* (Columbia: University of South Carolina Press, 1996).

2. Thomas Jefferson to John Adams, 1 June 1822, in Lester J. Cappon, ed., *The Adams-Jefferson Letters: The Complete Correspondence between Thomas Jefferson and Abigail and John Adams* (Chapel Hill: University of North Carolina Press, 1959), 577–78.

3. John S. Palmer to James J. Palmer, 16 November 1860, in Towles, ed., *A World Turned Upside Down*, 272–73.

This book would not have existed without the terrific anxiety that southerners felt about turning this generation of boys into men—their hopes and fears led them to write extensively. Fortunately, historical repositories throughout the Southeast have preserved these papers. My research is based on archival collections held at the Duke University Special Collections Library (DUL), Filson Historical Society (FHS), Georgia Historical Society (GHS), North Carolina Collection at the University of North Carolina (NCC), South Carolina Historical Society (SCHS), South Caroliniana Library at the University of South Carolina (SCL), Southern Historical Collection at the University of North Carolina (SHC), Tennessee State Library and Archives (TSL), University of Kentucky Special Collections Library (UKSCL), University of Tennessee Special Collections Library (UTSCL), and Virginia Historical Society (VHS). In the early twentieth century, state history journals such as *The Georgia Historical Quarterly*, *The Maryland Historical Magazine*, *The South Carolina Historical and Genealogical Magazine*, and *The Virginia Magazine of History and Biography* routinely published transcribed manuscript materials, which also aided my research efforts. Edited collections of family papers published by university presses were additionally valuable. Examples include Margaret Law Callcott, ed., *Mistress of Riversdale: The Plantation Letters of Rosalie Stier Calvert, 1795–1821* (Baltimore: Johns Hopkins University Press, 1991); and Louis P. Towles, ed., *A World Turned Upside Down: The Palmers of South Santee, 1818–1881* (Columbia: University of South Carolina Press, 1996). And I benefited from excellent papers' projects for John C. Calhoun (University of South Carolina Press), Henry Clay (University of Kentucky Press), Andrew Jackson (University of Tennessee Press), and Thomas Jefferson (Princeton University Press).

Important biographies and studies of individual southern families from this era include Edward Ball, *Slaves in the Family* (New York: Farrar, Straus, and Giroux, 1998); Emily Bingham, *Mordecai: An Early American Family* (New York: Hill and Wang, 2003); Robert J. Brugger, *Beverley Tucker: Heart over Head in the Old South* (Baltimore: Johns Hopkins University Press, 1978); Robert Dawidoff, *The Education of John Randolph* (New York: W.W. Norton, 1979); Drew Gilpin Faust, *James Henry Hammond and the Old South: A Design for Mastery* (Baton Rouge: Louisiana State University Press, 1982); Joanna Bowen Gillespie, *The Life and Times of Martha Laurens Ramsay, 1759–1811* (Columbia: University of South Carolina Press, 2001); Phillip Hamilton, *The Making and Unmaking of a Revolutionary Family: The Tuckers of Virginia, 1752–1830* (Charlottesville: University of Virginia Press, 2003); Anya

Jabour, *Marriage in the Early Republic: Elizabeth and William Wirt and the Companionate Ideal* (Baltimore: Johns Hopkins University Press, 1998); Russell Kirk, *John Randolph of Roanoke* (Indianapolis: Liberty Press, 1978); Paul C. Nagel, *The Lees of Virginia: Seven Generations of an American Family* (New York: Oxford University Press, 1990); and Robert E. Shalhope, *John Taylor of Caroline: Pastoral Republican* (Columbia: University of South Carolina Press, 1980).

Men's history is still a relatively young field, with much of the work centered on northern middle-class men and building on E. Anthony Rotundo's foundational book *American Manhood: Transformations in Masculinity from the Revolution to the Modern Era* (New York: Basic Books, 1993). The most important works on northern men include Stephen M. Frank, *Life with Father: Parenthood and Masculinity in the Nineteenth-Century American North* (Baltimore: Johns Hopkins University Press, 1998); Shawn Johansen, *Family Men: Middle-Class Fatherhood in Early Industrializing America* (New York: Routledge, 2001); Michael Kimmel, *Manhood in America: A Cultural History* (New York: Free Press, 1996); Anne S. Lombard, *Making Manhood: Growing Up Male in Colonial New England* (Cambridge: Harvard University Press, 2003); and Lisa Wilson, *Ye Heart of a Man: The Domestic Life of Men in Colonial New England* (New Haven: Yale University Press, 1999). Additional relevant comparative works include Mark C. Carnes and Clyde Griffen, eds., *Meanings for Manhood: Constructions of Masculinity in Victorian America* (Chicago: University of Chicago Press, 1990); David G. Gilmore, *Manhood in the Making: Cultural Concepts of Masculinity* (New Haven: Yale University Press, 1990); Laura McCall and Donald Yacovone, eds., *A Shared Experience: Men, Women, and the History of Gender* (New York: New York University Press, 1998); and John Tosh, *A Man's Place: Masculinity and the Middle-Class Home in Victorian England* (New Haven: Yale University Press, 1999).

Histories of adolescence have likewise centered more on the North than the South, and include John Demos, "The Rise and Fall of Adolescence," chapter 5, in Demos, *Past, Present, and Personal: The Family and the Life Course in American History* (New York: Oxford University Press, 1986); Harvey J. Graff, *Conflicting Paths: Growing Up in America* (Cambridge: Harvard University Press, 1995); Harvey J. Graff, "Early Adolescence in Antebellum America: The Remaking of Growing Up," *Journal of Early Adolescence* 5: 411–27; and Joseph F. Kett, *Rites of Passage: Adolescence in America, 1790 to the Present* (New York: Basic Books, 1977).

Studies of southern men have been largely subsumed by Bertram Wyatt-Brown's paradigm-setting *Southern Honor: Ethics and Behavior in the Old South* (New York: Oxford University Press, 1982). Further explorations of honor culture in the South include Edward L. Ayers, *Vengeance and Justice: Crime and Punishment in the Nineteenth-Century American South* (New York: Oxford University Press, 1984); Kenneth S. Greenberg, *Masters and Statesmen: The Political Culture of American Slavery* (Baltimore: Johns Hopkins University Press, 1985); Robert F. Pace, *Halls of Honor: College Men in the Old South* (Baton Rouge: Louisiana State University Press, 2004); Robert F. Pace and Christopher A. Bjornsen, "Adolescent Honor and College Student Behavior in the Old South," *Southern Cultures* 6 (Fall 2000): 9–28; and Bertram Wyatt-Brown, *The Shaping of Southern Culture: Honor, Grace, and War, 1760s–1880s* (Chapel Hill: University of North Carolina Press, 2001). Joanne B. Freeman explored honor nationally in *Affairs of Honor: National Politics in the New Republic* (New Haven: Yale University Press, 2001). Two very recent approaches to southern manhood which do not rely on the honor thesis are Stephen W. Berry II, *All That Makes a Man: Love and Ambition in the Civil War South* (New York: Oxford University Press, 2003); and Craig Thompson Friend and Lorri Glover, eds., *Southern Manhood: Perspectives on Masculinity in the Old South* (Athens: University of Georgia Press, 2004). Classic interpretations of southern men and culture preceding the Wyatt-Brown model and still resonant today are W. J. Cash, *The Mind of the South* (New York: Knopf, 1941); and John Hope Franklin, *The Militant South, 1800–1861* (Cambridge: Harvard University Press, 1956).

The more expansive and sophisticated field of women's history provided guidance for exploring the lives of the men in this study. The most significant studies of white women in the early national South include Cynthia A. Kierner, *Beyond the Household: Women's Place in the Early South, 1700–1835* (Ithaca: Cornell University Press, 1998); Catherine Clinton, *The Plantation Mistress: Woman's World in the Old South* (New York: Pantheon Books, 1982); and Elizabeth Fox-Genovese, *Within the Plantation Household: Black and White Women of the Old South* (Chapel Hill: University of North Carolina Press, 1988). For the colonial South, see particularly Kathleen M. Brown, *Good Wives, Nasty Wenches, and Anxious Patriarchs: Gender, Race, and Power in Colonial Virginia* (Chapel Hill: University of North Carolina Press, 1996). For black women in the slave South, see Jacqueline Jones, *Labor of Love, Labor of Sorrow: Black Women, Work, and the Family from Slavery to the Present* (New York: Basic Books, 1985); Deborah Gray White, *"Ar'n't I a Woman?": Female Slaves in the Plantation South* (New York: W. W. Norton, 1985); and Marie Jenkins Schwartz, *Born in Bondage: Growing Up Enslaved in the Antebellum South* (Cambridge: Harvard University Press, 2000). For slaveholding women, see Kirsten E. Wood, *Masterful Women: Slaveholding Widows from the American Revolution through the Civil War* (Chapel Hill: University of North Carolina Press, 2004). For northern women in the new nation, see Nancy F. Cott's foundational *The Bonds of Womanhood: "Women's Sphere" in New England, 1780–1835* (New Haven: Yale University Press, 1977).

The best books investigating how the American Revolution transformed the lives and expectations of white women and exploring the concept of republican motherhood remain Linda K. Kerber, *Women of the Republic: Intellect and Ideology in Revolutionary America* (Chapel Hill: University of North Carolina, 1980); and Mary Beth Norton, *Liberty's Daughters: The Revolutionary Experience of American Women, 1750–1800* (Boston: Little, Brown, 1980). See also Ruth H. Bloch, "The Gendered Meaning of Virtue in Revolutionary America," *Signs: Journal of Women in Culture and Society* 13 (August 1987): 37–58; and Rosemarie Zagarri, "Morals, Manners, and the Republican Mother," *American Quarterly* 44 (June 1992): 192–215.

Scholarly analyses exploring the broad consequences of the Revolution on the post-Revolutionary generation include most notably Joyce Appleby, *Inheriting the Revolution: The First Generation of Americans* (Cambridge: Harvard University Press, 2000), which interprets the South as aberrant; and Steven Watts, *The Republic Reborn: War and the Making of Liberal America, 1790–1820* (Baltimore: Johns Hopkins University Press, 1987). See also Jay Fliegelman, *Prodigals and Pilgrims: The American Revolution against Patriarchal Authority, 1750–1800* (Cambridge: Cambridge University Press, 1982); George B. Forgie, *Patricide in the House Divided: A Psychological Interpretation of Lincoln and His Age* (New York: W. W. Norton, 1979); Peter Charles Hoffer, *Revolution and Regeneration: Life Cycle and the Historical Vision of the Generation of 1776* (Athens: University of Georgia Press, 1983); Mark E. Kann, *A Republic of Men: The American Founders, Gendered Language, and Patriarchal Politics* (New York: New York University Press, 1998); Kann, *The Gendering of American Politics: Founding Mothers, Founding Fathers, and Political Patriarchy* (Westport: Praeger, 1999); and Sarah J. Purcell, *Sealed with Blood: War, Sacrifice, and Memory in Revolutionary America* (Philadelphia: University of Pennsylvania Press, 2002).

Family was the crucible for turning boys into men in the new nation, and southern families have attracted considerable scholarly inquiry. Important works exploring the eighteenth century include Daniel Blake Smith, *Inside the Great House: Planter Family Life in Eighteenth-Century Chesapeake Society* (Ithaca: Cornell University Press, 1980); Lorri Glover, *All Our Relations: Blood Ties and Emotional Bonds among the Early South Carolina Gentry* (Baltimore: Johns Hopkins University Press, 2000); Allan Kulikoff, *Tobacco and Slaves: The Development of Southern Cultures in the Chesapeake, 1680–1800* (Chapel Hill: University of North Carolina Press, 1986); Jan Lewis, *The Pursuit of Happiness: Family and Values in Jefferson's Virginia* (Cambridge: Cambridge University Press, 1983); Darrett and Anita Rutman, *A Place in Time: Middlesex County, Virginia, 1650–1750* (New York: W. W. Norton, 1984); and Michael Zuckerman, "William Byrd's Family," *Perspectives in American History* 12 (1979). For the early nineteenth century, see especially Carol Bleser, ed., *In Joy and in Sorrow: Women, Family, and Marriage in the Victorian South* (New York: Oxford University Press, 1991); Joan Cashin, "The Structure of Antebellum Planter Families: 'The Ties that Bound us Was Strong,'" *Journal of Southern History* 56 (February 1990): 55–70; Joan Cashin, *A Family Venture: Men and Women on the Southern Frontier* (New York: Oxford University Press, 1991); Jane Turner Censer, *North Carolina Planters and Their Children, 1800–1860* (Baton Rouge: Louisiana State University Press, 1984); Stephanie McCurry, *Masters of Small Worlds: Yeoman Households, Gender Relations, and the Political Culture of the Antebellum South Carolina Lowcountry* (New York: Oxford University Press, 1995); Brenda Stevenson, *Life in Black and White: Family and Community in the Slave South* (New York: Oxford University Press, 1996); and Steven M. Stowe, *Intimacy and Power in the Old South: Ritual in the Lives of the Planters* (Baltimore: Johns Hopkins University Press, 1987).

For child rearing approaches in the new nation, see also Gail S. Murray, "Rational Thought and Republican Virtues: Children's Literature, 1789–1820," *Journal of the Early Republic* 8 (Summer 1988): 159–77; and Bernard W. Wishy, *The Child and the Republic: The Dawn of Modern American Child Nurture* (Philadelphia: University of Pennsylvania Press, 1967). For raising southern sons, see Michael Zuckerman, "Penmanship Exercises for Saucy Sons: Some Thoughts on the Colonial Southern Family," *South Carolina Historical Magazine* 84 (July 1983): 152–66. As in gender history generally, the training of daughters has attracted far more scholarly attention than raising sons. See Anne M. Boylan, "Growing Up Female in Young America, 1800–1860," in Joseph M. Hawes and N. Ray Hiner, eds., *American Childhood: A Research Guide and Historical Handbook* (Westport: Greenwood Press, 1985), 153–84; Catherine Clinton, "Equally Their Due: The Education of the Planter Daughter in the Early Republic," *Journal of the Early Republic* 2 (April 1982): 39–60; Christie Anne Farnham, *The Education of the Southern Belle: Higher Education and Student Socialization in the Antebellum South* (New York: New York University Press, 1994); Anya Jabour, "'Grown Girls, Highly Cultivated': Female Education in an Antebellum Southern Family," *Journal of Southern His-*

tory 64 (February 1998): 23–64; Jabour, " 'College Girls': The Female Academy and Female Identity in the Old South," in Bruce L. Clayton and John A. Salmond, eds., *"Lives Full of Struggle and Triumph": Southern Women, Their Institutions, and Their Communities* (Gainesville: University Press of Florida, 2003), 74–92; Margaret A. Nash, " 'A Triumph of Reason': Female Education in Academies in the New Republic," and Kathryn Walbert, " 'Endeavor to Improve Yourself': The Education of White Women in the Antebellum South," both in Nancy Beadie and Kim Tolley, eds., *Chartered Schools: Two Hundred Years of Independent Academies in the United States, 1727–1925* (New York: RoutledgeFalmer, 2002).

 The best book explaining elite southerners' complicated relationship with evangelical Christianity in this period is Christine Leigh Heyrman's *Southern Cross: The Beginnings of the Bible Belt* (New York: Knopf, 1997). Other important analyses of the rise of evangelicalism in the South include John B. Boles, "Evangelical Protestantism in the Old South," in Charles Reagan Wilson, ed., *Religion in the South* (Jackson: University Press of Mississippi, 1985), 13–34; Boles, *The Great Revival, 1787–1804: The Origins of the Southern Evangelical Mind* (Lexington: University Press of Kentucky, 1972); Rhys Isaac, *The Transformation of Virginia, 1740–1790* (Chapel Hill: University of North Carolina Press, 1982); Janet Moore Lindman, "Acting the Manly Christian: White Evangelical Masculinity in Revolutionary Virginia," *William and Mary Quarterly* 57 (April 2000): 393–416; Cynthia Lynn Lyerly, *Methodism and the Southern Mind, 1770–1810* (New York: Oxford University Press, 1998); and Donald G. Mathews, *Religion in the Old South* (Chicago: University of Chicago Press, 1977). For the centrality of women in nineteenth-century evangelical Protestantism, see also Ann Douglas, *The Feminization of American Culture* (New York: Knopf, 1977); and Jean Friedman, *The Enclosed Garden: Women and Community in the Evangelical South, 1830–1900* (Chapel Hill: University of North Carolina Press, 1985). The early southern frontier was a key site for revivalism; the interior's distinctions from and connections with the tidewater are explored in Stephen Aron, *How the West was Lost: The Transformation of Kentucky from Daniel Boone to Henry Clay* (Baltimore: Johns Hopkins University Press, 1996); and Elizabeth Perkins, *Border Life: Experience and Memory in the Revolutionary Ohio Valley* (Chapel Hill: University of North Carolina Press, 1998). Masculine cultures are the central focus of Nathaniel Shiedley's dissertation, "Unruly Men: Indians, Settlers, and the Ethos of Frontier Patriarchy in the Upper Tennessee Watershed, 1763–1815" (Ph.D. dissertation, Princeton University, 1999). For additional work on regionalism within the South, see Edward E. Baptist, *Creating an Old South: Middle Florida's Plantation Frontier before the Civil War* (Chapel Hill: University of North Carolina Press, 2002); Elliott J. Gorn, " 'Gouge and Bite, Pull Hair and Scratch': The Social Significance of Fighting in the Southern Backcountry," *American Historical Review* 90 (February 1985): 18–43; and Christopher Morris, *Becoming Southern: The Evolution of a Way of Life, Warren County and Vicksburg, Mississippi, 1770–1860* (New York: Oxford University Press, 1995).

 The history of educational values and institutions in this era is quite expansive. For the role of formal education to the future of the Republic, see Bernard Bailyn, *Education in the Forming of American Society* (Chapel Hill: University of North Carolina Press, 1960); Lawrence A. Cremin, *American Education: The National Experience, 1783–1876* (New York: Harper and Row, 1980); Richard Beale Davis, *Intellectual Life in Jefferson's Virginia, 1790–1830* (Knoxville: University of Tennessee Press, 1972); Daniel Walker Howe, "Church, State, and Education in the Young American Republic," *Journal of the Early Republic* 22 (Spring 2002): 1–24; Carl F. Kaestle, *Pillars of the Republic: Common Schools and American Society, 1780–1860* (New York: Hill and Wang, 1983); Gilman M. Ostrander, *Republic of Letters: The American Intellectual Community, 1775–1865* (Madison: Madison House, 1999); and David W. Robson, *Educating Republicans: The College in the Era of the American Revolution, 1750–1800* (Westport: Greenwood Press, 1985). Additional works investigating educational institutions in this era include Roger L. Geiger, ed., *The American College in the Nineteenth Century* (Nashville: Vanderbilt University Press, 2000); J. David Hoeveler, *Creating the American Mind: Intellect and Politics in the Colonial Colleges* (New York: Rowman and Littlefield, 2003); Jurgen Herbst, *From Crisis to Crisis: American College Government, 1636–1819* (Cambridge: Harvard University Press, 1982); Howard Miller, *The Revolutionary College: American Presbyterian Higher Education, 1707–1837* (New York: New York University Press, 1976); and Donald G. Tewksbury, *The Founding of American Colleges and Universities before the Civil War, With Particular Reference to the Religious Influences Bearing upon the College Movement* (New York: Archon Books, 1965). For histories of particular colleges, see E. Merton Coulter, *College Life in the Old South* (Athens: University of Georgia Press, 1928); Mark A. Noll, *Princeton and the Republic, 1768–1822: The Search for a Christian Enlightenment in the Era of Samuel Stanhope Smith* (Princeton: Princeton University Press, 1989); Ronald Story, *The Forging of an Aristocracy: Harvard and the Boston Upper Class, 1800–1870* (Middletown: Wesleyan University Press, 1980); Mark R. Wenger, "Thomas Jefferson, the College of William and Mary, and the University of Virginia," *Virginia Magazine of History and Biography* 103 (July 1995): 339–74; and Thomas J. Wertenbaker, *Princeton, 1746–1896* (Princeton: Princeton University Press, 1946).

Discussions of student culture appear in Steven J. Novak, *The Rights of Youth: American Colleges and Student Revolt, 1798–1815* (Cambridge: Harvard University Press, 1977); and Jon L. Wakelyn, "Antebellum College Life and the Relations between Fathers and Sons," in Walter J. Fraser Jr., R. Frank Saunders Jr., and Jon L. Wakelyn, eds., *The Web of Southern Social Relations: Women, Family, and Education* (Athens: University of Georgia Press, 1985), 107–26. For southern students' experiences, see Daniel Kilbride, "Southern Medical Students in Philadelphia, 1800–1861: Science and Sociability in the 'Republic of Medicine,'" *Journal of Southern History* 65 (November 1999): 697–732; and Lorri Glover, "An Education in Southern Masculinity: The Ball Family of South Carolina in the New Republic," *Journal of Southern History* 69 (February 2003): 39–70. For military school life in the early South, see Jennifer R. Green, "'Stout Chaps Who Can Bear the Distress': Young Men in Antebellum Military Academies," in Craig Thompson Friend and Lorri Glover, eds., *Southern Manhood: Perspectives on Masculinity in the Old South* (Athens: University of Georgia Press, 2004), 174–95; and Stephen A. Ross, "To 'Prepare our Sons for All that May Lie before Them': The Hillsborough Military Academy and Military Education in Antebellum North Carolina," *North Carolina Historical Review* 79 (January 2002): 1–27.

An excellent and engaging exploration of refinement in American culture is provided in Richard Bushman, *The Refinement of America: Persons, Houses, Cities* (New York: Knopf, 1992). Additional important works highlighting this subject include Jay Fliegelman, *Declaring Independence: Jefferson, Natural Language, and the Culture of Performance* (Stanford: Stanford University Press, 1993); and Tamara Plakins Thornton, *Cultivating Gentlemen: The*

Meaning of Country Life among the Boston Elite, 1785–1860 (New Haven: Yale University Press, 1989); and for the South, Charlene M. Boyer Lewis, *Ladies and Gentlemen on Display: Planter Society at the Virginia Springs, 1790–1860* (Charlottesville: University Press of Virginia, 2001); and Michal J. Rozbicki, *The Complete Colonial Gentleman: Cultural Legitimacy in Plantation America* (Charlottesville: University Press of Virginia, 1998). The most expansive work on conduct literature is C. Dallett Hemphill's fine *Bowing to Necessities: A History of Manners in America, 1620–1860* (New York: Oxford University Press, 1999). Additional analysis is provided by John Kasson, *Rudeness and Civility: Manners in Nineteenth-Century Urban America* (New York: Hill and Wang, 1990); Sarah E. Newton, *Learning to Behave: A Guide to American Conduct Books before 1900* (Westport: Greenwood Press, 1994); and Arthur M. Schlesinger, *Learning How to Behave: A Historical Study of American Etiquette Books* (New York: Cooper Square Publishers, 1968). For the specific topic of letter writing, see William Merrill Decker, *Epistolary Practices: Letter Writing in America before Telecommunications* (Chapel Hill: University of North Carolina Press, 1998); Konstantin Dierks, "Letter Writing, Masculinity, and American Men of Science, 1750–1800," *Pennsylvania History* 65 (1998): 167–98; Tamara Plakins Thornton, *Handwriting in America: A Cultural History* (New Haven: Yale University Press, 1996); and Steven M. Stowe, "The Rhetoric of Authority: The Making of Social Values in Planter Family Correspondence," *Journal of American History* 73 (March 1987): 916–33.

Important works interrogating courtship in the nineteenth-century South include Jane Turner Censer, *North Carolina Planters and Their Children, 1800–1860* (Baton Rouge: Louisiana State University Press, 1984), chapter 4; Steven M. Stowe, *Intimacy and Power in the Old South: Ritual in the Lives of the Planters* (Baltimore: Johns Hopkins University Press, 1987), chapter 2; and Bertram Wyatt-Brown, *Southern Honor: Ethics and Behavior in the Old South* (New York: Oxford University Press, 1982), chapter 8. The rise of romantic love in southern marriages was most fully explored in Daniel Blake Smith, *Inside the Great House: Planter Family Life in Eighteenth-Century Chesapeake Society* (Ithaca: Cornell University Press, 1980), chapter 4. Northern courtship studies include Karen Lystra, *Searching the Heart: Women, Men, and Romantic Love in Nineteenth-Century America* (New York: Oxford University Press, 1989); and Ellen K. Rothman, *Hands and Hearts: A History of Courtship in America* (New York: Basic Books, 1984).

Two of the best and most recent overviews of marriage in America's past are Nancy F. Cott, *Public Vows: A History of Marriage and the Nation* (Cambridge: Harvard University Press, 2000); and Hendrik Hartog, *Man and Wife in America: A History* (Cambridge: Harvard University Press, 2000). Both authors discuss the history of divorce, a subject fully analyzed in Norma Basch, *Framing American Divorce: From the Revolutionary Generation to the Victorians* (Berkeley: University of California Press, 1999); Thomas E. Buckley, *The Great Catastrophe of My Life: Divorce in the Old Dominion* (Chapel Hill: University of North Carolina Press, 2002); and Glenda Riley, *Divorce: An American Tradition* (New York: Oxford University Press, 1991). Anya Jabour's *Marriage in the Early Republic: Elizabeth and William Wirt and the Companionate Ideal* (Baltimore: Johns Hopkins University Press, 1998) is a model case study.

The most thorough overview of American sexual ethics comes from John D'Emilio and Estelle B. Freedman, *Intimate Matters: A History of Sexuality in America* (New York: Harper and Row, 1988). See also G. J. Barker-Benfield, *The Horrors of the Half-Known Life: Male Attitudes toward Women and Sexuality in Nineteenth-Century America* (New York: Harper and Row, 1976). The fullest exploration of female sexual deviance in the early South is Victoria E. Bynum, *Unruly Women: The Politics of Social and Sexual Control in the Old South* (Chapel Hill: University of North Carolina Press, 1992). Other important studies include Martha Hodes, *White Women, Black Men: Illicit Sex in the Nineteenth-Century South* (New Haven: Yale University Press, 1997); and Joshua D. Rothman, *Notorious in the Neighborhood: Sex and Families across the Color Line in Virginia, 1787–1861* (Chapel Hill: University of North Carolina Press, 2003). Cynthia Kierner offers an exemplary interrogation of a sexual scandal in one of Virginia's leading families in *Scandal at Bizarre: Rumor and Reputation in Jefferson's Virginia* (New York: Palgrave Macmillan, 2004). The more widely known Jefferson-Hemings controversy is explored in Jan Ellen Lewis and Peter S. Onuf, eds., *Sally Hemings and Thomas Jefferson: History, Memory, and Civic Culture* (Charlottesville: University Press of Virginia, 1999). While this is an extremely difficult subject to recover in documents, explorations of homosexuality in this era include Martin Baulm Duberman, " 'Writhing Bedfellows': 1826— Two Young Men from Antebellum South Carolina's Ruling Elite Share 'Extravagant Delight,' " *Journal of Homosexuality* 6 (Fall/Winter 1980–81): 85–101; and Clare A. Lyons, "Mapping an Atlantic Sexual Culture: Homoeroticism in Eighteenth-Century Philadelphia," *William and Mary Quarterly* 60 (January 2003): 119–54. A pathbreaking article on women's homosocial lives by Carroll Smith-Rosenberg, "The Female World of Love and Ritual: Relations between Women in Nineteenth-Century America," *Signs: Journal of Women in Culture and Society* 1 (1975): 1–29, has recently been followed up by Karen Hansen, " 'Our Eyes Beheld Each Other': Masculinity and Intimate Friendship in Antebellum New England," in Peter Nardi, ed., *Men's Friendships* (London: Sage, 1992), 35–58; and Donald Yacovone, " 'Surpassing the Love of Women': Victorian Manhood and the Language of Fraternal Love," in Laura McCall and Donald Yacovone, eds., *A Shared Experience: Men, Women, and the History of Gender* (New York: New York University Press, 1998), 195–221.

Men's efforts to groom themselves for reputable careers is illuminated by Thomas Neville Bonner, *Becoming a Physician: Medical Education in Britain, France, Germany, and the United States, 1750–1945* (New York: Oxford University Press, 1995); Michael Grossberg, "Institutionalizing Masculinity: The Law as Masculine Profession," in Mark C. Carnes and Clyde Griffen, eds., *Meanings for Manhood: Constructions of Masculinity in Victorian America* (Chicago: University of Chicago Press, 1990), 133–51; and Anya Jabour, "Male Friendship and Masculinity in the Early National South: William Wirt and His Friends," *Journal of the Early Republic* 20 (Spring 2000): 83–111. For the role of the military in general and the War of 1812 in particular in men's careers and lives, see especially Steven Watts, *The Republic Reborn: War and the Making of Liberal America, 1790–1820* (Baltimore: Johns Hopkins University Press, 1987); as well Lawrence Delbert Cress, *Citizens in Arms: The Army and the Militia in American Society to the War of 1812* (Chapel Hill: University of North Carolina Press, 1982); and Donald J. Morzek, "The Habit of Victory: The American Military and the Cult of Manliness," in J. A. Mangan and James Walvin, eds., *Manliness and Morality: Middle-Class Masculinity in Britain and the United States, 1800–1940* (Manchester: Manchester University Press, 1987): 220–39.

Understanding the centrality of slavery to the South and the new nation begins with

Edmund S. Morgan's seminal *American Slavery, American Freedom: The Ordeal of Colonial Virginia* (New York: W. W. Norton, 1975). Attitudes toward slavery in the varied regions of North America are also elegantly explained in Ira Berlin, *Many Thousands Gone: The First Two Centuries of Slavery in North America* (Cambridge: Harvard University Press, 1998). For northerners' experiences with emancipatory programs and racial identity, see also Joanne Pope Melish, *Disowning Slavery: Gradual Emancipation and "Race" in New England, 1780–1860* (Ithaca: Cornell University Press, 1998). For the new field of whiteness studies, see David R. Roediger, "The Pursuit of Whiteness: Property, Terror, and Expansion, 1790–1860," *Journal of the Early Republic* 19 (Winter 1999): 579–600; Dana Nelson, *National Manhood: Capitalist Citizenship and the Imagined Fraternity of White Men* (Durham: Duke University Press, 1998); Lacy K. Ford Jr., "Making the 'White Man's Country' White: Race, Slavery, and State-Building in the Jacksonian South," *Journal of the Early Republic* 19 (Winter 1999): 713–37; and, for a critique of the model, Peter Kolchin, "Whiteness Studies: The New History of Race in America," *Journal of American History* 89 (June 2002): 154–73.

Foundational works on southern plantation culture include Eugene D. Genovese, *The Political Economy of Slavery: Studies in the Economy and Society of the Slave South* (New York: Vintage, 1967); Genovese, *The World the Slaveholders Made: Two Essays in Interpretation* (New York: Pantheon, 1969); Kenneth S. Greenberg, *Masters and Statesmen: The Political Culture of American Slavery* (Baltimore: Johns Hopkins University Press, 1985); James Oakes, *The Ruling Race: A History of American Slaveholders* (New York: Knopf, 1982); William Kauffman Scarborough, *Masters of the Big House: Elite Slaveholders in the Mid-Nineteenth-Century South* (Baton Rouge: Louisiana State University Press, 2003); and Jeffrey Robert Young, *Domesticating Slavery: The Master Class in Georgia and South Carolina, 1670–1837* (Chapel Hill: University of North Carolina Press, 1999). See also Dickson D. Bruce Jr., *Violence and Culture in the Antebellum South* (Austin: University of Texas Press, 1979); and John M. Grammer, *Pastoral and Politics in the Old South* (Baton Rouge: Louisiana State University Press, 1996).

The relationship between slavery and early national southern politics is rigorously explored in William W. Freehling, *The Road to Disunion: Secessionists at Bay, 1776–1854* (New York: Oxford University Press, 1990). Exemplary state studies include Lacy K. Ford Jr., *Origins of Southern Radicalism: The South Carolina Upcountry, 1800–1860* (New York: Oxford University Press, 1988); Manisha Sinha, *The Counterrevolution in Slavery: Politics and Ideology in Antebellum South Carolina* (Chapel Hill: University of North Carolina Press, 2000); and Christopher J. Olsen, *Political Culture and Secession in Mississippi: Masculinity, Honor, and the Antiparty Tradition, 1830–1860* (New York: Oxford University Press, 2000). Proslavery ideology is interrogated in works including Paul Finkelman, ed., *Defending Slavery: Proslavery Thought in the Old South. A Brief History with Documents*, Bedford Series in History and Culture (New York: Bedford, St. Martin's, 2003); and Larry E. Tise, *Proslavery: A History of the Defense of Slavery in America, 1701–1840* (Athens: University of Georgia Press, 1987). An engaging recent addition to the study of antislavery is Richard S. Newman, *The Transformation of American Abolitionism: Fighting Slavery in the Early Republic* (Chapel Hill: University of North Carolina Press, 2002).

Additional works used for understanding the broader context of the early national era include Robert H. Abzug, *Cosmos Crumbling: American Reform and the Religious Imagina-*

tion (New York: Oxford University Press, 1994); Richard D. Brown, *Knowledge Is Power: The Diffusion of Information in Early America, 1700–1865* (New York: Oxford University Press, 1989); Andrew Burstein, *America's Jubilee: How in 1826 a Generation Remembered Fifty Years of Independence* (New York: Knopf, 2001); Susan-Mary Grant, *North over South: Northern Nationalism and American Identity in the Antebellum Era* (Lawrence: University Press of Kansas, 2000); Michael Grossberg, *Governing the Hearth: Law and Family in Nineteenth-Century America* (Chapel Hill: University of North Carolina Press, 1985); Linda K. Kerber, *Federalists in Dissent: Imagery and Ideology in Jeffersonian America* (Ithaca: Cornell University Press, 1970); Louis P. Masur, *1831: Year of Eclipse* (New York: Hill and Wang, 2001); Henry F. May, *The Enlightenment in America* (New York: Oxford University Press, 1976); Charles Sellers, *The Market Revolution: Jacksonian America, 1815–1846* (New York: Oxford University Press, 1991); James Roger Sharp, *American Politics in the Early Republic: The New Nation in Crisis* (New Haven: Yale University Press, 1993); David Waldstreicher, *In the Midst of Perpetual Fetes: The Making of American Nationalism, 1776–1820* (Chapel Hill: University of North Carolina Press, 1997); and Gordon S. Wood, *The Radicalism of the American Revolution* (New York: Knopf, 1992).